Dear Reader:

The book you are abou   the
St. Martin's True Crime   *nes*
calls "the leader in tru   u a
fascinating account of   hat
has captured the nationa   her
of perennial bestselling   ose
SALT OF THE EARTH is the true story of one woman's tri-
umph over life-shattering violence; Joseph Wambaugh called it
"powerful and absorbing." Fannie Weinstein and Melinda Wilson tell the story of a beautiful honors student who was lured
into the dark world of sex for hire in THE COED CALL GIRL
MURDER. St. Martin's is also proud to publish two-time Edgar
Award–winning author Carlton Stowers, whose TO THE LAST
BREATH recounts a two-year-old girl's mysterious death, and
the dogged investigation that led loved ones to the most unlikely murderer: her own father. In the book you now hold,
SHADOWS OF EVIL, True Crime Library veteran Carlton
Smith studies a truly amazing case: a serial killer who turned
himself in for his crimes.

St. Martin's True Crime Library gives you the stories *behind*
the headlines. Our authors take you right to the scene of the
crime and into the minds of the most notorious murderers to
show you what really makes them tick. St. Martin's True Crime
Library paperbacks are better than the most terrifying thriller,
because it's all true! The next time you want a crackling good
read, make sure it's got the St. Martin's True Crime Library
logo on the spine—you'll be up all night!

Charles E Spicer

Charles E. Spicer, Jr.
Executive Editor, St. Martin's True Crime Library

AT APPROXIMATELY 6:30 P.M. THE FOLLOWING EVENING, Wayne Adam Ford, accompanied by his brother Rod, entered the lobby of the Humboldt County Sheriff's Department in Eureka, California. After spending much of the day with his older brother, Ford had decided to turn himself in, an act that his brother had encouraged all day. He identified himself by his middle name—"Adam"—as he had apparently been calling himself for some time.

Exactly what happened next wasn't made clear later, at least in the voluminous court documents that the life and times of Wayne Adam Ford would eventually spawn. For some reason, the Humboldt sheriff's deputies put their hands in Ford's jacket pockets, probably to search him. It was at that point that a deputy retrieved a small sealed plastic bag. Inside the bag was a piece of yellowish human flesh. . . .

SHADOWS OF EVIL

CARLTON SMITH

St. Martin's Paperbacks

FOR LIEUTENANT DAN NOLAN
KING COUNTY POLICE
1941–1990
THANKS FOR YOUR WISDOM AND YOUR FRIENDSHIP

SHADOWS OF EVIL

Copyright © 2001 by Carlton Smith.

Cover photograph courtesy of the San Bernardino County Sheriff's Department.

ISBN: 0-312-97887-1

Printed in the United States of America

St. Martin's Paperbacks edition / June 2001

St. Martin's Paperbacks are published by St. Martin's Press, 175 Fifth Avenue, New York, N.Y. 10010.

10 9 8 7 6 5 4 3 2 1

ACKNOWLEDGMENTS

The author wishes to thank the many people who helped make this book possible. In Eureka, California, the efforts of Kevin Robinson, of the Humboldt County Office of Conflict Counsel, and Rhonda Parker of the Humboldt *Times-Standard* newspaper, were instrumental in helping the author to assemble the facts necessary to understand the first critical days of the Ford investigation, as was Marco Ibarra at the Ocean Grove Lodge in Trinidad. Also helpful was Arcata resident Dan Ames, who provided valuable perspective on his former neighbor, Wayne Adam Ford. Humboldt County Sheriff's Detective Juan Freeman, while limited in what he could say by a court order, was nevertheless helpful in describing the environment in which some of the events described in this narrative transpired.

In Sonoma County, thanks are due to Deputy County Counsel Byron K. Toma, who intervened to obtain the release of important information from the Sonoma County Sheriff's Department, and to then Lieutenant, now Captain, Mike Brown of that department. Thanks are also due to Art Holquin of Santa Maria, California, who not only rescued a victim of violence one night in 1998, but also later found the time and courtesy to share his recollection of the events.

In the Central Valley of California, employees of the San Joaquin County Coroner's Office and the Kern County Coroner's Office were especially helpful and supportive, as were Sgt. John Huber of the San Joaquin Sheriff's Department, and Glenn Johnson of the Kern County Sheriff's Department.

In Las Vegas, Nevada, Metropolitan Police Department Sgt. Tirso Dominguez was of great assistance in tracking down records related to the last, sad days of Tina Renee Gibbs. Special thanks are also owed to several others in Las Vegas, who, for various reasons, have asked that their names not be used, but who greatly assisted in helping to reconstruct Tina's life and times before her death.

In San Bernardino and Riverside Counties, the support of Riverside *Press-Enterprise* Publisher Marcia McQuern in the lengthy battle over court documents was greatly appreciated, as were the efforts of *Press-Enterprise* reporter Tim Grenda in helping me keep track of the various court proceedings involving Wayne Adam Ford.

Thanks are also due to Melonee Vartanian of the San Bernardino County Superior Court administrator's office, who played a vital and difficult role in tracking down important legal documents pertaining to the victims, even as others insisted that the documents did not exist.

In Orange County, the firemen of Orange County Fire Department Station 29, on Culver Road in Irvine, California, provided invaluable assistance in tracking down at least some of the details of the traffic accident that was to play such an important role in Wayne Adam Ford's life. I also wish to thank the employees of what was formerly the B & M Towing Company of San Clemente, California, who provided their own perspectives on their former co-worker.

The author owes a great debt of gratitude to Wayne Adam Ford's first wife, identified in this book by the pseudonym Leigh, who shared her recollections of life with the young Wayne Ford, and of the events that had at least some sort of significance in what was to come later; without Leigh's freely shared memories, much about her former husband's mentality would forever remain a mystery.

I would also like to thank Deputy Public Defender Joseph Canty of the San Bernardino County Public Defender's Office, who, while adhering scrupulously to ethical guidelines, was nevertheless helpful in enabling me to understand a number of the procedural issues in the Ford case, as well as his counterpart, Deputy District Attorney David Whitney, for the same. State Department of Justice investigative profiler Sharon Pagaling Hagan was also helpful in describing some of the parameters of her work. *Los Angeles Times* reporter James Rainey was kind enough to share some of the circumstances surrounding his interview with Ford in October of 1999.

In addition, I wish to thank the Honorable Michael A. Smith of the Superior Court, County of San Bernardino, Department 19, who patiently put up with my seemingly innumerable motions and often whiny correspondence, and never laughed at my seat-of-the-pants efforts to gain public access to documents he had long previously believed to be outside the public domain; and who nevertheless ruled conscientiously and fairly throughout the long battle over the Ford files. Without Judge Smith's essential fairness, this book would not have been possible.

Special thanks are likewise due to court reporter Terry Wolfe, who under difficult circumstances provided timely and accurate transcripts of the proceedings against Wayne Adam Ford. Her good humor and friendship throughout the summer of 2000, as the struggle over the Ford files unfolded, is greatly appreciated.

Finally, but not least, I would like to express special gratitude to Evi Roberson, clerk of Department 19, for her invaluable, indeed irreplaceable assistance; always patient, and ever friendly, Evi Roberson is one of the unsung heroes of the justice system; on her unflagging efforts to keep things organized and moving, and on the efforts of others like her, the progress of justice truly rests.

All of these, and others, provided essential, even vital help in assembling what is known, at least so far, about the life and crimes of Wayne Adam Ford. Still, if there are any errors in this narrative, they are my responsibility alone.

Carlton Smith
San Francisco, California
December 2000

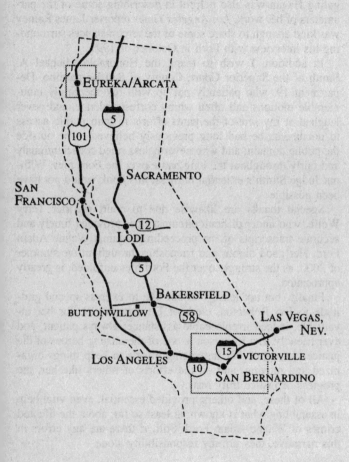

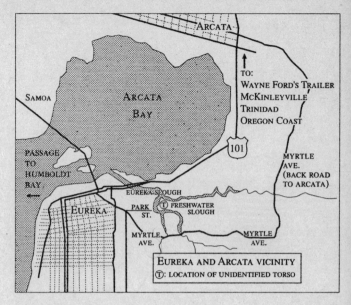

ARCATA

SAMOA

ARCATA
BAY

PASSAGE
TO
HUMBOLDT
BAY

EUREKA

101

TO:
WAYNE FORD'S TRAILER
McKINLEYVILLE
TRINIDAD
OREGON COAST

MYRTLE
AVE.
(BACK ROAD
TO ARCATA)

EUREKA SLOUGH

PARK
ST.

Ⓣ

FRESHWATER
SLOUGH

MYRTLE
AVE.

MYRTLE
AVE.

EUREKA AND ARCATA VICINITY
Ⓣ: LOCATION OF UNIDENTIFIED TORSO

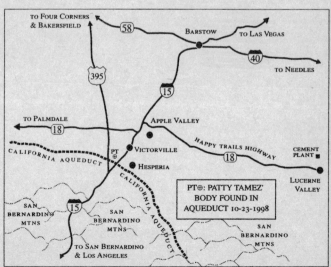

TO FOUR CORNERS
& BAKERSFIELD

58

BARSTOW

TO LAS VEGAS

40

TO NEEDLES

395

15

APPLE VALLEY

TO PALMDALE

18

HAPPY TRAILS HIGHWAY

CEMENT
PLANT

CALIFORNIA AQUEDUCT

PT⊕

VICTORVILLE

Hesperia

18

LUCERNE
VALLEY

SAN
BERNARDINO
MTNS

15

CALIFORNIA AQUEDUCT

SAN
BERNARDINO
MTNS

PT⊕: PATTY TAMEZ'
BODY FOUND IN
AQUEDUCT 10-23-1998

SAN
BERNARDINO
MTNS

TO SAN BERNARDINO
& LOS ANGELES

CONTENTS

CONTENTS

I
ADMISSIONS AND ARGUMENTS

1

True Crime

OVER THE PAST TEN YEARS I HAVE WRITTEN A DOZEN BOOKS about murder—the ultimate crime, as some have called it, because a life, once taken, can never be replaced.

Of these "dirty dozen," as I have sometimes called them, three involved sensational cases that to this date remain unsolved: the horrific Green River murders in Washington State, in which forty-nine women and at least two unborn fetuses were murdered by a single (or perhaps two) unknown killer(s) between 1982 and 1984; the eleven mysterious murders near New Bedford, Massachusetts, in the summer of 1989, which were so reminiscent of the depredations of the Green River killer; and the still-controversial death of JonBenét Ramsey on Christmas night in Boulder, Colorado.

In none of those cases were authorities able to identify a prosecutable suspect; and in the absence of a suspect, the writing of the facts of the case was made far more difficult by the understandable desire of law enforcement officials to keep secrets necessary to positively identify the perpetrator.

Six other books involved cases in which charges had been brought, but which had not yet gone to trial, at least at the time of writing: these included the murder of Olympic wrestling champion Dave Schultz by the wealthy madman John Du Pont in 1996; the assassinations of the father, mother and sister blamed on would-be multimillionaire heir Dana Ewell in 1992; the serial murders of his wife, two children, and mother, all charged to Jack Barron of Sacramento from 1992 to 1995; the killings of four women charged to motel handyman Cary Stayner near Yosemite National Park in 1999; the wanton, sexdriven murder allegedly committed by James DaVeggio and his female accomplice Michelle Michaud in 1997; and finally, the four murders attributed to Wayne Adam Ford in this book, which took place in 1997 and 1998.

Of these six cases that were unresolved at the time of writing, Du Pont was later found guilty but insane. Ewell and his college acquaintance–accomplice, Joel Radovcich (cq), were later found guilty but spared the death penalty by a Fresno County jury for the murders of the Ewell family; Jack Barron was likewise found guilty in Sacramento County for the serial killings of his own family, but spared the death penalty by negotiated agreement. Stayner pled guilty to murdering Yosemite naturalist Joie Armstrong after the U.S. Government agreed not to seek the death penalty, and still awaits state justice in Mariposa County for the deaths of Yosemite tourists Carole Sund, Juli Sund, and Silvino Pelosso as of this writing, as do DaVeggio and Michaud in Alameda County, where authorities are seeking the death penalty for both. As for Ford, as the year 2000 nears its end, a trial date remains far in the future.

In only three of the twelve murder cases had a jury reached a verdict before I began writing, and in two of those three, the defendants were either acquitted by a jury or had the charges dismissed by prosecutors.

Based on this record, I am sometimes asked: *Why write anything at all, before the final verdict is in?*

The answer is simple: justice in America, at least as practiced in the current legal environment, is extraordinarily slow. Today, especially in California, it may take three years, or even longer, before a complex case comes to trial.

Despite these delays, prosecutors and defense lawyers alike earnestly wish to keep the facts of such cases out of public awareness for as long as possible, while they argue their legal points, even as the months and years after an arrest unfold. They believe that *any* publicity may be deleterious to a fair trial; as a result, they believe that the public should be kept in the dark about what happens when someone is murdered, a crime is then charged, and the legal system begins its inexorable if excruciatingly slow grind to a conclusion, even as years elapse before a resolution.

I believe this is wrong. I believe the public is entitled to know *what* happened, *how* the police dealt with the event, *how* the government attempted (or is attempting) to prosecute it, and *how* the accused attempted (or is attempting) to defend himself.

And, if it's at all possible to know, I believe the public is entitled to know the theories of *why* such a crime took place—because, by knowing what may have caused such horrors, we might be able to prevent them in the future.

Most certainly I do not believe that the public should be shut out of this information for years, as this fundamentally important function of democracy—justice—goes forward. After all, the authority to charge an individual with a crime is the most potent power in the government's possession, and its use should never be lightly dismissed, especially by legal advocates, as "none of the public's business."

When the government charges a person with a crime, all of the immense power of the State has been focused on a single individual; and when this happens, we must always demand that the government rigorously follow the law. To permit the government to arrest, charge and convict someone in secrecy is surely the fastest and most slippery slope down to a police state. That is why I have persisted in writing about criminal cases even before a verdict has been delivered.

I especially do not concur with the view, so often advanced by the legal authorities involved in these most notorious cases, that, once such publicity occurs, it will be impossible to impanel an unbiased jury to decide the guilt or innocence of the accused.

Indeed, after having attended nearly one hundred highly publicized criminal trials over the past thirty years, I believe that even a juror exposed to extensive publicity has the capacity to take his or her oath seriously: to judge the case based upon the evidence presented in court, and *on nothing else*.

All that this requires is awareness on the part of the juror of what is evidence acceptable in a court of law, and what is not—which implies an understanding of the easily grasped rules of evidence, and which in any case is the responsibility of the judge to interpret, and to instruct.

No matter what the lawyers may argue, this is not brain surgery, nor even rocket science. Instead, it is, as the rules of evidence make clear, only simple, common sense; and it is the very heart of the notion that, in the United States of America, the final power always rests with the people.

Nevertheless, it seems to be an article of faith among lawyers, both prosecutors or defenders, that the ordinary person is incapable of making these discriminations. In my view this only illustrates the elitism which has afflicted our legal practitioners over the past few decades.

In stark contrast to the firmly held and often-expressed beliefs of such legal luminaries as Abraham Lincoln, Harlan Stone, Oliver Wendell Holmes, Hugo Black, Earl Warren, William Brennan, Lewis Powell and other stalwart defenders of the Constitution over the last two hundred years of American juridical experience, *today's* lawyers believe that the average person cannot possibly understand the complexities of a convoluted criminal case. In essence, they believe that the nuances of the law are best left to the experts—namely, *them*.

Again, I do not agree. The average person, I am convinced, can easily distinguish between what they read in a newspaper or see on television, or what they read in a magazine or book, and what they hear, see or read as sworn testimony in a court of law.

And the average person can quite readily grasp the rules of court: that the issue they are being asked to decide must be decided *only* on the information they receive while sitting in the jury box, and on nothing else—no prejudices, no outside reading, no extralegal influences. In short, I believe the people are not nearly as stupid as the lawyers like to think they are.

In that sense, what has been presented in the books I have written—these "dirty dozen"—is not much different, at least in philosophy, than that which is published in a newspaper, or broadcast by a television station; except that it is *better*—better by being more complete, placed in context, and including facts that the mainstream media usually overlook, or indeed, never obtain at all, in their rush to get to the next story.

For this reason, I have never attempted to call myself a writer; rather I am a journalist, collecting the information that is available and presenting it in such a way, that, hopefully, by the time a case finally reaches trial, the reader will have a well-grounded understanding of the issues presented in the case.

My jocularity about the "dirty dozen," above, is, of course, an emotional defense.

In my life as a journalist I have covered, written about, or investigated well over 200 murders, beginning in August of 1969 with the slaying of Sharon Tate and her companions in their death house in the Hollywood Hills; over the years I have written about parents killing children, children killing parents, murders over drugs, murders over money, murders for so-called "kicks"; and even accidental murders, as I believe the JonBenét Ramsey case may well have been.

Over these thirty years I have seen crime scenes that were indoors, in which the bloodspatter on the walls stood as a most visceral signpost of the emotions that preceded the act, or outdoor crime scenes which told unspeakable tales of loneliness and desolation. Even now I can recall a trip through the Sacramento County morgue, where scores of toe-tagged bodies awaiting post-mortem examinations lay stacked in gray plastic body bags, one on top of the other, tier on tier all the way to the ceiling of the "cold room"; and where five murder or suicide autopsies were then underway nearby. I will hear the whine of the bonesaws and the look and smell of the newly dead for the rest of my life.

In the dozen books I have so far written, a total of eighty-six people were murdered. Eighty-six people, people who were alive as you and I, one day; but gone forever the next.

Eighty-six lives, wiped out, cut short: real people with real friends, with families, with feelings, with pets; with problems, with joys, with dreams, with hopes, suddenly robbed of the chance to breathe, to live, to love, to laugh and to forgive.

Over the past three decades I have encountered scores of parents, children, husbands, wives, lovers and friends of the dead, and there was never one who did not feel the inconsolable pain that comes from being told that someone they loved had their life taken by another person, and always, for no good reason.

After so many killings, after so much pain, I readily confess to be weary of death.

All death, whether that inflicted by an accused perpetrator, or by the government—in other words, by *us,* in the form of capital punishment. No matter who is killing, killing is wrong. And especially so in the case that is the subject of this book, Wayne Adam Ford, who has been said to have confessed to at least four murders, two of them involving his victims' dismemberment.

For there should be no mistake: if not for the government's insistence that Wayne Adam Ford should be put to death for his alleged crimes, the charges against him would have been settled years ago.

And it is not just the moral ambiguity of society acting exactly like that which it deplores that is so troubling about this, or even the expense—although, by the time the Ford case is finally determined by all the courts, perhaps a decade into the future, millions of taxpayer dollars will have been spent on a case that could easily have been settled almost immediately with Ford's willing plea of guilty, if then followed by a sentence of life without parole.

If only an agreement *not* to seek the death penalty had been offered to Ford by *us,* things might have been much different; but it is the futility of trying to kill someone for killing that remains, for me, as one of the most disturbing aspects of the life and desperate times of Wayne Adam Ford. And why?

Because, as the reader will discover, it was not until Wayne Adam Ford presented *himself* for arrest—turned himself in—that anyone, anywhere, had the slightest idea that he was a possible serial murderer. In other words, if Ford hadn't delivered himself for justice, he likely would still be killing today.

In coming forward, Ford admitted that he had been doing wrong, and needed to be stopped before he killed again. But, in seeking to execute him for his admissions, the authorities are sending exactly the wrong message to the score or so of others who, somewhere in America, are even now doing exactly the same thing that Wayne Adam Ford claimed to have done—murdering desperate young women who are easy targets of opportunity.

Isn't executing Wayne Adam Ford for confessing his sins the same as telling other serial killers to stay in the shadows? That is, "If you come out and confess, we will kill you"? And isn't that the same as encouraging or at least permitting these unknown others to keep back, and thereby to go on killing? What sort of incentive for solving the hundreds of other unsolved serial murders in the United States does the execution of Wayne Adam Ford provide? Is this justice, or is it vengeance?

Or is it simply politics: the all-too-base desire to be seen as doing something about which it is far too late to do anything, as the dead would readily agree?

So many dead, so many stories: where does one end and the other begin?

This has always been the charge against those, like me, who have tried to tell those still living what has happened.

Why write anything at all? When all is said and done, isn't this book nothing more than an attempt to cash in on the fright, the pain, the sadness; of the evil that permitted these events to happen?

Over the past few years I have spent many nights thinking about these questions. What, indeed, are the ethics here? What are the issues: for the survivors, for the perpetrators, for the prosecutors and defenders? For the public? For the writer, or even journalist?

These are complicated matters, and not easily answerable. A police lieutenant in one of the dirty dozen cases once tried to answer these questions, at least for me:

"You do it," he said, "because that is what you do."

In other words, he went on, it was my responsibility to tell the story—of the perpetrator, of the victims, of the police—to tell something of the history of our lives.

And, he concluded, it was useful—for people to understand what happened, to whom it happened, and why. Otherwise, he said, no one would know.

And as the years have passed since that police lieutenant—a good friend, now dead—provided this benediction, I have tried to see each of the criminal cases I have written about in terms of what it contributes to our understanding of the social contract that binds us, that underlies our acceptance of the rule of law: *first*, that the public has a right to know what happened; *second*, that the survivors have a right to the same knowledge, unfiltered from the spinning of those, such as prosecutors or defenders, who often have a political interest in how the information is portrayed; and *third*, that the *public* itself has an interest in observing the government's efforts to prosecute, especially when its criminal justice machinery threatens to take someone's liberty, or most of all, his life.

As a journalist, I have a sacred obligation: to collect the facts, to put them into some sort of coherent order, and to let the people decide; and that's what I've tried to do in this book.

I must say it hasn't always been easy, and it certainly wasn't in the case of Wayne Adam Ford. By the time I finished this book, I had traveled thousands of miles by road and air, from the misty hills of the northern California coast to the barren wastelands of the Mojave Desert, from the glitter that is Las Vegas to the barrios of San Bernardino County, and scores of other places in between. I spent thousands of dollars from my own savings, toiled for weeks in law libraries, pored over thousands of pages of difficult-to-obtain documents, and logged more hours on the telephone than a telemarketer. I tried to get the story, the one that would otherwise have never come to light. I did it for my friend, the cop, who had told me to do it because it had to be done.

2

Contending

I FIRST SAW WAYNE ADAM FORD IN A COURT IN SAN BERnardino, California, early in the year 2000, more than two years after he had initially presented himself for arrest in Eureka, California, with a rather grisly piece of evidence in his jacket pocket to support his story.

By the time I got my first look at him, I was on my third trip to San Bernardino County, in what had been until then, and would be for some time to come, a futile effort to find some of the legal documents that might recite, at least officially, just what it was that Ford was supposed to have done; and why the authorities believed that he was the one who had done it.

Clad in a red jail jumpsuit, shackled hand and foot, bearded, the frowning Ford at first impression seemed to be a larger, well-muscled version of Charles Manson. From my seat in the small courtroom, it seemed to me that Ford's eyes glittered with suppressed malice and the potential for an explosion of rage. Throughout the proceeding, he sat quietly, observant and patient, yet still giving off an aura of tightly coiled energy.

Even some of those in law enforcement saw something attractive in him; as one female sheriff's deputy in Kern County told me, Ford had an animal magnetism that seemed to draw women to him.

"I could see why a woman would get into a car with him," was how she put it, and all she'd seen of Ford was a photograph. Clearly, there was something here of the wild man, and the supposed power of woman to soothe the savage breast, that ran through Ford's encounters with women, and through all of the fatal encounters that had brought him to this place in his life.

The immediate problem in writing about Ford was that almost all of the important records related to his arrest had been rendered legally unavailable, through one stratagem or another, as I soon discovered.

Yet the case itself presented some cutting edge issues worthy of exploration.

For one, there was the issue of legal jurisdiction, which was not so simple. Ford had presented himself for arrest in Humboldt County, California, on the evening of November 3, 1998, and had subsequently been charged with one count of murder in that county, although he had supposedly confessed to committing similar crimes in three other counties, elsewhere in California.

How then did the case wind up in San Bernardino County, more than 740 miles to the south, and in a far different legal environment than the one Ford had apparently expected to encounter when he first turned himself in, in a jurisdiction in which prosecutors had historically almost never sought to impose the death penalty?

The authorities in Humboldt County, in the far north of the state of California, had agreed not to seek to kill Wayne Adam Ford—provided that he confessed exactly, and in detail, to every homicide he had ever committed. And this Ford soon agreed to do.

In San Bernardino County, by contrast, death penalty cases were quite common; and in the case of Ford, the authorities in San Bernardino were adamant—if *they* had their way, Wayne Adam Ford would die.

This unexpected change of venue was due to a law that came into force in California two months after Ford had turned himself in.

Authored by a California State Senator, Richard Rainey, a Republican from Walnut Creek in the San Francisco Bay area, the new law gave prosecutors the right to consolidate murders committed in one or more counties into a single trial in one county, provided that the murders could be shown to have been "connected together in their commission."

This was the state's newly enacted so-called "serial killer" law, which promised a legal remedy for the complexities of prosecuting such crimes in multiple jurisdictions, and increased efficiencies in the delivery of justice.

Exactly what "connected together [sic] in their commission" meant, in actual practice, wasn't clear; since the law had never been used before, it would be up to the courts to interpret. Ford's was to be the first test case, even though the crimes he was accused of committing had taken place well before the effective date of the legislation, which was January 1, 1999.

So, one of the main issues in the Ford case was: just *how* were the crimes connected together, and did they qualify for consolidation and prosecution in a single county? In addition, was it possible to go backward in time and make the new law apply to crimes that had actually taken place before the law went into effect?[1]

When, in October of 1999, nearly eleven months after Ford had been arrested, I first inspected the San Bernardino court's file, I found it remarkably barren of the sort of basic supporting information necessary to charge any crime at all, let alone *four* different murders somehow "connected together in their commission."

All that could be unearthed was a simple, straightforward declaration of a San Bernardino County detective. One LeRoy Sapp had apparently sworn under penalty of perjury that he had probable cause to believe that Ford had committed four murders, based upon "the official police reports attached hereto and incorporated herein."

I asked the court clerk where the "official police reports attached hereto and incorporated herein" might be found.

---

1. Even as I was getting my first look at Ford, a judge was ruling that the new serial killer law applied to his case, even if the crimes had taken place before the legislation had gone into effect.

The clerk had no idea. I went to the arraignment judge, intending to ask her if she knew where the "official police reports attached hereto and incorporated herein" might be found, and was there blockaded by the judge's bailiff, sidearm on her hip, who told me that the "official police reports attached hereto and incorporated herein" were *never* provided to the public, at least not in the county of San Bernardino.

"We don't do that here," the bailiff gravely assured me.

Thus, almost a year after he was first arrested, there appeared to be nothing, at least in the publicly accessible record, stating officially and exactly *why* Ford had been accused of murder; even the names of Ford's supposed victims were secret, let alone the information of where, when, how or why they were allegedly killed; or why anyone had any reason to believe that Ford was the person who had killed them.

As to whether the crimes "were connected together in their commission," it appeared that the public was just going to have to take the San Bernardino County District Attorney's Office's word for it—in that office's view, they were; but the district attorney's office had provided nothing to publicly support that position.

Beyond that, the unresolved question of whether San Bernardino County had any right to take jurisdiction over a murder that had originated in Humboldt County hung from the case like an albatross of potential reversal.

Even *if* Ford was eventually convicted in San Bernardino, it might easily be argued that Senator Rainey's new law—which might have the effect of denying a defendant a jury of his peers in one or more cases—was unconstitutional. In the Ford case, those arguments might be applied to victims found in the counties other than San Bernardino. Rainey's legislation aside, was it really possible to try an accused serial killer in one jurisdiction, when his alleged crimes had taken place in far distant counties, hundreds of miles away?

To some, the United States Constitution was clear, no matter what Rainey and his legislative allies had enacted: anyone accused of a crime was constitutionally entitled to a fair trial before a jury of peers, which was almost always defined as those who lived in the same *vicinage* as the crimes.

In Rainey's opponents' view, the word "vicinage" meant the victim and accused perpetrator's locality, and not some arbitrary political jurisdiction that might extend hundreds of miles. In short, the eventual trial of Wayne Adam Ford was about to become a legal landmark: could the Constitutional right of a defendant to a trial by peers be *administratively* extended from one county to another, over more than seven hundred miles, despite a defendant's objections?

And if it could, could it also eventually be extended beyond one state's boundary lines to yet another state? If it was possible to legislatively extend a criminal vicinage, was it therefore possible that the entire Constitutional concept of a trial by one's peers was about to be eviscerated? If this concept was upheld, could defendants charged in Alaska eventually be judged by juries in Florida? Could juries in Maine decide the guilt of people in New Mexico? Once the principle of vicinage was breached, could there be any end to venue shopping by ambitious prosecutors?

None of these issues were clear; and as a result, the matter of *People* v. *Wayne Adam Ford* began to loom ever larger in my mind as a potentially crucial constitutional case as the twenty-first century began.

I made two more trips to San Bernardino over the next several months, each time attempting to breach the "we-don't-do-that-here" wall of secrecy that seemed to surround the essential facts of the case. I eventually learned that the "official police reports attached hereto and incorporated herein" comprised a bit over 1,500 pages of police investigation reports, including nearly 400 pages of transcripts of law enforcement interviews with Ford himself—statements which, if newspaper accounts and the scanty court records available to the public could be believed, seemed to indicate that Ford had confessed to all four murders.

All of my efforts to induce the court clerk to locate these reports to turn them over to me for inspection, as a member of the public, were rebuffed; until finally, late in February of

2000, I learned that in *all* criminal cases in San Bernardino County—not just the Ford case—*all* probable cause documents, such as police reports, or affidavits in support of arrest or search (which stand as the basic factual grist of any public accounting of the criminal justice system everywhere in America), were routinely hidden from the public eye by the San Bernardino County court clerks.

When pressed, none of the clerks seemed to know why this was, or who, in fact, was responsible for it.

Several months elapsed as I attended to other pressing matters; when those were concluded, I returned to the mystery and challenge of the San Bernardino Ford documents. I resolved to try to break down the walls of secrecy surrounding the case.

Ordinarily, a non-party seeking to obtain court records withheld from public scrutiny does best to hire legal counsel; the hired attorney then seeks to intervene in the case on behalf of the non-party, and demonstrate to a judge just why the withheld documents should be made available to the public.

This intervention has most often been mounted on behalf of the news media over the past half century; in fact, there is a long record of United States Supreme Court cases establishing the rights of public access to court records going back to at least 1915, many of them brought by newspapers or broadcasters. And the courts have consistently held that the right of public access to court documents is grounded in common law, and thus pre-exists even the United States Constitution.[2]

But lawyers are expensive. In fact, experts in the field of First Amendment law and related decisions can cost as much as $400 an hour, and given the complexity of many of the issues, and the tenacity of prosecutors and defense lawyers in wanting to keep things secret, a great many hours might be required before the records could be pried loose.

---

2. See e.g., Ex Parte Uppercu, 239 U.S. 435 (1915), in which the U.S. Supreme Court held that the right of access to depositions and exhibits filed in a court case is a general public right, one which extends even to those who are not parties to the original litigation.

Accordingly, I contacted representatives of several newspapers in Southern California, including *The Los Angeles Times*, for whom I once worked, and the Riverside *Press-Enterprise*. The *Press-Enterprise*, in fact, was well known for pursuing such public access cases; two of the most critical Supreme Court decisions relating to public access to court records involved the *Press-Enterprise*. I hoped to interest either or both newspapers in initiating the litigation that I now realized would be necessary to liberate the hidden documents, reasoning that they at least had the deep pockets I lacked.

Alas, neither newspaper seemed particularly interested in intervening. As it was later explained to me, paying the freight of a high-powered lawyer to take on a public documents case really required a sort of journalistic calculus: was the story that might result from the papers to be disclosed worth the cost of litigation, including the $400-an-hour lawyer?

My argument was, of course, that it *was* worth the expenditure, if for no other reason than to establish the principle of public access to fundamental court documents—a principle that seemed to have escaped the San Bernardino County courts entirely. The newspapers, at least initially, did not agree: for a large case, say involving a celebrity like O. J. Simpson, it would be worth doing battle, they suggested, but not for a relatively minor case such as that involving Wayne Adam Ford. On such cost–benefit rationales does the protection of our constitutional public liberties lie.

At length, not having the resources to hire a lawyer to intervene on my behalf, I resolved to do it myself.

After all, I reasoned, there was ample precedent; all that was really required was for me to read the cases, understand the principles laid down, and try to make an argument that would hold water, given the particular circumstances of the Ford case.

I took myself to the San Francisco Law Library, and began to read the law books. One of the truly delightful things about American justice is that it relies to a great extent on precedent. Thus, one case provides a raft of citations which lead a reader to other, similar cases. Eventually, after enough reading, the fundamental principles of public access to criminal proceedings became clear: the public has a general right to attend *all* criminal proceedings, and to review *all* documents in a court's files, unless a judge, for reasons of "compelling government interest," decides that access should be limited.

Because any such limitation does violence to the Constitutional concepts of openness of government operations, exceptions should be "narrowly tailored" to meet the specific interest, and established "on the record" in open court. Also, before ordering any closure, a judge must find that there are no alternatives that would achieve the same objective. The prospect of publicity alone is insufficient to warrant closure of proceedings, particularly in jurisdictions that can draw juries from a large population. (San Bernardino County has a population of about 1.8 million.)

Additionally, all documents contained in the court file in California are by statute considered to be open to the public.[3]

Based on this quick familiarization with the law, the cases and the principles, I began a series of interventions in the San Bernardino County court that lasted through most of the summer, and entailed seven different trips to court, with the attendant expenses. In May of 2000, I filed a motion to compel the clerk to disclose the 1,500 pages of investigative reports, including the transcripts of Ford's interviews with detectives, supplemented by a memorandum outlining higher court rulings on the subject of public access to court records.

At first my efforts were greeted by a mixture of indignation and amusement by both the prosecution and defense in the Ford case. Both sides had long assumed that such information was *not* public information. But after considering my filings and my oral arguments, the judge assigned to the Ford case, the Honorable Michael A. Smith of the San Bernardino County Superior Court, ruled that the documents were subject to public disclosure.

"Perhaps the way we've always done it may not be in con-

---

3. California Government Code Section 68150 *et seq.*

formity with what is expected," the judge observed.

However, Judge Smith also ruled that the transcripts of Ford's interviews with various law enforcement officers after his arrest in November of 1998 should be sealed to protect Ford's right to a fair trial. Judge Smith noted that the legal admissibility of these purported statements was still in question, and that release of the statements might endanger Ford's right to a jury untainted by knowledge of the transcripts' contents. He ordered that the 1,500 pages of investigative reports be publicly released, but after removal, or redaction, of Ford's purported statements to any law enforcement officers from the time of his arrest forward.

Despite this partial advance toward the required public disclosure, I was not satisfied, particularly when court clerks in the various satellite courthouses of San Bernardino County refused access to court records related to Ford's supposed *victims*. Eventually I obtained an order from Judge Smith granting access to these records as well; and still later, when the San Bernardino authorities dismissed their criminal information against Ford and replaced it with a grand jury indictment, I was able to convince the court that the law also required public disclosure of the transcripts of testimony before the grand jury.

In one final effort, I also attempted to uncover the written correspondence between the district attorneys of the four counties where Ford had allegedly committed his murders, under the notion that if one county had deferred prosecution to a second under the new serial killer law, the rationale for the decision ought to be subject to the state's public records law.

There, however, Judge Smith drew the line, holding that any such correspondence was privileged under the law.

These records, while not perfect by any definition, were nevertheless sufficient to assemble at least some sort of accounting of the events that led to Wayne Adam Ford's surrender and prosecution; if the key witness—Ford himself—was not to be heard from, at least it would be possible to know pretty much what had in fact happened.

What follows, therefore, is the often gruesome, sometimes shocking, occasionally even poignant story of a person some were to call "the serial killer with a conscience"; but who, as the facts the authorities so ardently endeavored to suppress actually suggest, might more honestly have been characterized as a sad case of the demented in pursuit of the desperate.

II
HUMBOLDT COUNTY, CALIFORNIA
NOVEMBER 1998

1

The North Coast

THE WINTER ALWAYS COMES EARLY ON CALIFORNIA'S North Coast. It is a land mostly forgotten by roads, by freeways, by airports, by the usual modes of high speed transportation that have shrunk the spaces of the industrialized world.

On the North Coast, in the semi–no-man's-land between Oregon and California, the world's clock runs on a slower tick, driven by the seas that roll in, uninterrupted and majestic, across the thousands of unsurveyed miles of the world's most unfathomed ocean, the loneliest ocean in the world, the North Pacific.

From the fog-shrouded mountains of the barely discoverable subset of North Coast geography called the King Mountains, sometimes called the Lost Coast—that strip of isolated mountainous land beyond all highways, shadowing westward into the unknown and beyond any modernity—along the hundreds of other scalloped coastal coves and inlets, down through innumerable fir- and redwood-shadowed ravines, the encompassing country of the North Coast lives as a place apart, a throwback to an America that lived before the marketers, the franchisers, the focus-group organizers, the calculators of the statistically average American. It is a place where the individualist still reigns, where the notion of live-and-let-live remains firmly fixed in the community ethic; a place where, when a person is told, "you can't get there from here," he or she is being told the literal truth, not just in geographical terms, but in dimensions of the human soul.

For all practical purposes, there is only one road into and out of the North Coast, and that is U.S. Highway 101, the so-called Redwood Highway, a road that runs north from the Golden Gate through Marin and Sonoma Counties, through Cloverdale, Willits, Ukiah and the marijuana capital of the West Coast, Garberville.

Past Garberville the highway crests over the 4,000-foot passes of the Coast Range, and then begins a plunge into the moisture-laden, fog-bound redwood forest, following the sinuous canyon of the Eel River, bottoming out past the small towns of Rio Dell, Fortuna and Ferndale, all lead-ins to the North Coast's largest town, Eureka, and all of them existing in a climate different, both literally and figuratively, from anywhere else in California.

With about 30,000 residents, and boasting a sizeable stock of surviving Victorian homes, Eureka is large enough to have its own suburb: the college town of Arcata, home of California State University at Humboldt.

Arcata, with a year-round population of about 15,000, stands as the major progressive cultural depository on the North Coast, the sort of place where ecologically minded students might gravitate to wear earrings, smoke ganja and rail at the ecological depredations of the timber interests, before growing old enough to realize that survival requires compromise; Arcata is likewise the college town where liberal parents might send their children, knowing them to be committed to environmental activism but still vulnerable to the vicissitudes of moral choices presented by the big city, and therefore better off put away from temptation.

Still farther to the north up Highway 101 lies another scattering of small towns, among them McKinleyville, and Trinidad, a coastal resort town of extraordinary beauty, followed by Orick and Klamath. Beyond those small towns lies the most northern municipality in California, Crescent City. It was in Crescent City that the last known tidal wave to hit the continental United States struck in 1964, as part of the great Alaska earthquake of that year; Crescent City bears the scars of the historic tsunami to this day. After Crescent City comes

Oregon, and an even sparser population on the North Pacific Coast—Brookings, Pistol River, Gold Beach, Ophir, Port Orford, Bandon, Coos Bay, Reedsport, Newport, and so on, up the coast to Astoria, Oregon, where in 1804, the explorers Lewis and Clark first brought the United States of America to the Pacific Rim.

All in all, the North Coast is cool, fog-shrouded, highly individualistic, and almost a perfect place for someone to hide out, if even from himself.

It was in such a place, in Trinidad, eighty-some–odd miles south of the Oregon border, that on the night of November 2, 1998, a 36-year-old man found himself wrestling with his conscience—indeed, it was the sort of wrestling match that might have defeated even the Biblical Jacob. For one thing, this was no struggle between a man trying to decide whether to confess unfaithfulness to his wife or girlfriend, or even a doubt about the existence of God.

For Wayne Adam Ford, a 36-year-old former United States Marine, it was literally a question of his own life or death—either in this world, or the next. As was befitting such a major decision, Ford decided to have a drink on the question. Or even several.

"It's either get drunk or blow my brains out," Ford told Marco Ibarra, the bartender at the Ocean Grove Lodge. And with that, Ibarra poured Ford the first of many rum-and-Cokes, followed, sometime later, by a number of Brandy Alexanders.

The bar at the Ocean Grove was rustically typical of many North Coast wayside stops. The bar top was scarred from many decades of spillage and cigarette burns. The back of the bar was cluttered with the sort of flotsam and jetsam typical of many working-class hangouts along the Coast: illuminated beer signs, packages of nuts, a machine that continuously grilled hot dogs, a popcorn popper; above the bar a television droned mindlessly, the sound turned down to near inaudibility. In one corner of the barroom there was a jukebox, and in another, a wood-burning stove. In an open space in front of a large pair of windows looking over a wooden veranda there was a pair of pool tables.

Ibarra had seen plenty of drinkers in the years that he'd managed the Ocean Grove, including quite a few who said the sort of thing that Ford had just said. People had bad days, he later explained. They often shot their mouths off, threatening themselves or others. It didn't mean anything, usually. But still, Ibarra could tell that the husky, neatly groomed man in front of him was in some serious psychic pain.

The man in Ibarra's bar was over six feet tall, and a solidly muscled 190 to 200 pounds. He was clean-shaven, but with a neatly trimmed mustache, and wore a black tee-shirt, Levi's jeans and work boots. Marco couldn't place him, but he soon formed the impression that the man had been in the bar before.

The afternoon wore on, and Ford continued to drink. At one point, Ford and Ibarra played a few desultory games of eight-ball on one of the pool tables. Around six, Ford asked Ibarra if the lodge had any vacancies. Ibarra rented him the cheapest room in the house, a small cabin facing the roadside, for $38.50. Ford asked Ibarra for directions to a telephone. "I want to call my brother," he said. There was a telephone in the bar, but Ford apparently wanted one with some privacy.

Ibarra showed Ford the telephone booth just outside the bar. Ford placed his call, and afterward came back in the bar and ate two Polish hot dogs, before starting in on the brandies. A bit later, Ford went to the room he had just rented. He sat on the bed and stared out the window, waiting for his brother to arrive. Ibarra thought he didn't seem drunk at all.

At approximately 6:30 p.m. the following evening, Wayne Adam Ford, accompanied by his brother Rod, entered the lobby of the Humboldt County Sheriff's Department in Eureka, California. After spending much of the day with his older brother, Ford had decided to turn himself in, an act that his brother had encouraged all day. He identified himself by his middle name—"Adam"—as he had apparently been calling himself for some time.

Exactly what happened next wasn't made clear later, at least in the voluminous court documents that the life and times of Wayne Adam Ford would eventually spawn. For some reason, the Humboldt sheriff's deputies put their hands in Ford's jacket pockets, probably to search him. It was at that point that a deputy retrieved a small sealed plastic bag. Inside the bag was a piece of yellowish flesh that the deputy recognized as a female human breast with large brown nipple still attached.

Ford was immediately arrested, and hustled off to the cells of the Humboldt County Jail. Later, a Humboldt County Sheriff's Department detective would attempt to talk to him, only to be stymied by the prisoner's request to consult with an attorney before agreeing to an interview. The detective exited the interview area, and sought out Rod Ford, who was still in the outer lobby. Until the moment that Adam had been arrested, Rod Ford had never had a clue as to what his younger brother had done to cause himself so much pain, and to lead to his arrest.

Frustrated by "Adam's" reluctance to speak freely, Humboldt County Detective Juan Freeman wanted Rod Ford to know what was happening. After this brief conversation, Rod asked to speak to his brother, either of his own volition or because of persuasion by the police, depending on whom one believes. The difference was crucial, at least legally, because shortly thereafter, "Adam" agreed to speak to Freeman; and as the details poured out over the next three days, Freeman and his colleagues in the sheriff's department were as horrified as they were elated: they had apparently caught themselves a bona fide serial killer.

2

A Right to Counsel

THE DAY AFTER FORD'S ARREST, NOVEMBER 4, 1998, Rhonda Parker, a reporter for the *Times-Standard*—"the North Coast's daily newspaper since 1854"—made her way to the four-story, cement-gray Humboldt County courthouse on I Street, just a block or two west of the newspaper's office in Eureka.

There Parker picked up whispers that something extraordinary had taken place the evening before. She soon pieced together the essentials of the story: a man with a human breast in a plastic bag in his jacket pocket, had presented himself for arrest. In Parker's mind, based upon the demeanor of the people in the sheriff's department offices that afternoon, it was clear that the deputies felt that they had scored a major coup.

In the newspaper the following day, Parker laid out the bare facts:

Trucker linked to torso case, the newspaper headlined.

"A long-haul trucker from Arcata has apparently confessed to murdering four people, including a young woman whose torso was found floating in a slough near Eureka last fall," Parker wrote. The severed breast Ford had been carrying was from a more recent victim, and was not from the headless body that had been found in the slough the year before, Parker added. Parker contended that her sources, one of them apparently Humboldt County Sheriff Dennis Lewis, claimed that Ford had told investigators that he turned himself in because his conscience had been bothering him. Ford, Parker added, had been employed by a long-haul trucking outfit headquartered in Arcata. Ford's truck driving had taken him throughout the western states, she said.

Parker contacted the trucking company owner, who expressed shock at Ford's arrest. Certainly he'd never had any reason to believe that his employee was a serial murderer.

"He seemed like a normal kind of guy," the employer told Parker. "I wouldn't have expected any problems from him. He was kind of quiet but he wasn't weird or anything."

Parker's story was picked up by the Associated Press and given national distribution. Within a matter of hours scores of print and broadcast journalists were making their way to Eureka; the bizarre angle of the severed breast assured the story national circulation.

One person who paid particularly close attention to Parker's report was Eureka attorney Kevin Robinson, a supervisor in one of the county's three separate public defender agencies. Robinson thought it very strange that a man could have allegedly confessed to four murders in Eureka, while his own first inkling of the matter had come from a newspaper. Ordinarily, Robinson knew, he would have heard about such a case from official sources, such as the police, the prosecutor's office, or at least one of his fellow public defenders. No one seemed to know who was representing Ford, if anyone. For such an important case, to Robinson, this seemed wrong.

Later, Robinson recalled that after he read the newspaper's report, he'd asked one of his associates to go over to the jail to see whether Ford had been provided with the opportunity to talk to an attorney. In Robinson's recollection, the associate had returned to the office, saying that the sheriff's department wouldn't allow Ford to see anyone. However, still later, the associate told Robinson that his recollection was faulty, that he hadn't gone to see Ford after all.

Ford's initial appearance before a magistrate, required by law to take place within forty-eight hours of arrest, was at first set for that day, Thursday. For some reason, however—perhaps because it was still two hours short of the 48-hour maximum when court adjourned for the day—the legally required proceeding was postponed to the following day.

Later that same Thursday, Robinson himself tried to visit Ford at the jail, only to be told by the sheriff's deputies that Ford was "unavailable." Robinson left the jail, fuming; he guessed that the Sheriff's personnel might be illegally denying Ford access to legal representation. In California, if a jailer prevents an attorney from seeing a prisoner who has asked for legal counsel, the jailer is guilty of a misdemeanor. The critical question was whether Ford had ever asked to consult a lawyer.

By the next day, Friday, November 6, the third-floor courtroom of Superior Court Judge W. Bruce Watson was jammed with news people who had made their way over the Coast Range down to the fog-shrouded North Coast, including television camerapersons and still photographers. All watched and recorded as the by-now-notorious Ford was led in for his first appearance in court, where he met Robinson for the first time.

Deputy District Attorney Worth Dikeman read the particulars of the complaint, which charged only a single count of murder, that of the unidentified "torso" victim whose headless remains had been found in the slough near Eureka the previous year. Dikeman asked Ford if he understood the charge against him.[4]

"Yes," Ford said.

Now Judge Watson asked Ford whether he had a lawyer.

"I keep asking for one," Ford said.

"Would you like to speak to an attorney?"

"Yes, sir."

"Do you have money to hire an attorney? Money available?"

"I can't hire an attorney," Ford said.

With that, Watson appointed Robinson to represent Ford. Robinson entered a plea of not guilty on Ford's behalf.

There were several interesting things about this situation, at least some of which would come back to haunt the efforts to prosecute Ford over the coming months and years. For one,

4. Transcript of *People* v. *Ford*, Humboldt County Superior Court, CR985444S, November 6, 1998.

if, after Ford's arrest on the evening of November 3, he had actually asked to speak with an attorney but was prevented from consulting one by law enforcement, any subsequent statements by Ford, including confessions, might be rendered inadmissible in a trial. That was one reason Judge Smith in San Bernardino County had ordered Ford's supposed statements withheld.

It certainly sounded as if Ford *had* been denied access to legal counsel, based upon his own statement in court—"I keep asking for one"—as well as Robinson's own experience in being denied access to Ford the day before.

Secondly, the complaint against Ford was for only one count of homicide, because only one murder, that of the still-unidentified victim in the slough, had taken place in Humboldt County. Even if evidence tying Ford to three other murders could be found, they could not be tried in Humboldt County, which would not have jurisdiction; at that point, the state's new serial killer law had not yet taken effect.

Robinson, glancing around the courtroom crowded with so many news people, realized the sensational nature of the charges against Ford probably meant that he would have to contend with a news media blizzard in the coming weeks. He advised the court that he would be asking for a gag order on the court and law enforcement personnel to keep the publicity down. Watson agreed to consider such an order the following week.

In the meantime, however, people were free to say what they wished about the case; and with so many newspaper and TV reporters in town, a lot of people were soon saying a lot of things. One of them was Robinson himself. Asked by a reporter why his client had pleaded not guilty if he had already confessed, Robinson almost lost his temper. "Because," he snapped, "that's how the process works."

Over the weekend and into the first part of the following week, under the pressure of the competing news media, a number of details about Ford and his alleged crimes became known.

It was soon learned that while Ford had been in custody on

November 4 and 5—when Robinson, at least on the latter day, had been trying to see him—he had made confessions to detectives from three other jurisdictions in California: San Joaquin County in central California, Kern County in south central California, and San Bernardino County in eastern Southern California. To the representatives of each of those counties, it was reported, Ford had confessed to murdering a woman. It thus appeared that Ford had killed at least four women, one by one, over a period of a year. Who Ford claimed to have killed, just where he had killed them, and why, along with his reason for subsequently turning himself in, quickly became the focus of the news media's inquiries.

Drawing on a press briefing provided by officials of the sheriff's department, apparently augmented by investigators from the other agencies who had streamed in over the previous two days, the news outlets identified the victims: the severely chopped-up and eviscerated torso of a 20- to 25-year-old woman found in Eureka's Freshwater Slough in October of 1997; Tina Renee Gibbs, 26, last seen in Las Vegas, Nevada, in late May of 1998 and found in the California Aqueduct near Buttonwillow, just west of Bakersfield, on June 2, 1998; Lanett Deyon White, 25, last seen in Fontana, California, on September 23, 1998, found in an irrigation ditch near Lodi, California, on September 25, 1998; and Patricia Tamez, 29, last seen in Victorville, California, on October 22, 1998, found the following night in the California Aqueduct near Victorville. It had been Tamez' breast that Ford had been carrying in his jacket pocket when he was arrested.

But the law enforcement officials thought there might be other victims as well.

"Everyone is taking a look at him because his method of killing matches so many cases," the *San Francisco Chronicle* quoted a Kern County Sheriff's detective, Sgt. Glenn Johnson. "These four that he has told us about may just be the tip of the iceberg."

Johnson's department had been trying to solve the Gibbs murder since June, and until Ford had turned himself in, had only the vaguest leads to follow.

Johnson said that Ford appeared to have picked up his victims as hitchhikers; but here it appears that Johnson was perhaps being a bit disingenuous; by this point the various investigators had already established that the three identified victims, all known drug users, were likely to have entered Ford's vehicle for purposes other than getting a ride. Gibbs, at least, had a well-documented background in prostitution, while investigators from San Bernardino knew that Tamez likely had experience there as well. As for White, the circumstances of her disappearance, as the San Joaquin County detectives had learned a month before, strongly suggested that she had encountered her killer while working as a prostitute; Ford's confessions appeared to confirm this.

Johnson, and others, added a particularly gruesome detail: Ford had claimed that on at least two occasions he had driven hundreds of miles over several days with a dead victim in the sleeper portion of his big rig truck. The effect was to create an image of the Trucker From Hell, barreling down the highway with a corpse riding shotgun in the rear.

This assertion only fueled the curiosity about Ford, and sent the news people scurrying in new directions. The *Chronicle*, for example, discovered that Ford had been born in Petaluma, California, just north of San Francisco Bay, the son of a man who had been part of the Army Security Agency's secret signals listening post at Two Rock Ranch. Reporters for the paper soon turned up Ford's father, Gene Ford, long retired from the Army, who lived near Napa, California. Gene declined to say much of anything about his son's predicament.

"It's devastating enough as it is," he said, "and I have nothing to say." With that, Gene Ford walked away.

Reporters delving into Ford's life in Arcata soon discovered that he had recently been divorced, and that he was the father of a two-year-old son. His ex-wife and the child lived in Las Vegas, the reporters learned. Several neighbors and acquaintances, among them Ford's employer at the long-haul trucking firm, said that Ford had often complained that his ex-wife wouldn't permit him to see the boy.

By Saturday, in fact, Ford's relationship with his former

wife had metamorphosed into a quasi-motive. Humboldt County Coroner Frank Jager, one of a number of officials who gave the news media interviews, told *The San Jose Mercury News* that Ford had said his treatment by his ex-wife "was kind of the last straw for him." Ford claimed his ex-wife had interfered with his visits to their son, Jager added.

"His anger toward her was growing every day," Jager said, "and he felt if he didn't turn himself in, he might end up taking some of his anger out on her, which would leave his son an orphan. He was concerned about his son."

Jager said he'd formed the impression that if Ford hadn't turned himself in, he would eventually have killed his ex-wife, the same way he'd killed the others.

This information set off a media scramble to find the ex–Mrs. Ford in Las Vegas. But they were too late: having been warned of what was coming, representatives of Ford's ex-wife had already obtained a judge's order sealing the record of the divorce. When some reporters nevertheless managed to locate the former Mrs. Ford's address, neighbors threatened to call the police and have the reporters arrested if they didn't get lost.

Still others tracked down Ford's relatives in the Eureka area. Two reporters from *The Mercury News* interviewed some of the unnamed relatives, who claimed to have visited Ford in jail over the weekend. The relatives told reporters Tracy Seipel and Julia Prodis Sulek that Ford didn't want a trial—he wanted the death penalty.

"He said he was really sorry for what he had done," the reporters quoted one of the relatives as saying, "and he wanted his family to try and see his son and give him lots of hugs and kisses. He says he knows he has done wrong and . . . he says he wants the death penalty, and to get this over with. I think he wants to punish himself."

The unnamed relative seemed to suggest that Ford's problems with women stemmed from a bad relationship with his mother, according to the reporters. Ford's mother had left his father when Ford and his brother were young, the relative said.

"She turned her back on the boys [Wayne and his brother

Rod] when they were younger," the reporters quoted the unknown relative. "It's another sore subject. She hurt Wayne when he needed her."

Humboldt County Coroner Jager seemed to confirm this information about Ford's mother.

"It was extremely sensitive," Jager said, describing his own interview of Ford on Friday. Whether Jager's interview took place before or after Ford was represented by Robinson wasn't made clear by the reporters. Jager said that when he brought up the subject of Ford's mother, Ford began shaking.

"I was a little concerned he might flip out at that point because he was so upset about his mother. He absolutely did not want to talk about that."

Jager added some more insight into Ford's personality, at least as Jager perceived it.

"This seems to be a recurring pattern in his life," Jager said. "He would form attachments to women and they would dump him. That seemed to bother him a lot."

Jager added that Ford seemed filled with remorse and shame. Jager thought this was quite different from other murder suspects he had interviewed in the past. Ford claimed to have dismembered the first victim with a saw and a knife, burying the head and other body parts on the bank of the Mad River, which ran down to the ocean not far from his Arcata trailer, and from which they had apparently washed out to sea. Ford had kept two thighs from the October 1997 "torso" victim in his freezer, before burying them at a campsite near Trinidad shortly before turning himself in, Jager said.

Meanwhile, the unnamed relative claimed that Ford had told him that his ex-wife in Las Vegas had denied him the right to visit his son, which upset Ford enormously. "He would say she hurt him badly. He'd cry over it all the time. We'd tell him to try to get over it," the unnamed relative said.

Thus, by early in the week following his arrest, there had already been two possible motives suggested for Ford's actions: first, he was angry with his mother for allegedly abandoning him when he was a child; and second, he was mad at his wife for preventing visitations with his son.

As it would turn out, however, neither situation was particularly germane to Wayne Adam Ford's unhappy life, or most especially, his violent times.

3

Profiles

THROUGHOUT MOST OF THE NEXT WEEK, THE REPORTERS kept the focus on the man with the breast in his pocket; the man who'd kept severed body parts in his freezer; the man who'd driven hundreds, if not thousands of miles in a big rig with corpses of naked women as his traveling companions. The macabre nature of the alleged crimes, topped by the weird circumstances of his arrest, made Ford front-page news.

Already, several other police agencies had tried for a piece of the action on Wayne Adam Ford. One was the Sonoma County Sheriff's Department, which announced that, in August of 1998, a young prostitute working in Santa Rosa had been abducted, tied up, beaten, raped and robbed by a man in a black truck similar to that driven by Wayne Adam Ford. After the attack, the man had put the young woman out of his truck, alive, somewhere on Highway 101 near Healdsburg, California. A passerby had come to her assistance. Lieutenant Mike Brown told the news media that Ford had confessed to that attack, and that the young woman had identified Ford as her attacker.

By Tuesday, November 10, police officials were raising the possibility that Ford might have committed far more than just the four murders he had reportedly confessed to.

Kern County's Sgt. Glenn Johnson said Ford had admitted to picking up at least five women at a truck stop on Highway 58 in east Bakersfield. Johnson said Ford had said he'd tied the women up and had rough sex with them, and later threw them out of his truck, in a pattern that appeared to match the attack on the woman in Sonoma County. Ford wasn't sure whether any of the unknown five were still alive when he left them behind.

"We have to give his confession some credibility," Johnson said, "because the information on at least four deaths is panning out." Johnson said his department would expand their efforts to see whether there were other victims who hadn't yet been discovered. According to Humboldt County Sheriff Dennis Lewis, there were at least two other known murders in a jurisdiction he did not identify that appeared to be similar to those of the four victims already acknowledged by Ford. Finally, two detectives from Oakland were said to be on their way to Eureka to interview Ford in connection with two dismemberment murders there.

"The chance that he stopped at just four is slim," Johnson told the *San Francisco Chronicle*. "But we have to compare our notes to figure this all out."

Figuring this all out was on the minds of the news reporters, as well. Some worked to develop a quick portrait of Ford, scouring neighbors, co-workers, relatives and even casual acquaintances for attributes and anecdotes; the public soon learned that Ford had recently become interested in religion, that he occasionally attended church, that he had been influenced by the owner of a Eureka store that sold religious supplies; others recalled Ford's fondness for Garth Brooks' songs, and said he had taught himself to sing and play the guitar, and hoped one day to make a career as a country singer.

Ford's past was also brought into the picture: he was reported to be a U.S. Marine Corps veteran who'd received a medical discharge years before; afterward he'd delivered newspapers for a living in Orange County, and had driven a school bus for handicapped children there; he'd been a karaoke dj at a Japanese restaurant in San Clemente, and although he appeared to have no significant prior criminal history, he'd once been jailed for shooting a junkyard dog for no apparent reason. Others discovered that he'd driven a taxicab in Las

Vegas, that he'd worked as a tow-truck driver, a motorcycle mechanic, a lube-and-oil man, and a car salesman. Taken together, Ford seemed to be an unnaturally bright man with a lot of capabilities, who simply had gotten nowhere in his life— and who then, at the age of 36, had suddenly burst into the public awareness as a horrible serial killer.

Some reporters went to academia for answers. The *Chronicle* lassoed Mike Rustigan, a criminologist from San Francisco State University. Rustigan said he was very surprised that Ford had turned himself in, and that he had confessed.

"It's almost without precedent," Rustigan told the newspaper. "Usually they delight in trying to outwit the police, and they have absolutely no sympathy for their victims. To see genuine remorse in a guy capable of such savagery is extremely surprising." Rustigan went a bit further when he told *The San Jose Mercury News* that the fact that Ford had remorse for his actions was "truly an exception in the annals of serial killers."

Not to be outdone, the afternoon *San Francisco Examiner* called on its own expert, Jack Levin, a professor of criminology and sociology at Northeastern University in Boston, Massachusetts. Levin's take on Ford was slightly different from Rustigan's.

"He fits the profile of a serial killer motivated by the thrill," Levin told the newspaper. "Most serial killers are sexual sadists. But Ford is different in that he is not a sociopath. He feels out of control and doesn't want to kill again."

Thus, by the middle of the week following his voluntary surrender and his detailed confessions, Wayne Adam Ford would forever be known as a unique specimen: "the serial killer with a conscience," as some newspaper headline writers quickly dubbed him.

Was Ford really "a serial killer with a conscience"? Was such a person even possible, or was the very idea an oxymoron? Why did he kill? Why had he turned himself in? Who, really, were his victims? Why them? And most of all, even more than the possible reasons for his purported confession: why did Ford's pattern of murder—his so-called *modus op-*

erandi—go against every known paradigm of any other serial murderer known to history?

In other words, why was the worst crime in the beginning? And why was that October 1997 dismemberment horror followed with progressively less violent killings, and even interspersed with a number of non-fatal attacks, at least until the partial dismemberment of Patty Tamez in October of 1998?

Was there, in fact, something psychologically significant about the month of October in Wayne Adam Ford's life?

People like Pierce Brooks, the original expert in serial murder, formerly of the Los Angeles Police Department, and his intellectual descendants at the Federal Bureau of Investigation's Behavioral Science Unit at Quantico, Virginia, have long maintained that serial killers inexorably follow an escalating curve of violence: in other words, a serial killer's first killing is likely to be less gruesome than his last.

This tends to be particularly true with dismemberment killers; normally, the dismemberment gets worse as the killings progress. The classic example of this is the Jack the Ripper murders in England of the late nineteenth century, where the dismemberment grew more grotesque as the number of murders mounted. But this was hardly true of the crimes claimed by Wayne Adam Ford.

In the Ford case, the murders began with the *worst* dismemberment, that of the torso found in the slough in Eureka in October of 1997. The crimes then seemingly abated for more than eight months, followed by Gibbs (no dismemberment), the non-fatal rapes, then the White murder (no dismemberment), and finally the Tamez murder in October of 1998 (partial dismemberment).

Instead of describing an upward curve of violence, the Ford murders plotted out almost backward; even more peculiar, there were non-fatal attacks right in the middle of the series. Since this was not typical of the ordinary serial murderer, did it mean anything at all?

In retrospect, there *was* a meaning in the pattern of the victimization: the fact that it didn't seem to make any difference to Ford (at least at the time of the murders) that some lived, some died, had significance that wasn't readily apparent, either to the police or the academicians.

It wasn't the act of killing that seemed to motivate Ford, as it usually is with other serial killers; indeed, the deaths appeared to be a mere by-product of his behavior. It was only later that the fact that some *had* died seemed to have impressed on Ford the notion that he had some sort of problem, and needed help.

After first making efforts to conceal his actions—the first dismemberment, for example, and the scattering of the body parts—he eventually brought himself to the authorities' attention in the most macabre way. It was, as Levin suggested, the act of a man who knew he was out of control, and who wanted someone, anyone, to simply take over responsibility for his life. Jager, in his interview with Ford, noted that Ford, just before turning himself in, had experienced "a difficult time doing analytical functions, remembering addresses, that sort of thing."

But as it would turn out, this was hardly the first time Wayne Adam Ford had had such difficulties with his thinking and other aspects of his mental health. Was Ford in his right mind when the murders were committed? That question, it appears, wasn't initially considered by those striving to execute Wayne Adam Ford, or even explain his behavior; it was only later, as more facts came to light, that anyone considered it to have any meaning. By that time, it would seem entirely likely that, by turning himself in, Ford may have committed less an act of conscience than one of self-preservation.

There was, of course, an afterthought about Wayne Adam Ford; this one was delivered by a columnist for *The San Jose Mercury News* on November 14, 1998, one Sue Hutchison.

Hutchison observed that to write about Ford was to become part of the problem; her objection was to the celebrity that attended Ford's surrender. "It's also demoralizing," she wrote, "to know that when a 36-year-old trucker walks into the Humboldt County Sheriff's office with a woman's severed breast in a bag, he's going to be treated like a rock star. And a lot of people who are repulsed by the crimes are nevertheless going to gobble up every bit of information about him."

Hutchison found the whole thing fundamentally wrong.

"What about the victims?" she asked. "Is anyone interested in who they were? It's likely that some of the four women Ford has confessed to killing had lives just as hard and troubled as he says his has been . . . Ford may be a textbook example of the boogeyman, but the slain women don't fit the 'pristine victim' stereotype. And that means a lot more people are going to be interested in hearing his life story than theirs." In the end, Hutchison argued, giving Ford precedence in publicity over those he had murdered was to get everything backward; in a way, it was to reward notoriety at the expense of the pathetically desperate women who had become his victims.

III
WAYNE

1

Origins

WAYNE ADAM FORD WAS BORN ON DECEMBER 3, 1961, the second son of Calvin Eugene Ford, then 24, and his wife, Birgette Danzigger, who herself had been born in Berlin, Germany, in early January 1942, less than a month after the United States entered World War II. Gene Ford was born in Tulsa, Oklahoma, but had grown up on the North Coast, and joined the U.S. Army in the late 1950s when he was still quite young. It appears that he met Birgette while stationed in Germany, when both would have been teenagers. Their first child, Calvin Rodney Ford, who would become known as Rod, was born in 1959, also in Germany.

Because Ford's lawyer, San Bernardino County deputy public defender Joseph Canty, declined to allow Ford to be interviewed,[5] it wasn't possible to assemble detailed and pri-

---

5. Ford did provide an interview to a reporter from the *Los Angeles Times* in October of 1999, but this took place without Canty's knowledge. Afterward, Canty was furious, and tried to obtain a court order forbidding San Bernardino County jail personnel from providing the news media with access to Ford. Although this was denied, I felt honor-bound to accept Canty's insistence that no interviews be conducted with his client without Canty's presence, and these Canty declined to permit, even when I offered to allow Canty to sit in on the questioning. Likewise, Canty did not respond to a list of written questions I submitted through him to Ford; I can only assume he discussed the list with Ford, and that, together, they decided to maintain their silence. Likewise, a letter to Ford's brother Rod seeking an interview drew no response.

mary source information on Wayne's childhood and upbringing.

As a result, information about Ford's early life remains fairly sketchy. Most of what is now publicly known about his upbringing comes from Ford himself in communications with his first wife, Leigh, his former girlfriend, Anaya, and his second wife, Lucie.[6]

Contrary to the Eureka Ford relatives' impressions, at least in Leigh's recollection, Ford appeared to get along quite well with his mother, Birgette. In Leigh's recollection, it was his father, Gene, whom Wayne did not get along with. While Wayne did not like to talk very much about his years growing up, Leigh sensed there had been considerable antagonism between father and son. The whole subject of his relation with his father seemed to make Wayne angry, Leigh recalled. On one occasion, shortly after their marriage in May 1981, when Leigh pressed him for some detail about his relationship with his father, Wayne became so angry he smashed his fist into a wall, breaking several bones in his hand.

It was Leigh's impression, from her talks with Wayne, that Wayne's father was emotionally remote, and extremely controlling not only of his sons, but also of his young wife. Leigh recalled Wayne telling her that when he was a small boy, his father had locked him out of the house for an entire night because of some sort of childhood transgression; this appeared to be a punishment that had had a traumatic effect on young Wayne, at least as Leigh perceived it.

It seemed to be a given among the Fords of the North Coast—Gene's brother Jimmy, and sisters Dorris (cq) and Vicki—that neither Wayne nor Rod received much in the way of love from their father *or* their mother.[7] Vicky's husband Dale believed that Wayne had always longed for recognition and acceptance from his father, but never got it.

---

6. Leigh, Anaya and Lucie are pseudonyms used by the author to protect the privacy of the three women.
7. Interview of Ford family members by Eureka Police Detective Dave Parris, January 8, 1999, Report #3c98-10245.

According to the family members, the relationship between Gene and Birgette (spelled "Brigetta" on some documents) seemed to be rocky throughout the 1960s, when both Rod and Wayne were children. Sometime in 1971, the marriage finally broke apart, with Birgette gaining custody of at least Wayne by order of the Sonoma County Superior Court in July of 1971, when Wayne would have been nine years old. It appears that Wayne may have lived with his mother for some period of time after the divorce, but Birgette, then only 28 years old or so, soon decided to make a drastic change in her life.

According to some accounts, Birgette may have joined the Peace Corps, eventually traveling to India for service there. This would account for the Ford family stories contending that Wayne had been abandoned by his mother; some thought Birgette should have put aside her own desires and stayed behind to care for Wayne. In any event, custody of Wayne was taken over by Gene, then living in Napa, California. Gene later remarried.

Sometime in perhaps the mid-1970s, when Wayne was 14 or so, he was caught breaking into a store in Napa and referred to juvenile court.[8] Because records of juvenile offenses are routinely destroyed in the state of California after ten years, there is no way to know for certain exactly what happened. It appears, however, that Wayne was given a probationary sentence, with a promise of expungement if he kept his nose clean.

Subsequent to his juvenile arrest, Wayne went to live with his Uncle Jimmy in Eureka. In Jimmy's view, Wayne seemed to have no obvious problems—at least, if believing that neither of his parents cared very much for him wasn't a problem. But it does seem that there may have been some emotional disturbances lurking under Wayne's apparently placid exterior: at one point, Uncle Jimmy recalled, Wayne ran away from home and went to Arcata. According to Jimmy, Wayne felt guilty about violating his juvenile probation, so he called the juvenile probation agency to turn himself in. Juvenile probation called

---

8. Interview of Ford's uncle, Jimmy, by Detective Parris, as cited above.

Jimmy, who went to Arcata to pick Wayne up.

This may seem like an ordinary case of teenage angst, at least until one realizes that a bit over twenty years later, Wayne was again in Arcata and similarly turned himself in. In both cases one might discern a cry for help from someone who felt his life had gone out of control.

Despite his half-hearted attempt to run away from his uncle's house in 1976, Wayne must have successfully completed his course of probation and had his crime expunged from the record, because when he enlisted in the Marines a few years later, his enlistment sheet showed no crimes, and Wayne himself claimed no arrests, and no convictions.

At some point in 1977 or so, Birgette returned to the Sonoma area; it appears that she had also remarried, according to Sonoma court records. That year, Wayne moved in with his mother in Santa Rosa. He dropped out of high school and went to work as a laborer for a construction company. In early 1978, Wayne was in a car accident, and broke his foot. Birgette filed a claim with the driver's insurance company on Wayne's behalf. The company agreed to pay Wayne's medical bills, and to turn over about $1,600 to Birgette for her use in buying a car for then 16-year-old Wayne.

Two weeks after his seventeenth birthday, in December of 1978, Wayne enlisted in the Marines. In joining the Corps, Wayne said his objective was to earn enough money to pay for a college education. Despite his lack of a high school degree, he scored more than 91 percent on the Corps' enlistment aptitude test. He was clearly very bright, if still very raw.

On January 17, 1979, Wayne reported for active duty in the United States Marines; eventually, he would spend a bit over five years as a Marine, and by the time he got out, he would be a changed man.

2

USMC and the Accident

BY OCTOBER OF 1980, WAYNE HAD BEEN A U.S. MARINE for twenty-two months. His journey from a callow youth of 17 to a skilled fighting man was remarkable. Judging from Wayne's Marine Corps personnel records, he had adjusted exceedingly well to the rigor of the highly disciplined Corps. His fitness reports were uniform in their praise of his intelligence and his abilities; all in all, it appeared that Wayne was well-launched on a promising military career. Most significant, in marked contrast to his next few years in the Marines, Wayne had absolutely no disciplinary problems. On paper, at least, it appeared that Wayne was a perfect Marine—dedicated, focused, enthusiastic and smart—exactly the sort of enlistee the Corps craved. As far as the Marines could see, Wayne's future was unlimited.

Wayne's first duty post was at the Marine Corps Air Station at El Toro, in Orange County, California. His military speciality was in defending against nuclear, biological and chemical warfare. Protecting a Marine air wing from such types of attack demanded someone who was calm, careful and quite methodical, a person capable of learning and applying the often complex protocols of coping with poison gasses, radiation or virulent viruses and bacteria, and Wayne was eminently capable, at least in the views of his superiors.

By that fall, Wayne had grown into the strapping man he was to be: a bit over six feet, close to 200 pounds. He routinely graded out at the top of his unit in physical fitness, capable of running for miles, performing hundreds of push-ups on command—in sum, lithe, agile and strong. Wayne's excellent record brought quick promotions—first to private first class, followed nine months later, when he was still just 18 years old, to lance corporal.

In addition to his Marine duties at the El Toro base, Wayne also had a part-time job at a pizza parlor in nearby Irvine. It was there, through a mutual friend, that he met a beautiful young woman, Leigh, who was a student at the nearby University of California at Irvine in late October of 1980.

It was, Leigh said years later, Wayne's hard-muscled taciturnity that originally intrigued her. "I was at a period in my life where I was attracted by the macho ploy," Leigh observed. "You know, the silent type."

Gazing back across the divide of almost two decades, after a second marriage and two daughters of her own, Leigh had grown into a wisdom that would have been missed by the 18-year-old she was when she first met her husband-to-be. Whereas in 1980, Leigh had seen a handsome young man of 19, polite and well-groomed, who kept himself under control, by 1998, when she was eventually interviewed by the police, Leigh had reached a rather more insightful perception of Wayne.

When she first met him, Leigh was later to realize, Wayne was just a boy—a boy in a man's body, true, but a boy just the same. At the time, his macho demeanor had seemed mysterious, even powerful; it was only in looking back that Leigh could realize that Wayne was silent only because he had nothing to say. Having armored himself inside a stoic, ultra-masculine exterior, Wayne ran away from emotions as fast as his carefully crafted persona could carry him.

In retrospect, to Leigh, this seemed to be the consequence of Wayne's upbringing in an environment in which a remote, controlling father dominated his young wife and two sons. Wayne had feelings, but all roads to expression of them, save for lust and anger, were blocked.

When she tried to find out more about Wayne's family— her own family was very important to Leigh—Wayne seemed to clam up even more; it was as if the whole subject was off-limits.

And Wayne very quickly exhibited a peculiar sort of contradictory behavior toward Leigh herself. After a few dates, and after Leigh had made it clear she was interested in him, Wayne did not call her for more than a week. When she saw him next, Leigh asked why he hadn't called. Wayne told her he'd forgotten her telephone number.

"Wayne was kind of stand-offish," Leigh was to recall. "And so it was interesting, because he was treating it like he could take it or leave it."

But just when Leigh decided that Wayne wasn't really interested in her, he showed up one day at her apartment in Irvine—almost a fifteen-mile hike from the base at El Toro, as Leigh later calculated.

In psychological terms, this early ambivalence by Wayne probably has significance; in some important aspects, it was to foreshadow a pattern of behavior that was eventually to have fatal results. Even at this stage of his life, Wayne was exhibiting evidence of a serious psychic conflict: his desire to be with Leigh was at war with his fear of intimacy, and with all of intimacy's threats of vulnerability—for Wayne, to love was to leave oneself unprotected; better, in Wayne's secret heart, never to love at all.

But all of these realizations were still in Leigh's future that October of 1980; what she could only see then was that a handsome young Marine seemed smitten by her, and that was enough.

By early December, the relationship between Leigh and Wayne had advanced, and Wayne was beginning, slowly, to emerge from his shell. On the night of Saturday, December 6, Wayne and Leigh went for a late dinner at Orange Hill Restaurant, a fashionable dining spot in the hills overlooking the city of Tustin, not far from the El Toro Marine base.

Shortly before one in the morning, as Leigh was driving with Wayne southbound on the Santa Ana Freeway, I-5, heading toward the off-ramp that would take them back to Leigh's UCI-area apartment, they passed two cars off to the side of the freeway. It was clear they had just been involved in an accident. Leigh stopped her car, and Wayne got out to check the condition of the two drivers. One man appeared to be seriously injured. Wayne ran back to Leigh, who was still behind the wheel of her own car, and told her to get help. Leigh drove off to find a telephone.

It took Leigh some minutes to find a phone, and when she was done, she was somewhat disoriented. She drove around for a time trying to find her way back onto the freeway. Eventually she made it back to the scene of the accident.

"By the time I got there," she recalled, "there were fire trucks, policemen . . . I start looking for Wayne, and I can't find him. And I'm asking the firemen, 'Big, tall Marine, have you seen him? You know, a jarhead, you can't miss the haircut.' "

But no one seemed to know what had happened to Wayne.

"They kept asking me if I'd seen the third car," Leigh recalled. "And I said, 'Well, I was the third car.' And they were saying, 'No, no, the red car.' " Leigh had no idea what the firemen were talking about. Eventually she left the scene; she had no idea where Wayne had gone.

The next morning, Leigh heard from their mutual friend that Wayne was in a Tustin hospital; it turned out that after she had gone for help, another car had indeed come by. This one had hit Wayne and a second man, knocking them both over an embankment down into a ditch thirty or forty feet below. By the time she had gotten back to the accident scene the night before, Wayne and the other man had already been taken to the hospital, where Wayne was now in intensive care with severe injuries to his head, face and left side. In all, he would be in intensive care at Tustin Community Hospital for nine days.

The human brain is by far the most fragile organ of the body. About three pounds of pinkish-gray tissue, comprising about 10 billion electro-chemical cells, the brain is composed of three basic parts: the cerebrum, the cerebellum, and the brain stem, also known as the medulla oblongata. The cerebrum, representing about 85 percent of the total weight of the brain, is further divided into lobes: the frontal, parietal, temporal, occipital and insula lobes, one each on each side of the brain, and each having responsibility for specialized tasks. The frontal lobes, for example, are thought to be the center of consciousness, thinking, judgment and memory, while the other lobes deal with such phenomena as language, spatial orientation, abstract reasoning, and visualization.

It is difficult to conceive of any other organic evolution on the planet, going back to the Earth's origins, that has anywhere near the complexity of the human brain; as compared to other animals in the history of the fossil record, the human brain stands (so far) as the very acme of biochemical sophistication. That such a complicated construction could be made so compact, and so adaptable to environmental conditions, is in itself the story of the success of the human species.

As it has evolved, the brain exists as the control center for every type of life-sustaining action: from the automatic equipment that enables us to breathe (whether we want to or not) to the higher functions that lead to sublime poetry, music, logic, abstract imagination and reasoning, that three-pound lump of tissue enables us to exist, and more, enables us to climb out of ourselves and think of the universe that exists beyond our immediate physical needs. Even more remarkable, the entire gizmo is contained within a hard shell, the skull, designed to protect it in case things go wrong.

But if the skull is our protection, it is also one of our great weaknesses. Because the brain essentially floats freely within the skull cavity—doubtless for reasons of fluidity, temperature control and survivability—it remains vulnerable to violent forces. A severe impact, for example, can send the entire brain bouncing from one end of the skull to the other; these so-called contrecoup injuries can decimate the complicated bioelectrical connections inside the brain in ways that even the brain surgeons do not totally understand.

When, for example, an adult male, standing on an embankment, with his back turned to an onrushing car, is struck—and then falls a considerable distance into a drainage ditch, where he is subsequently discovered unconscious—the chances are that the man's brain has sustained a rather considerable rattling; that is, the banging of the entire organ from one side of the skull to the other, and back again. On just about any given Sunday, television viewers watching a pro football game will recognize the phenomenon: the announcers will say that so-and-so "had his bell rung"; what they are really talking about is a concussion; what's only becoming clear now is that a concussion, even a so-called minor one, causes some amount of brain damage. And when one is knocked unconscious, the brain damage is yet more severe. When one is put into a coma—at least from a head injury resulting from a violent collision—the damage is greater yet, depending on the severity and length of the coma.

When Wayne was hit by "the red car"—how anyone knew it was red was a mystery twenty years later, since almost all of the records of the incident had by then disappeared—he'd had his back turned to it; he probably never knew what hit him. By the time the paramedics from the Orange County Fire Department arrived on the scene, at the Myford Road overcrossing of I-5, shortly after 1:30 a.m. on December 6,[9] Wayne was lying in the ditch below the embankment, completely unconscious.

Wayne was quickly rushed to Tustin Community Hospital, one of two establishments authorized to accept trauma victims in the immediate vicinity. Eventually, the hospital would go out of business, and the facility would be converted to a nursing home. But in 1980, it would be the primary caregiver to Wayne in the aftermath of the hit-and-run—responsible for his various examinations and surgeries as the next week unfolded.[10]

---

9. Orange County Fire Department log, traffic accident #27925. Years later, the accident report of the fire department had been destroyed, as had records of the California Highway Patrol, and of the hospital where Wayne was taken; thus, the facts about Wayne's injuries, and his diagnosis and treatment could only be reconstructed by anecdote.

10. Unfortunately, California law requires hospitals to retain their medical records for only seven years; by the time Wayne's injuries became vital to his defense, the records no longer existed.

Two decades after his hospitalization, there would be controversy over the extent of Wayne's injuries. This was partly due to his own statements; in his interview with the reporter from *The Los Angeles Times* in October of 1999, Wayne appeared to have claimed that he had been in a coma for nine days as a result of the accident. Leigh, however, remembered it quite differently. In her recollection, Wayne was conscious the following morning, and was even fairly talkative.

As Leigh recalled the story, after leaving the accident scene, she had driven around the area for some time, looking for Wayne, without success. Eventually she returned to her apartment in the university area. Given the fact that Wayne had once walked fifteen miles to see her, Leigh thought it entirely possible that he had simply left the accident scene and walked back to the Marine base. Still, the whole thing was puzzling.

The next morning, however, one of Leigh's roommates at the UCI apartment phoned her to say that the hospital had been calling. This was when Leigh learned that Wayne had been hit by a car and seriously injured. Leigh went to Tustin Community Hospital; she was sure she wouldn't be allowed to see Wayne. But when she arrived, a nurse told her that Wayne had been demanding to talk to her for hours, or at least, ever since he had regained consciousness.[11]

When she got in to see Wayne, Leigh saw that he was a mess. The car that clobbered him had sent him soaring into the ditch, where he had landed on his face. Wayne's four front teeth had been knocked out, and most of his upper lip had nearly been torn off. He'd broken his upper mandible. The

---

11. The question of exactly when Leigh first saw Wayne would later become important; while Leigh told police in 1999, and the author in 2000, that she saw Ford the morning after the accident, she also said that she met Wayne's mother at the hospital, and that Birgette had been there first. This seems to suggest that it might have been at least one day, or perhaps more, before Leigh actually saw Wayne for the first time after the accident, which in turn could buttress Wayne's assertion that he was in a coma for a number of hours, or maybe days; this in turn would lend support to Ford's assertion that he suffered brain damage as a result of the car wreck, because the longer one is in a coma, the greater the likelihood of brain damage.

doctors had spent much of the night extracting bits and pieces of his broken teeth from his mouth. Wayne told Leigh that if he'd been a prisoner of war, and had been made to undergo the broken-tooth extraction operation as a torture, he would have told the enemy anything they wanted to know, the pain was that bad.

"I mean," Leigh said later,[12] "his whole face was like a balloon. It was swollen so bad, his lip, they'd sewn it back . . . but it had to have been two inches thick, all swollen and everything."

It was that same day that Leigh was introduced to Wayne's mother. Having been notified that Wayne was in the hospital, Birgette had immediately come to Southern California to be with her son, which perhaps stands as evidence that Wayne's mother was hardly the uncaring, abandoning figure later depicted by her ex-husband's relatives to the news media.

The later loss of the medical records from Ford's stay at the hospital was most unfortunate, not least from the point of view of Ford's defense lawyers. Leigh was to later recall that the bill for treatment of the injuries had come to more than $10,000, which was paid by the Marine Corps' insurance agency, Champas; but her anecdotal description of Ford's injuries were certainly consistent with the sort of trauma that one might expect to be accompanied by a severe head injury. However long Ford had been knocked out—whether hours or days—it was still clear that the blow from the hit-and-run red car (which was never identified by any police agency) had put Ford's lights out, for at least some substantial period of time.

---

12. Interview with Leigh by Humboldt County Detective Juan Freeman, January 14, 1999.

3

Brain Damage

ALMOST TWO DECADES LATER, WELL AFTER FORD HAD turned himself in as the serial killing truck driver from hell in 1998, the issue of Ford's injuries in the December 6, 1980, accident was to become critical, probably even vital evidence in the case against him. As Ford explained to *Los Angeles Times* reporter James Rainey in the unauthorized interview of October 1999, while he might have killed the women he was charged with murdering, and while he might have to spend the rest of his life locked up, he didn't deserve to die. His 1980 head injury, Ford told Rainey, had caused him to do what he had done, and so, he wasn't legally responsible. Shrinks in Humboldt County, hired by Kevin Robinson, had told him this was so, Ford added.

Rainey (no relation to the state senator of the same last name) then dutifully contacted David Whitney, the San Bernardino County Deputy District Attorney who was scheduled to try Ford for the four murders. Whitney told Rainey that Ford's claims of a head injury might easily be discounted; such assertions, Whitney told Rainey, were "de rigueur" in death penalty cases. But Whitney admitted he didn't have enough information yet (in October of 1999) to know whether Ford's claim was valid.

Rainey then contacted criminologist Mike Rustigan from San Francisco State University. At this point Rustigan appeared to fall back a bit from his earlier claims that Ford's remorse was something new in the annals of serial killerdom.

He told Rainey that Ford's head injury defense was typical of multiple killers.

"Before," Rustigan told Rainey, "he was apparently saying that his wife leaving him triggered his rage; it was a psychological explanation. And now he is focusing on brain damage. It looks like they're flailing for a defense."

But was this really bunkum—the idea that a head injury might make somebody homicidal? I wasn't sure that such claims were at all typical of serial killers, whatever Rustigan believed. I didn't remember Ted Bundy making any such claim, or John Wayne Gacy, or any of the serial killers I had written about. I kept coming back to the fact that Ford's pattern of murder was quite atypical. Most serial killers murder for the thrill of killing; the more I learned, the more it seemed to me that Ford's crimes had almost nothing of the anticipation and planning that bona fide serial murderers usually demonstrated.

I contacted a forensic psychiatrist in Seattle, an expert on mental illness and the law, who had testified for both the prosecution and defense in previous criminal cases, and asked if it was really possible that a head injury could alter behavior, even to the extent of turning a law-abiding person into a serial killer.

My friend the psychiatrist assured me that it was, at least in theory, possible. But, he warned, the entire area was subject to confusion. Where did the anti-social personality end and the head injury begin? It was difficult, my friend stressed, to say which, if either—or anything—was the actual proximate cause of murderous behavior. The science of mental assessment was far too rudimentary as yet to delineate such boundaries.

My friend referred me to an authority in the field: Dr. William Alwyn Lishman's textbook, *Organic Psychiatry: the Psychological Consequences of Cerebral Disorder.*[13] My friend the shrink assured me that Lishman's book was the standard,

13. Dr. William Alwyn Lishman is Emeritus Professor of Neuropsychiatry at the Institute of Psychiatry, London; and, among other qualifications, Honorary Life President of the British Neuropsychiatry Association.

and that it dealt extensively with the behavioral effects of head injuries such as that claimed by Ford.

I went to the San Francisco Public Library in search of Professor Lishman's book; not surprisingly, it wasn't in the collection. I called the University of California at San Francisco, operators of the local medical school, and discovered that the text, in paperback, was available at the university bookstore for the price of $114.

This is nuts, I thought, as I wrote a check to the university for $123 (tax included). *I probably won't even be able to read the thing.* The big fat paperback looked impressive, but after all, was it really worth that much money, at least for my purposes?[14]

But in all fairness to Professor Lishman, his book wasn't that impenetrable (even if it was expensive). Indeed, *Organic Psychiatry* had an entire section on head injuries, and their behavioral consequences. When I was done reading, I thought about recommending it to both Whitney and Rustigan, neither of whom, obviously, had read it.

The way Lishman explained it, there are all kinds of things that can go wrong with your brain. And what's worse, often no one can be sure exactly why.

Lishman readily admitted that it was difficult, sometimes even impossible, to distinguish between behaviors caused by psycho-social factors such as character disorders, and those caused by brain injuries. Aberrant behavior that might be attributed to some sort of brain injury could, in fact, have preexisted the injury. The only way to separate the two, Lishman

---

14. Dr. Lishman's book, *Organic Psychiatry*, Blackwell Science Ltd., Oxford, United Kingdom, third edition, 1996, runs to over 900 pages, and comprises Lishman's review of all manner of organic psychiatry, including clinical examination protocols, and information about specific disorders, including head injury, epilepsy, brain tumors, encephalitis, consequences of stroke, Alzheimer's, chemical imbalances, vitamin deficiencies, drug and alcohol disorders, Parkinson's disease, and scores of other brain problems I'd never heard of before, and wasn't sure I wanted to, given some of the dire consequences outlined by Lishman.

contended, is to find out as much as possible about the patient's life and behavior before the injury in an effort to determine whether the patient was predisposed to the aberrant behavior even without the injury.

Still, Lishman noted, "The psychological disturbances which result from brain pathology [i.e., injury or illness] often share common ground which cuts across differences in background, personality and social situation." In other words, two people with vastly different upbringings and social orientations, but both with the same kind of head injuries, may still show the same sort of aberrant behavior, suggesting that such head injuries may be the cause.

"Brain damage," Lishman noted, "often results in changes of temperament, or changed patterns of reaction to events and to other people. As a result, behavioral tendencies which have previously been enduring characteristics of the individual are found to be altered. Areas typically affected include the control of emotions and impulses, and aspects of motivation and social judgment." Frequently, Lishman added, such "organic personality change" may be the result of injuries to the frontal lobes of the brain.

"Most characteristic [of frontal lobe injuries] is disinhibition, with expansive over-familiarity, tactlessness, overtalkativeness, childish excitement," Lishman noted. "Social and ethical control may be diminished, with a lack of concern for the future and for the consequence of actions . . . sexual indiscretions and petty misdemeanors may occur, or gross errors of judgement with regard to financial and interpersonal matters. Sometimes there is marked indifference, even callous unconcern, for the feelings of others . . ."

In addition, a person with an injury to the frontal lobes may suffer from an impaired ability to concentrate and to get things done. His memory may be deficient. He may have problems with insomnia, or with involuntary oversleeping. Motivation may become diffuse as a feeling of ennui invades all aspects of life.

This is not to say that a person with a frontal lobe injury has been rendered less intelligent; often people with head injuries perform as well on standardized intelligence tests after the injury as they did before, Lishman said. The damage is less to the intellect than it is to the quality of character, it appears.

By far the most common causes of frontal lobe injuries are blows to the head, such as the one Ford surely must have sustained in the Myford Road accident. Lishman noted that in 1992 in the United States alone, more than a million people sustained head injuries severe enough to require hospitalization, "and from these 30,000 to 50,000 persons have such serious intellectual and behavioral dysfunction that they are unable to return to normal life."[15]

Head injuries are so common, in fact, that the medical people have even developed a term for one of the most frequent pathologies that result: *frontal lobe syndrome*.

"In the typical case [of frontal lobe syndrome]," Lishman wrote, "the personality of the patient is more profoundly and obviously affected than his cognitive functions. The striking changes in well-marked examples are in the area of volitional and psychomotor activity, habitual mood and social awareness and behavior."

Often people with frontal lobe syndrome have difficulty completing tasks—reminiscent of Jager's report that Ford had been having difficulty with analytical functions and memory. "In consequence the capacity to function independently in daily life can be profoundly affected," Lishman noted. "Yet, when vigorously urged, or constrained by a structured situation, the patient may function quite well."

The most obvious effects of frontal lobe syndrome occur in the areas of relations with other people, according to Lishman. "Typically the patient is less concerned with the consequences of his acts than formerly. Loss of 'finer feelings' and social graces form part of a general coarsening of the personality. In interpersonal relationships there is a lack of normal adult tact and restraints, and a diminished appreciation of the impact of his behavior upon others. Disinhibition is sometimes

---

15. Lishman attributed his statistics to the National Head Injury Foundation.

apparent in the sexual sphere with lewd remarks, promiscuity or the emergence of perverse tendencies . . ."

Just how does a brain injury actually affect behavior? No one at present is entirely sure, although a number of theories have been advanced, according to Lishman. One possibility is that the disruption of brain cells due to injury removes the sort of learned restraints on behavior that have accumulated through socialization over the years.

In cases where the injury has created a contrecoup effect— the bouncing of the brain from one side of the skull to the other—the damage may occur because nerve cells in the brain have literally been stretched.

"Acceleration injuries," Lishman reported, "as in the impact of a car with the head, or deceleration injuries, as when a motorcyclist hits a wall after flying through the air, cause swirling movements throughout the brain . . . the resulting rotational and linear stresses tear and damage nerve fibres throughout the brain."

As the cells stretch and rip during the bouncing, the axial connections leading to adjacent cells are severed, causing the nerve cell to essentially curl in on itself; eventually, the cell withers and dies. When the cell dies, the fragment of information stored within it—whether part of a memory of a sound, a feeling, an odor, or an abstract idea—is essentially wiped out.

Thus, if some theorists are correct, one of the results of a brain injury may be the effective erasure of a lifelong series of patterned responses to stimuli; while the higher intellect may remain intact, the social "brakes" on behavior, the bioelectrical "circuits," learned through a complex system of socialization going back to the earliest years of consciousness, may be essentially ripped out. In the most extreme form, it may be as if a person has been reborn, with all the intellectual awareness of an adult, but with all the social consciousness of an infant. In many ways, this is the very definition of a psychopath, albeit one created by an accident, rather than one by lifelong conditioning.

According to Lishman, the severity of the brain damage

might be gauged by the length of unconsciousness. Studies of thousands of people, in both Great Britain and the United States, seem to indicate that the longer a person is out, the greater the likelihood of brain damage. In cases in which a contrecoup injury induces a coma lasting a week or longer, according to the studies, the chances of serious behavioral disorder upon return to consciousness are greater than 70 percent. But even momentary loss of consciousness may create significant brain damage, Lishman reported; it all depends on where the injury might have occurred, coupled with the patient's previous mental state.

In another section of his text, dealing with the effects of alcohol on the brain, Professor Lishman noted that there is a "well-known increased susceptibility to severe intoxication in the presence of brain damage." Lishman also noted that brain-damaged people who consume excessive amounts of alcohol "may be particularly liable" to display violent behavior. Afterward, the person frequently has no memory of this behavior. Likewise, Lishman noted that brain-damaged people are more likely to suffer from alcoholic blackouts than people without brain damage.

Lishman's discussion about the causes and effects of brain damage—particularly head injuries—on behavior was quite helpful, at least in the abstract. What I now wanted to know was whether there was any empirical evidence: if anyone had established that head injuries and murder might be connected.

My psychiatrist friend in Seattle now steered me to another source—Dr. Dorothy Otnow Lewis, et al. Dr. Lewis is a professor at the New York University School of Medicine. In a study conducted with four other mental health professionals in 1986, Dr. Lewis examined the "psychiatric, neurological and psycho-educational characteristics of 15 death row inmates in the United States."[16]

In this study, Dr. Lewis and her associates examined the lives of fifteen people who had been sentenced to death in the

---

16. Lewis, Pincus, Feldman, Jackson and Bard, *American Journal of Psychiatry*, July 1986.

United States between 1976, when the death penalty was re-instated, and 1984. Most of the subjects were selected because they had exhausted almost all of their appeals, and were therefore subject to execution. In other words, the criteria for inclusion in the study was established by circumstance, rather than by background.

Strikingly, *all fifteen* of the condemned subjects examined by the Lewis team (thirteen men and two women) had sustained significant head injuries at different times in their lives prior to their capital crimes. Almost all of the subjects of the study exhibited evidence of brain dysfunction, most frequently blackouts in which events took place that the subject had no memory of. Often the convict had either attempted suicide, or had expressed a desire to commit suicide prior to the crime(s) which had led to incarceration. Many had experience with mental health professionals at various times before the crimes leading to their conviction.

"To date," Lewis reported, "very little has been known about the neuropsychiatric status of persons condemned to death. In fact, most studies have been conducted by lawyers and sociologists and have focused on the racial characteristics of condemned individuals and their victims rather than on clinical issues . . . [T]o the best of our knowledge, there have been no systematic clinical investigations of the neuropsychiatric status of individuals condemned to death."

If Lishman and Lewis were right, it seemed to indicate that brain injuries could indeed precipitate homicidal action. Such people might not be legally insane under the prevailing standard—in other words, they knew the difference between right and wrong—but appeared to lack some sort of internal mechanism that ordinarily prevented people from killing.

This indeed threatened to open a vast gray area in the study of murder. One might understand and roundly condemn a killing for profit, such as in an armed robbery, or a paid assassination; or excuse a demonstrably crazy person who heard voices and saw visions that led him to kill; but if Lishman and Lewis were right, there might be a huge middle ground of murderers who were legally neither sane nor insane, but who might still be said to have some form of mitigating brain damage—damage that could have permitted otherwise law-abiding people to commit the ultimate crime.

In turn, this probably accounted for the resistance to the idea of brain damage by prosecutors such as David Whitney—"de rigueur in death penalty cases"—because, if there was empirical evidence suggesting that many murders in the United States might involve some degree of brain injury, a gigantic area of reasonable doubt, at least about intent, might be established. Such a finding could in turn make it far more difficult to gain convictions, especially in death penalty cases.

And this in turn was political, because convictions (the more the better) and steadfastness for the death penalty, had become the standard of electability for district attorneys, at least in California by the late 1990s. In an era in which being "tough on crime" was the standard employed by those who sought to be elected to public offices that administered the principal organs of justice, making crimes such as those Wayne Alan Ford had been accused of into simple matters of right and wrong was politically critical—as was the elected official's commitment to their prosecution.

Did someone kill someone? If they did, should they be given the death penalty? Saying yes to both questions had, by the late 1990s, become an important way of maintaining incumbency, particularly for an elected prosecutor pledged to protect the public from depredations such as those attributed to people like Wayne Adam Ford; punishing accused serial killers was a sure path to voter approval. It was entirely easy to stand up and say one was against murder; and *enormously easy* to say that such apparently wanton *multiple* murderers should die.

It was a great deal harder politically, however, to publicly acknowledge there might be mitigating circumstances associated with such crimes, or to accept the fact that under certain circumstances, *anyone* might have been in the position of Wayne Adam Ford—that is, if one believed in the findings of shrinks like Lishman and Lewis.

Under these circumstances, to admit an entirely new area of legal dispute, about the relevance of brain damage, especially when the political environment ardently wishes a case to be a simple matter of right or wrong, can be, to say the least, unwelcome.

Almost all of the people I met on the road of finding out more about Wayne Adam Ford utterly rejected the notion that there might be any excuse for his crimes. They wanted to see him die.

As one court reporter [not named anywhere in this book] once put it to me, "Why should we pay to support him [in prison] for the rest of his life?"

Ford had killed, went her reasoning, and therefore should *be* killed. All the psychiatric mumbo-jumbo about head injuries, brain damage, blackouts, involuntary actions, was just so much teary do-gooderism, just the sort of thing that slick defense lawyers used to pull the wool over people's eyes. The sooner Wayne Ford was dead, the better, she told me; and a great many in California agreed with her.

I saw this sentiment as both understandable and flawed. Most people were sickened by the level of violence in America: the mindless wastage of lives; killing the killers seemed to be one way to Just Say No. The real problem remained, however: for every one we killed, there would be others to take their place, unless we began to understand what made them tick.

But of course, none of these things are quite so simple. As applied to Wayne Adam Ford, the question was: was there any evidence at all that Wayne had suffered brain damage in the hit-and-run accident; and even if he did, what evidence was there that the brain damage had played a significant role in the murders he was accused of?

It's one thing to theorize, and another to inventory, as Lishman and Lewis had done; it's quite another thing entirely to sift the facts for evidence. It was for that reason, among others that I became so adamant in my insistence that "the People," as the prosecutors called themselves, ought to lay out the known facts of the murders blamed on Wayne Adam Ford; to the extent that the circumstances behind the crimes could be obscured, it was an advantage to the prosecution, in that any information that tended to mitigate Ford's crimes might be publicly suppressed.

I had no desire to see Wayne Ford walking free; indeed, the prospect was chilling. Whatever else one believed about him, the facts seemed to indicate that he was a killing machine; letting him loose seemed the height of foolishness, because he was almost certain to kill again. But killing Ford in retaliation did not seem to me to be the answer. And even Ford himself seemed to agree that he should not be freed, when he had told *The Los Angeles Times*' James Rainey that he should be locked up for the rest of his life.

The essential question, to me, was whether there had been significant evidence of brain damage in Wayne Adam Ford in the years prior to the murders. In one way, this was pertinent to the issue of whether Ford should be executed. But in a far larger sense, it was pertinent to whether any of the murders Ford was accused of could have been prevented. And as some of the documents I so laboriously prised out of the San Bernardino Courts were to reveal, there *was* such evidence, if one only knew what to look for. One of the first places Ford's brain damage was to manifest itself was in his forthcoming marriage to Leigh.

4

Leigh and Wayne

IN THE MIDDLE OF DECEMBER OF 1980, FORD CHECKED OUT of Tustin Community Hospital, accompanied by Leigh. Leigh took Wayne to her apartment near the university. As she recalled the events, much later, her three roommates were absent for Christmas vacation.

For the next two weeks or so, Wayne stayed at Leigh's UCI apartment, while she took care of him. Wayne was incredibly sore from the bashing he'd experienced being blindsided by the still-unidentified red car. Leigh had to help him to the bathroom, and to prepare food he could get down, given the sorry state of his mouth.

Later Leigh was to observe that the experience of her taking care of Wayne had brought them "closer together." But in another sense, she didn't really know him very well at all. Interacting with Wayne in a situation in which he was significantly dependent on her had the effect of making him seem more vulnerable, and thus softer to Leigh. And in another sense, Wayne received from Leigh the sort of mothering that he hadn't enjoyed since he was a small boy, which seems to have also affected him as well.

Shortly after Christmas, Wayne and Leigh flew to northern California, where they visited Wayne's mother, her boyfriend from India, and Wayne's brother Rod. It doesn't appear, from Leigh's recollection of this trip, that they visited Wayne's father, Gene, in Napa; Leigh does recall seeing some of Wayne's relatives from Eureka, including, possibly, Uncle Jimmy. After

perhaps a week in the Santa Rosa area, Wayne and Leigh
returned to southern California, this time driving a 1953 Chevy
Wayne had bought from his brother Rod. The car was almost
ten years older than either of them.

After the first of the year, Wayne went back to the Marines,
while Leigh returned to school. The two continued dating, and
sometime around February began talking about getting married.

It is fair to point out that in the aftermath of the December
accident, Leigh did not observe any particular behavior on
Wayne's part that might have suggested that he had sustained
brain damage; but if many of the symptoms of frontal lobe
syndrome involve changes in personality, it also has to be
observed that Leigh barely knew Wayne before the wreck. If
there *were* changes in his personality, in other words, it wasn't
likely that she would have been able to recognize them.

And any alterations in Wayne's behavior would likely have
been masked by the circumstances: that Leigh was taking care
of Wayne, which had the effect of making him seem vulnerable. It was only later that Leigh learned there was more—or
less—to Wayne than she had first thought. But that wasn't
readily apparent as she mothered him in the aftermath of the
accident. Still, at least on the surface, in the first months of
1981, Wayne seemed to be a good match. He was handsome,
and he was smart. He also seemed ambitious, to Leigh.

Perhaps significantly, there is no evidence in Wayne Ford's
Marine Corps records that indicates that anyone in his chain
of command knew anything about the wreck, or Wayne's injuries. That probably was deceptive: undoubtedly Wayne's superiors must have known *something* of the events of early
December. Still, in the absence of any Marine record indicat-
ing follow-up medical treatment, it seems likely that the Marines considered the injuries Wayne had sustained to be less
than serious. So what if he'd had his bell rung? They were
Marines—the few, the proud—and getting knocked out for a
substantial period of time may have been seen as the sort of
thing any real Marine might be relied upon to endure with no

ill effects. Certainly there was no notation in Ford's records that some of his future problems as a Marine may have stemmed from brain injuries received as a result of the accident. But the symptoms would eventually become quite apparent, even if no one in the Corps recognized them, then or later. Knocked silly or not, Wayne continued receiving superior fitness reports from his superiors throughout 1981.

By May of 1981, Wayne and Leigh had agreed to be married. As Leigh later explained it, her parents would never have supported the marriage if they had known of it in advance. This had nothing to do with Wayne, but was instead about Leigh: they wanted her to go to college and get a degree before thinking about marriage.

Wayne, however, convinced Leigh. He had a plan, he said. Servicemen with wives were entitled to an extra allowance; once they were married, the additional allotment would kick in. All they had to do was keep the marriage secret from Leigh's family until the fall of 1981, and in the meantime they could pocket the extra allowance. No harm, no foul, said Wayne, and on May 2, 1981, Wayne and Leigh were married secretly in Las Vegas, Nevada—a city that would later loom large in Wayne's personal history.

"And," Leigh said later,[17] "what our little plot was—because he was leaving for a six- or eight-week training course in Alabama—our little plot was, he gets more money if he is married. So we would get married on the sly. We'd run off and get married, we'd collect the increased dollar amount, I would stay at school, go home for the summer, and then, when I came back, we would have a big wedding."

The "plot," however, quickly ran aground. First, Leigh's sister tumbled onto the secret when one of Leigh's roommates told her. Leigh's sister told her parents, and Leigh was soon in the parental doghouse.

"So, anyway," Leigh said later, "it didn't turn out that way.

---

17. Interview of Leigh by Juan Freeman, January 14, 1999. Unless otherwise indicated, all of the quotes attributed to Leigh in this chapter were contained in this interview.

My sister caught us. My sister found out and told my mother."

Leigh's mother and father registered their disappointment by giving Leigh what amounted to the silent treatment. Leigh and Wayne took a small apartment in Tustin, while Wayne prepared to go to Alabama for much of the summer, where he was due to be trained as an instructor in nuclear, biological and chemical (NBC) warfare.

Within a week or so of the marriage, Leigh began to perceive some changes in Wayne's personality.

"Something was starting to change," Leigh recalled. "His attitude, his demeanor. He became more demanding, more domineering, just within this short period of time."

Along with this, Wayne's habitual taciturnity continued unabated. It was as if, now that he was married, he found himself involuntarily drawn into patterns of behavior that mimicked his father's.

One night, as Wayne and Leigh were sharing a bottle of wine, the conversation turned to Wayne's mother and father.

"My feeling, as a result of the conversation, was that his [father] was awfully mean to him as a child growing up." Leigh tried to press Wayne for more information.

"And he was trying to get me to shut up. And I didn't. And he basically went to kind of like threaten me, by taking a swing at me. I know he wasn't actually like aiming at me, just trying to take a swing at me to tell me to shut up. And he ended up hitting a stud in the wall, and broke the knuckles in his right hand. So [he] shattered all the knuckles, and he ended up going to Alabama with a cast on his hand."

In June, Wayne left for Fort McClellan, Alabama, but not before Leigh's family relented enough to host a wedding reception for the young couple. Leigh could tell they were still mad at her.

Worse, Leigh had discovered that she was pregnant.

Alone, sick from the pregnancy, Leigh missed her parents more than she could say. "I had basically, from eloping, almost alienated my family. They were barely talking to me, and I wasn't about to tell them that I'd a made a mistake. It just wasn't me, I couldn't do that."

Soon a long-distance dispute flared up between Leigh, in Santa Ana, and Wayne, at Fort McClellan. Leigh was supposed to draw Wayne's pay, and then send him money.

"For whatever reason the money I sent him didn't get there on time . . . and he calls me ranting and raving. And he went out and hocked his wedding ring so that he could get money to go out and have a beer with the guys." Leigh didn't know what she was more hurt by, Wayne's ranting, or the fact that he'd hocked his wedding ring for beer.

By August of 1981, Wayne had returned from Fort McClellan, now as a certified NBC instructor; he had passed the instructors' course as an honors graduate. But Wayne wasn't at all happy to learn that Leigh was pregnant.

"So he came home and told me he wasn't about to have kids right now. And I had to have an abortion. And I told him I didn't want to have an abortion. And he said, 'Well, I'm leaving, then.' And I felt like I had no choice. So he ended up taking me in [to the abortion clinic].

"And at one point they ask you, 'Is anyone forcing you to do this?' And I sat there and looked at the woman and said, 'What if I said yes?' She said, 'Then we couldn't do the abortion.' "

Leigh got up and left the interview room. Wayne was in the waiting room.

"I just walked right past him into the hall," Leigh said. "And he followed me out into the hall, and goes, 'What?' And I was crying and everything and I said, 'I don't want to do this.' And he grabbed me by the arms and said, 'Get back in there.' So I went back in and [had] the abortion."

As Wayne and Leigh tried to settle into their married life, the tensions mounted. In addition to working as a Marine NBC instructor at El Toro, Wayne took a series of part-time civilian jobs in the area. Consequently, he was gone for long periods each day, and often at night. When they were together, Wayne became increasingly abusive to Leigh, frequently pestering her for sex.

"He wouldn't take no for an answer," Leigh said. "He

would force the issue, and if I didn't comply, I would be verbally abused to the point where, after a period of time, it was like, well, if I have sex with [him] right now, [he] won't bug me for the next three hours. And it was like a constant barrage of . . . it was like my whole life at home had to do with sex."

Wayne soon made her stay nude while they were at home. He was constantly approaching her with sexual demands.

"It's like if I sat down and watched TV or something like that, he would feel free to come up and start suckling on a breast. I mean it was just a constant barrage of this, like it was all I was there for. That I was an object of his pleasure."

Wayne seemed to believe that it was Leigh's role in life to please him. It was her role to perform all the duties of shopping, cooking and cleaning, even though she had a full-time job. Once he'd finished with his NBC classes at El Toro, Wayne spent most afternoons in a video game parlor. Then, after spending a fair amount of money, he would complain to Leigh that they were too short of cash to buy things she considered necessities.

Once Leigh got home from work, the barrage would being anew.

"I had to cook a three-course meal. I couldn't just cook vegetables. I had to cook vegetables in a cheese sauce with this and that, you know? I mean, it all had to be a very elaborate meal. And if it wasn't perfect or right, he got angry. The thing was, I could never get angry back at him, because then I'd get in trouble. So a lot of times, he would have me cooking naked. And if I tried to say no, like if he wanted to have sex and I said no, he wouldn't out and out rape me. He would just . . . mentally torture me."

At times Wayne would keep Leigh up to three and four in the morning, pestering her, until she would finally give in.

Wayne took particular pride in showing Leigh off. When they went out with other people, he wanted her to wear revealing clothing. Leigh felt uncomfortable, but Wayne insisted.

Wayne's obsession with sex, in particular with the female

breast, would become more and more pronounced over the years, as we shall see. At one point he obtained a deck of playing cards from a Hollywood sex shop that showed women with bound breasts; he insisted on replicating the poses with Leigh. Another time, he cut holes in a white sheet, so that just her breasts would be exposed. On yet another occasion, he made a wax impression of Leigh's breasts.

Taken together, these recollections by Leigh might serve as potentially strong evidence of the sort of personality "coarsening" or perversions expected from one who had suffered from a brain injury such as frontal lobe syndrome. The fixation on the breasts was clearly pathological, especially in the symbolic severing represented by the sheet and the wax impression.

As compliant as Leigh was with most of this behavior, Wayne was hardly committed to monogamy.

In January of 1982, Wayne and several other Marines decided to take a short vacation at Big Bear Lake, a resort in the mountains north of San Bernardino. The Corps had a cabin there for use by the enlisted personnel.

Leigh had to work, so she stayed home. But before Wayne left for the weekend, Leigh gave him some towels, her best. "I remember I told him, 'These are my good towels, don't lose them, and don't screw around on me while you're gone,' because I already had the idea that he wasn't going to be able to go five days without having sex. So it was half-joking, half-serious.

"Friday night I get a phone call from the guys who were there. 'Leigh, has Wayne called you?' And I said 'No.' And they said, 'If he calls, tell him to come back.'

"And I said, 'Come back from where, what happened?' And they go, 'Well, we can't tell you, just if he calls, tell him to come back.' "

About 11 that night, Wayne called Leigh. Leigh wanted to know what had happened.

"To this day it amazes me," she said, "because he didn't think what he did was wrong. He just knew he was going to get caught, and that's why he'd run."

As Wayne told the story, he and one of the other Marines had picked up two young girls, both 15, and brought them back to the cabin. Wayne, at least, then had mutual oral sex with one of the girls. But when Wayne's friend was returning the girls to the village, they passed one of the girls' boyfriends on the road. The girl then claimed that Wayne had raped her.

The San Bernardino County Sheriff's Department had then come to the cabin to arrest Wayne. Wayne went out the back door to escape. He wandered around in the woods for hours before finally deciding to call Leigh.

Eventually, Wayne was arrested, and the case was set for trial. But Wayne and Leigh hired a lawyer, who was able to pressure the girl and her parents into dropping the complaint, based on the fact that the girl had been playing hooky from school when the incident took place, and that the parents might be criminally liable for failing to control their child.

But if Ford had no understanding that what he had done was wrong, he certainly appreciated that he might be sent to jail and dismissed from the Corps if he was convicted. For the next six months, until the complaint was dropped, Wayne was very tense and nervous, according to Leigh.

Sometime in April of that year, Wayne's mother and her Indian boyfriend came to live with them at an apartment complex in Santa Ana; Wayne obtained a civilian job managing the complex.

As far as Leigh could tell, Wayne and Birgette seemed to get along well. Leigh liked her, and was grateful to her in one way: with Birgette and her boyfriend around, Wayne's insistence that she cook naked and otherwise always be available for sex abated.

And in another way, Birgette was supportive of Leigh.

"If you keep treating her that way," Wayne's mother told him one day, after he had berated Leigh for some imagined transgression, "you're going to lose her, the same way your father lost me."

5

Destruction

EVENTUALLY BIRGETTE AND HER BOYFRIEND MOVED OUT, IN part because of some of Wayne's comments about the boyfriend, which Birgette felt were racist. "And they were," Leigh recalled—remarks about cleanliness and diseases, and statements that the boyfriend shouldn't be handling the food. Wayne's insensitivity might be seen as further evidence of the coarsening that often accompanies brain damage.

So, too, does Wayne's continued insistence in showing Leigh off in sexually revealing ways. Once, there was a pool party at the apartment, attended by a number of Wayne's fellow Marines.

"Everybody's at the swimming pool," Leigh recalled. "I spent the entire day in the house, ironing his uniforms and spit-shining his shoes. And there was just so much to do . . . that I never had a chance to go outside. But he bought me this bathing suit, I'll never forget it, because it was white, and it [was] really skimpy. And it had like a gold patch right at the crotch. And there was just like a bra, straight across . . . but when it got wet, you could see right through it. And so, like at the end of the day, when I got finished, I came out in the bathing suit, and it's fine if it isn't wet, but he made me go into the pool to get it wet, so that everybody could see, you know?

"He constantly wanted to show everybody, not only 'Look what I got,' but 'Look what I get to have.' It was a manliness type of issue."

A "manliness type of issue." What did this mean? There were perhaps three ways to look at this, a theme that would be echoed in all of Wayne's subsequent relationships: Was Wayne so insecure in his own masculinity that he felt the need to parade his sexual prowess in front of other men? Was he so insecure in his relationships with women that he could only feel safe by demonstrating his dominance? Or was it some sort of evidence of the personality coarsening associated with brain damage? Again, the issue was whether the pathological behavior pre-existed the head injury; and, even if it did, the question remained: how much of this behavior was purely psychological, and how much was the result of the destruction of vital brain cells? As Professor Lishman suggested, it was difficult, perhaps impossible to know with certainty.

By the fall of 1982, the relationship between Leigh and Wayne was wearing extremely thin. While he insisted that Leigh wear revealing clothing while she was with him, when she was at her job—away from Wayne's supervision—he insisted on entirely different garb.

"He made me wear like real baggy clothes to work every day," Leigh recalled. "I had to, you know, look real dowdy. Pants couldn't fit tight, stuff like that." But when she was out with Wayne, she added, it was a different story. Then Leigh had to show everything off. It was as if Wayne got validation by being around a woman who might be sought after by other men.

The entire effect was exasperating to Leigh.

"During this whole time . . . because of the verbal abuse and . . . I had to have a tight rein on my emotions, so that I didn't totally have a breakdown," Leigh said. "I kind of like lost all my personality. I was just a walking zombie. But when I started working at this new place, I [had] twenty guys telling me, 'Oh, you're a really nice person.' 'You're this, you're that . . .' my confidence all of a sudden started to build."

As the fall turned into winter, Leigh grew more defiant to Wayne's bullying ways. She met another man at work, Bob. Bob was everything that Wayne wasn't: warm, sensitive, car-

ing and prone to extolling her. Inevitably, Leigh became con-
flicted: on the one hand, she wanted her marriage to Wayne
to work; but on the other hand, Bob began to seem infinitely
more reliable.

"Anyway," Leigh said later, "my breaking point came
about a week before Christmas. And this was the first year I
had convinced Wayne to get a Christmas tree. For some reason, he was totally against Christmas. We'd spent two Christ-
mases together, and we never had a Christmas tree."

In Leigh's recollection, Wayne had never even bought her
a Christmas gift. For an isolated 20-year-old girl, one who had
once been so close to her now-estranged family, for whom the
holiday of Christmas had meant so much, going without a real
Christmas in this new and strange world that had become her
lot in life must have been the epitome of loneliness. Convinc-
ing Wayne to accede to the idea of letting her have a Christmas tree had to have been as happy an occasion as it was sad.

"So," Leigh continued, "this was the first year I convinced
him to let him let me put up a Christmas tree."

About a week before Christmas, Leigh came home from
work. By now she and Wayne had moved to a place in San
Dimas, California; the small house had a glass window in the
upper portion of the front door. When Leigh came home, she
looked in through the glass window.

"So I come walking up to the door, and like always I got
up on my tiptoes to peek in, it was a habit. That's how I
always did it, I always peeked in, and then opened the door.
Well, he was wrapping my presents. He'd gone out and bought
me like, twenty presents, and he was wrapping them. And he
saw me peek in. And he opens the door, drags me in, and
makes me sit there, and open all of my presents . . . [and here
Leigh lost her composure] . . .'cause I'd 'ruined everything.' "

This was it, for Leigh. It was too much to be blamed for
everything that went wrong, especially when it was something
that meant so much to her.

"You know, I couldn't handle it anymore. So, I can't really
remember exactly what happened, but, he calls me one day at
work, and he says, 'I want to see a marriage counselor.' I

mean, I was angry, and I told him I wanted to leave, and all this stuff . . .

"And when I would do that, he would get very apologetic and contrite, and say, 'I'm sorry,' you know? So he calls me up, and he says, 'Will you [come] down here and go to marriage counseling with me?' "

Leigh agreed. Wayne wanted her to wear his favorite blouse, one that was sheer and tended to have transparent qualities. She refused to wear the blouse.

A few days later, Leigh went to Orange County for the counseling session. The counselor talked to each separately for half an hour, and to them together for a bit.

"She's trying to communicate to Wayne what I'm telling her, or my feelings . . . And as he's sitting there the veins on his neck start . . . popping out."

Wayne was about to blow his top.

"He is fuming, and I couldn't see it," Leigh said. "And she [the counselor] goes, 'Okay, our time is up, you know, blah blah blah. And she grabs me by the arm, and she pulls me over, [and tells me] 'I'll have someone drive you home. I don't want you going home with him.' And I said, 'No, no, I'll be fine.' "

Leigh did not believe that Wayne would ever be physically violent with her, an opinion the counselor obviously did not share. Leigh and Wayne left together, and went to the movies together that night.

But one of the counselor's suggestions was that they stay apart for about a week as a cooling off period. Wayne agreed to this. He said he'd stay on the base, while Leigh could stay at the house in San Dimas. The next day, Wayne went to the base and Leigh went to her job.

"So I went to work the next day, and I told Bob what went on. And he goes, 'Well, since there's nobody home, why don't you come to dinner with me?' So I said, okay." Leigh and Bob and several other people from Leigh's job went out to dinner.

Later that night, Bob drove Leigh home. But outside the

house Leigh noticed a car she thought Wayne might be driving.

"I said, 'Don't stop,' because it was like ten, or ten-thirty. I knew if I walked in the house right then I would be toast, you know?"

Leigh had Bob drive down the street to a telephone booth. She called her sister, and asked if she could come stay with her. "She goes, 'Leigh, what's going on? Wayne's been calling here like every ten minutes for the past three hours.' " Leigh's sister told her that Wayne was drunk, and that he had been threatening Leigh. Contrary to his promise to stay the week at the El Toro base, Wayne had come home.

Leigh later found out that Wayne had arrived that evening with two dozen roses as a peace offering. When Leigh hadn't appeared as expected, because she'd gone to dinner with Bob and her co-workers, Wayne had begun drinking. As the evening unfolded, Wayne changed into his camouflage uniform, and secreted himself in the bushes outside the house with his bow.

"And at the time," Leigh said, "he was really into archery, I mean, he was good enough to split arrows . . ."

About one in the morning, Wayne called Leigh's sister's house once more. He was drunk. Leigh told him she'd see him in the morning. The next day, Leigh returned to the house in San Dimas, and Wayne was furious because she hadn't returned that night. He was certain that she'd spent the night with a lover.

Leigh tried to convince Wayne that, whatever their problems were, there was no one else, but Wayne refused to believe her.

By the middle of January, Leigh had reached the end. She was ironing, again, when it finally hit her.

"Look," she told Wayne, "I want a divorce."

Wayne was very calm, she recalled. He said, "Okay." And then Wayne asked her if she wouldn't mind staying around until he found someone to replace her.

*   *   *

"Well," Leigh told Wayne, "I don't think that would work out too well." Wayne agreed, and for the first time, Leigh saw his preternatural calmness as "kind of frightening."

Wayne and Leigh then agreed to split up their possessions, including several pieces of furniture that Birgette had given them, which Wayne wanted.

"That's fine," Leigh said. They calmly divided the rest of their belongings, until they came to their two motorcycles. Wayne wanted both of them, but Leigh wanted to keep her own.

"I said, 'I want my motorcycle.'

"He said, 'Why?'

"I said, 'Because I have friends that ride.' "

That did it. Wayne exploded. Leigh wasn't supposed to have any friends, and certainly no one capable of riding a motorcycle.

Wayne grabbed Leigh and dragged her to the telephone. He made her call Bob.

"So I call up Bob, poor guy, I mean, at the time, he's still married to someone else," Leigh recalled. Bob came on the line.

"Wayne wants to talk to you," Leigh told him.

Bob was concerned. He wanted to know whether Leigh was all right.

When Leigh assured Bob she was okay, Wayne took up the telephone. He invited Bob to have breakfast with them at a restaurant not far from their house.

Bob was certain that Wayne was going to try to kill him. After he hung up, Wayne came into the bedroom and raped Leigh, leaving bruises and burns on her back and wrists.

"Then," Leigh said, "he tells me to get dressed, and we walked down to the restaurant." Leigh wasn't sure what was going to happen.

"So, I'm sitting there hunkered down in the booth in the restaurant. Like hiding."

Wayne was quite calm. "He proceeds to have this conversation with Bob," Leigh recalled. Wayne wanted to know if

Bob could introduce him to a new woman, "preferably one with big breasts.

"Bob's just like, flabbergasted."

Bob fumbled for words, according to Leigh. He hemmed and hawed: " 'Gee, Wayne, I don't know, offhand, but I'll keep my eye out.'

"I mean, it was like a perfectly normal conversation. And I'm sitting there, so Bob gives me his car keys. And he says, 'Go drive to your house, get some clothes, and I'll take you away.' " Leigh left the restaurant by herself.

When she was gone, Bob and Wayne also left the restaurant. Bob was pretty sure that Wayne was going to try to punch him out. That was one reason that Bob had given Leigh the car keys—to get her away from the fight, when it took place.

As Bob later told the story to Leigh, he and Wayne stopped outside the restaurant.

"So, you want to fight?" Bob asked, according to Leigh.

"Oh no, man," Wayne told Bob, according to Leigh. "I'm happy for you."

So Leigh and Wayne reached their parting; for Leigh it was sad, representing the death of her idealization of Wayne. For Wayne, it appears, it was just confusion.

Because, for both Leigh and Bob, it wasn't the end of Wayne. She and Bob eventually moved in together, at an apartment in South Pasadena, but somehow Wayne always found them. Wayne continued calling Leigh at work.

"He would say, 'I saw you last night with him.' " Wayne made it clear that he had been following Leigh. " 'I saw you last night. You drove down this street, you turned here, Bob kissed you at the traffic light, you went to dinner at this restaurant.' He was following me. Like every day."

This went on for weeks. Then one day Wayne came to Leigh's job.

"It was raining," Leigh recalled, "and he walked into my office, grabbed me by the arm, and dragged me out . . . we're standing in the rain. He's got me by both arms, and he's like yelling at me. And I keep looking, because about that time, Bob's going to pick me up."

Wayne wanted to know if Bob was coming for her. "He goes . . . 'Are you looking for him? If he comes here I swear to God I'll kill him. He'd better not come anywhere near.' "

Suddenly Bob drove up. He parked the car and came walking up the ramp to where Wayne and Leigh were. Leigh remembered Bob looking at Wayne.

" 'You got a problem?' " she said Bob asked Wayne.

"And Wayne just goes, 'No, I just thought maybe we could get a cup of coffee or something, and talk.' " Leigh noticed that Wayne had their wedding rings pinned to his jacket.

Wayne, Bob and Leigh went to a nearby coffee shop.

"And we talked to him for a while," she remembered, "and it didn't make any sense." What Leigh remembered most from the strange encounter was Wayne describing to Bob the various sexual experiences he'd had with Leigh. Leigh felt very upset at this, but Bob remained calm, like this was no big deal.

In the months afterward, Wayne occasionally would seek Leigh out.

"He would come to the apartment where I was living," she remembered, "and write [on] my windows. Like, letting me know he was there."

Eventually she and Bob moved to Cathedral City, near Palm Springs, and then Indio, to get away from Wayne. That didn't prevent Wayne from accosting Leigh's sister to demand her address. Her sister refused to tell Wayne where Leigh was, but that didn't stop him.

In April of 1984, Wayne went AWOL from the Marine Corps to find Leigh.

"We were in Palm Springs," she remembered, "like at a sporting goods store one day. I look across the street, I say, 'Oh shit, it's Wayne.' And Bob's going, 'No way.' " But Leigh was sure it was. "We get in the car, we [drive] around the block, sure enough, there was Wayne . . ."

Leigh and Bob returned to the trailer park where they were living, in effect to hide out. About one in the morning, Wayne knocked on their door. He had checked every trailer park in Cathedral City until he'd found them.

Eventually, Leigh was able to complete her divorce from Wayne. It took more than a year, because Wayne refused to cooperate. It would eventually become permanent in August of 1984.

Later, Leigh remained convinced that Wayne had really loved her, from the beginning to the end; it was just that he was incapable of letting his feelings come through. For the young Wayne, at least to Leigh, a good part of defining himself was taking on the masculine roles he had unconsciously inherited from his distant father. Breaking through to the real Wayne, if there was one somewhere inside beneath all the macho poses, had finally defeated her. In the end, it was more trouble than it was worth.

6

Semper Fi

THE FAILURE OF HIS MARRIAGE WITH LEIGH OBVIOUSLY WAS something of a watershed in Wayne Ford's life. From January of 1983, his career in the Marines began to go sideways. But the troubles of Wayne the Marine actually predated the troubles of Wayne the husband by nearly a year, and may in fact have been related to injuries he sustained in the Myford Road car accident.

Judging from the reports filed by his superiors,[18] and Wayne's own responses to those reports, it appears that Ford's difficulties with authority figures escalated continuously throughout 1982, into 1983, before reaching a culmination in 1984.

Based upon those reports, it appears that at least initially, Ford continued to do well as an NBC instructor at the El Toro base, reaching the rank of full corporal a month before he and Leigh were married, on April 2, 1981, and sergeant on April 1, 1982.

At that point, nineteen months after the accident, things began to go wrong for some reason. Despite his earlier glowing fitness reports, Ford apparently ran afoul of his immediate superior, a warrant officer, in early 1982. As it happened, the officer who had given him glowing reviews from late 1981 to

---

18. Ford's Marine Corps record was included in the documents filed in support of Ford's arrest on the four homicides in San Bernardino County, June 29, 1999, recovered by the author as described in this book.

early 1982 now found Wayne's performance wanting.

In a fitness report covering the period April 1 to September 30, 1982, Warrant Officer Jeffrey A. Canales wrote, "Sgt. Ford has been an instructor at the NBCD School for over a year. Potentially he has the ability to be an outstanding Marine, however at times he proves to be a bit temperamental. In the past Sgt. Ford was recommended for Meritorious Sgt. and NCO of the Quarter. As an instructor, his classes can range from good to outstanding. His attitude can range from very positive to average to ill-tempered and untactful. Sgt. Ford appears to lack enthusiasm and the support normally associated with a Sgt's acceptance of appropriate orders. Sgt. Ford's lack of tact becomes an obvious problem which makes it hard for him to get his point across. Sgt. Ford scored a first class on his last PFT [personal fitness test]. Sgt. Ford has the talent to be an asset to the NBCD field but his present attitude leaves a lot to be desired. The feeling of this command is that Sgt. Ford cannot be recommended for promotion to the next rank at this time."[19]

Wayne, in a written response in October of 1982, professed shock at Canales' about-face. He traced Canales' less-than-sterling fitness report to Wayne's request for a transfer from the school to a field unit. This transfer request is not otherwise reflected in the Marine Corps record. Just why Wayne wanted a transfer remains unexplained.

Nevertheless, Ford complained. He suddenly went from the best of the seventeen sergeants in the air wing to next to the last, at least in the non-coms' ratings. He took exception to being called untactful. The only explanation he could think of, he said, was when Canales asked him what he thought of how the school was being run.

"I gave my answers in a straight-forward and honest manner," Wayne wrote. Wayne insisted that his attitude hadn't changed, only Canales' opinion of him had, once he'd asked

---

19. Ford's U.S. Marine Corps records, included in the reports in support of Ford's arrest in San Bernardino County, case FSB 023161.

for a transfer. After all, hadn't Canales just recommended him to be NCO of the quarter?

Wayne's lieutenant colonel investigated the dispute. He entered his findings later that fall:

"1/ The fitness report, as written, is justified.

"2/ Sgt. Ford was put up for NCO of the Quarter at the insistence of the CO of the Unit. He was not actually a good candidate. The award was being used in an effort to get him to work to his full potential.

"3/ That Sgt. Ford is really a somewhat immature personality who has the ability to present himself as an ideal Marine, when he wants to. His problems appear to be a lack of consistence and a cockey [sic], defensive attitude."

In early 1983, even as the marriage with Leigh was coming apart, Ford was again nominated by his superiors as "NCO of the quarter," a highly sought-after honor. This time, despite his previous dispute with Canales, he got it. But by April, after Leigh had left him, things really began to go wrong.

Leigh moved out of the San Dimas house on January 15, 1983. Wayne reenlisted on January 17, two days later. On April 5, Wayne received a truck driving license from the Marines. Three days later, April 8, he was in the El Toro clinic for psychiatric problems. The admission form recorded:

"20 y/o w[hite] m[ale] who states he feels that his situation is helpless and feels hopeless and would like to die, although he has made no plans to do so. Has had two motorcycle accidents in as many days. [Unintelligible] markedly depressed."

Under "provisional diagnosis," the El Toro clinician wrote, "suicidal ideation."

Under "consultation report," the clinician wrote: "Patient states that his performance started to deteriorate 18 months ago [i.e., in November 1981, one year after the accident] with the departure of two good supervisors. His marriage began declining shortly afterwards, resulting in separation in January. He complains of apathy, insomnia, poor concentration, 20# wt. loss and nightmares. He expressed suicidal thoughts but no plans. He admits to alcohol abuse recently. Two days ago, he went UA [unauthorized absence], feeling hopeless."

Three months after Leigh's departure from his life, Wayne had gone over the hill, as they said in the service. The UA corresponded in time to Leigh's description of Wayne accosting her at her work.

The El Toro clinician continued:

"No past psych history. Medical history reflects psychosomatic GI [gastrointestinal] problems. Military record was clear until recently. Family history was unremarkable.

"Mental status exam revealed a [unintelligible] Caucasian male in fatigues. Behavior was cooperative. Mood was depressed and blunted affect. There was no indication of thought disorder. Speech was coherent. Sensation was intact. Insight and judgment were limited. He denied drug abuse.

"D[iagnosis]: Depressive reaction.

"Recommend: P[atien]t Was transferred to [Naval Hospital Long Beach] for admission to Ward 2 South."

Ward 2 South was the Long Beach hospital's psych ward.

Strikingly, there was no mention of Wayne's 1980 head injury or hospitalization in this April 1983 medical report. Apparently, either Wayne had not thought to tell the clinician about it, or the clinician didn't consider it significant.

Ten days later, on April 18, 1983, Ford was formally charged with being AWOL for his rainy visit with Leigh and Bob; he received a reprimand and counseling, but no further punishment.

He signed a statement acknowledging the reprimand, promising to do better, and was denied a further promotion for the time being.

From here on, Wayne's career as a Marine began to seriously decline.

In a fitness report for the period April 1 to June 10, 1983, Wayne's CO reported, "Sgt. Ford has not performed up to his potential during this reporting period. A fine instructor, who provides cogent briefings/classes on NBC, Sgt. Ford has allowed his lack of maturity to adversely affect his performance as a Marine NCO." The Corps attributed Wayne's problems to the end of his marriage with Leigh. Again there is no mention of the head injury.

Things went even more wrong in May of 1984, when Wayne went AWOL again for three days, May 16, 17 and 18, 1984 [significantly, a little more than three years from the date of his marriage with Leigh; this absence corresponds with Leigh and Bob's sighting of Wayne in Indio], and compounded his troubles by misrepresenting himself as his commanding officer over the telephone to another Marine. As a result, Wayne was eventually busted to corporal and fined a month's pay.

On May 22, 1984, following his AWOL surrender, Wayne again appeared at the El Toro clinic for more psychiatric treatment. The documents received from the Marines and incorporated into the 1999 arrest warrant include a notation "See Command Request Attached," but no such document was provided in the material appended to Ford's 1999 arrest. Again, there is no recognition of the possible effects of the Myford Road accident.

After referring to the earlier consultation of April 8, 1983, the clinician's note reads:

"P[atien]t. States that he has a 'chemical imbalance' that impairs his judgment under stress. He has lost his temper unreasonably after twice being reprimanded for being late. He continues to have trouble with his estranged wife and he feels that his supervisor is out to get him. He denies alcohol or drug abuse. He complains of insomnia, poor appetite, and depression.

"Psych. history was significant for brief hospitalization one year ago at NHLB [Naval Hospital Long Beach] for depressive reaction due to similar problems.

"Mental status exam revealed an alert, cooperative Caucasian male in no distress. There was no evidence of thought disorder.

"D[iagnosis]: Adjustment Reaction with mixed features, Personality Disorder, with explosive and immature features.

"P[atien]t. found fit for duty. He will be followed in outpatient treatment. Admin separation should be considered if he becomes [unintelligible]. Patient will be given a trial of anti-depressant medication."

In an attached "chronological record of medical care," a note dated June 13, 1984, indicates that in the follow-up treatment, Wayne didn't take the medication. "P[atien]t. Did not take [unintelligible] due to fear of an inability to wake up in time to get to work. He has been on leave. S[ubject] feels he can cope better with work pressure. Motivated for continued service.

"O[rientation]: alert, cooperative

"A: Personality Disorder with mixed features, adjustment reaction, resolved.

"P[rognosis]: P[atien]t found fit for overseas duty. Further treatment is not desired or indicated. P[atien]t. will consult chaplain."

On June 27, 1984, Wayne was cleared for overseas assignment to the Japanese island of Okinawa.

But clearing Ford for further duty was far short of discerning the extent of his potential mental problems. Even before Ford shipped out for his overseas duty, his superiors at El Toro continued to express doubts about his fitness.

In a fitness report dated July 2, 1984, Wayne's commanding officer reported, "Sgt. Ford's shortcoming is inconsistent job performance as a Marine NCO. He allows outside personal problems to affect his military professionalism. To this point in his career he has not shown the ability to correct this trend, thus limiting his potential as a Marine. His low markings in judgment and potential reflect his inability to correct his known problem areas and his failure to mature professionally up to his level of capability."

Wayne responded in writing: "Though this report appears adverse due to a complex personal situation, I now definitely feel that my problems are a thing of the past. As noted by the ... comments concerning my regular duties, I definitely feel that I have the capability to fully become a mature NCO and to continue to contribute to the Marine Corps."

Two months later, Wayne was shipped out to Okinawa, where he promptly went nuts.

*   *   *

On September 27, 1984, shortly after arriving on Okinawa, Wayne was admitted to the Naval Hospital on the island for psychiatric observation. The clinical resume:

This was the first Naval Hospital, Okinawa psychiatric admission for this 22 year old separated Caucasian male, SGT/USMC, with five years, eight months continuous active duty . . .

HISTORY OF PRESENT ILLNESS: The patient reportedly became upset when confronted by his Commanding Officer following his unit's failure of inspection the day prior to admission. The patient stated that his commanding officer refused to listen to his reasons for failure of the inspection and consistently orally reprimanded him. Orally reprimanding him in front of the other Marines. The patient stated that he has little recall of the sequence of events following the oral reprimand. Medical records indicate that the patient was found in his barracks in a corner in a fetal position refusing to answer any questions. He was taken to an outlying medical clinic but during his examination there he reportedly became violent and left against medical advice. He was apprehended several hundred meters from the medical clinic and had to be forcefully restrained and brought to the hospital.

Patient was reportedly hospitalized at Naval Hospital, Long Beach, in 1983 for a 'depression' but narrative summary for this hospitalization was not in medical records. Patient was also seen by psychiatry at El Toro in May of 1984 and given a diagnosis of Adjustment Reaction with Mixed Features, Personality Disorder with Explosive and Immature Features . . .

PAST MEDICAL HISTORY: Past medical history revealed that the patient is the youngest of two siblings from a broken southern [sic] California family. The patient dropped out of high school but later got his GED. He enlisted into the Marines for educational purposes. He has been charged once for UA where he received a reduction in rank as a result of same. He denied any drug alcohol abuse.

PHYSICAL EXAMINATION: The patient's physical examination was within normal limits.

LABORATORY DATA: Indicated laboratory and x-ray examinations were within normal limits. Toxocology [sic] screen was negative.

MENTAL STATUS EXAMINATION: Mental status examinations reveal a well developed, well-nourished male who was in four-point restraints who was very angry, hostile, and uncooperative. The patient's speech was loud and abrasive. He then informed the Medical Officer that he would answer no further questions and became mute for several hours. After several hours of silence, the patient continued the interview. He denied any auditory or visual hallucinations. He denied suicidal or homicidal ideations. The patient's memory for recent and remote events was fair, and he was now better able to recall the events surrounding his admission. His judgment and insight were poor. His speech was not pressured. He was not suspicious or paranoid. His associations were not loosened. He did not have a fixed delusional system. He denied any form of thought blocking or thought broadcasting.

HOSPITAL COURSE: The patient was admitted, examined, observed and evaluated in individual, group and milieu settings. Early in the patient's hospital course because of a past history of over-aggressiveness and violent behavior, he was placed in a stimulus free environment for his protection as well as that of the staff and other patients. He was also placed on a neuroleptic [generally, a psychotropic drug such as Haldol or thorazine] for his agitation. Several attempts were made to try to maintain patient without the aid of neuroleptics. Each attempt was deemed a failure and the patient is now being maintained on Haldol 10 mg PO BID.

DISCHARGE DIAGNOSIS: 1. Borderline Personality Disorder, Severe, as manifested by intense and inappropriate anger and lack of control of anger, marked shifts in mood from normal to depression. Irritability, anxiety. Depression when alone and chronic feeling of emptiness or boredom.

2. Atypical Psychosis manifested by frequent psychotic breaks, unmarked by hallucinations or a fixed delusional system, not caused by a mind altering drug.

3. Rule-out schizophrenia. Rule-out Paranoid Disorder.

RECOMMENDATIONS FOR FUTURE CARE: The patient is to be medically evacuated to Naval Hospital, San Diego for further care and disposition. Accepting physician at Naval Hospital, San Diego is Dr. John Sentell.

Eventually, Wayne's medical records from El Toro caught up with him in San Diego, where he was apparently being treated by Dr. Sentell.[20] The extent of treatment received by Ford remains unclear, as does the question of whether his physicians were aware of the possible consequences of the car accident.

Wayne was released from the Marines in January of 1985. His discharge document indicates that he received an honorable discharge, "at the convenience of the government—character and behavior disorder."

---

20. Attempts by Ford's defense team to locate Dr. Sentell's records of treatment of Ford in the San Diego Naval Hospital in 1984–1985 were apparently unsuccessful, at least through October of 2000. Representatives of Ford's defense team believed the records may have been routinely destroyed by the USMC.

7

A Preliminary Assessment

AFTER READING THE DETAILS OF LEIGH'S INTERVIEW WITH Detective Freeman, and after analyzing Ford's Marine Corps records, I was faced with the question: was any of this evidence that Ford had indeed suffered brain damage as a result of the accident in December 1980?

There were, in fact, a substantial number of observed behaviors that might be consistent with the symptoms of frontal lobe syndrome as described by Professor Lishman:

- Ford seemingly became obsessed with sexual matters in the aftermath of the accident, including perversions involving bondage and separation of body parts (from the totality of the relationship), indicated by the holes in the sheets, the focus on body-part bondage, the wax mold of Leigh's breasts, and Ford's incessant pestering of Leigh for sexual relations;
- There was a marked coarsening of Ford's personality in the months following the accident, to the extent that he interacted with his young wife in crude, demanding terms, even to the extent of putting her on display (the see-through bathing suit with the gold crotch being a prime example); his demands as to her dress and demeanor at home; and including the insult of his mother's boyfriend with racist remarks;
- His relationships with his Marine Corps superiors precipitously declined after the wreck, to the extent that

Ford was repeatedly faulted for inattention to detail, for inappropriate behavior with commanders, for insubordination, for oversleeping, boredom, irritability, lack of emotional control, and for sloppy attention to his duties, despite his earlier superior performances, all symptoms cited by Lishman for head-injured patients;

- Ford's two motorcycle wrecks in early 1983 seemed to indicate a self-destructive wish, also not uncommon in brain-damaged patients, according to Doctors Lishman and Lewis;

- Ford's own statements to medical personnel, from 1983 to his involuntary restraint in Okinawa in 1984, appeared to parallel many of the symptoms predicted by Lishman for brain damage; these included Ford's inability to handle stressful situations throughout 1983 and 1984, which culminated in his bizarre behavior on Okinawa, which in turn led to his hospitalization in the psychiatric ward in San Diego.

At this point, I again contacted my psychiatrist friend in Seattle, and provided him with a fairly detailed precis of Wayne Ford's life and medical history, at least as described by the documents that had come into my possession. The Seattle psychiatrist, after studying this material, opined that it was entirely possible that Ford had indeed sustained the sort of brain damage described by Lishman. At least on the surface, he said, based upon my description of the events and reports described by Leigh and the Marines, Ford was a possible qualifier for a brain damage defense.

The main thing the defense attorneys should do, my psychiatrist friend advised, was subject Ford to neuropsychiatric analysis. A court-appointed psychologist wouldn't do, because the usual court-appointed expert would probably find ample evidence of Ford's anti-social personality, but might miss entirely any of the organic causes.

What someone like Ford needed, my friend suggested, was an expert in the ways possible brain injuries affected the emotions. This would require a physician board-certified in both psychiatry and neurology, a rare double expert—the neuro-psychiatrist. Such a medical expert should probably order so-phisticated tests to determine whether Ford indeed had evidence of brain damage, such as a PET or CAT scan of the brain.

If there *had* been brain damage, such a scan was likely to reveal it in terms of dead areas within the brain's electro-magnetic pattern.

Still, in the absence of any personal interview with Ford, and without such tests, my friend was reluctant to come to any definitive conclusion as to whether Ford's 1981 accident was principally responsible for Ford's murderous behavior. Much would depend, he suggested, on the pattern of Ford's behavior in the years before, and *after* the accident.

8

Anaya

A S INDICATED, FORD WAS DISCHARGED FROM THE MARINES in January 1985. His plans to replicate his father's service career, and to earn enough money for a college education, had been destroyed by his psychological collapse on Okinawa. From being NCO of the Quarter, a highly trained Marine specialist, a 19-year-old sergeant on the rise, Ford had been reduced to a civilian nobody. No one appeared to have, at least from his available Marine records, the slightest notion that he might have sustained significant brain damage as a result of the Myford Road accident, least of all Wayne himself.

The year 1985 is perhaps the least documented in Ford's adult life. Based on assertions later made by law enforcement sources, it appears that Wayne may have spent some time in the Big Bear Lake area, in the mountains above San Bernardino. Leigh also recalled that at one point in 1985 Wayne showed up at her grandparents' ranch in Chino, where her uncle was working; Wayne was again looking for Leigh. Apparently Wayne told Leigh's uncle he was a police officer. Leigh's relatives told Wayne they had no idea where she was, and Wayne left.

Outside of that appearance, however, it seems that Ford kept a fairly low profile that year; it was only the following year that Wayne next came to the attention of the authorities.

On January 15, 1986, according to the state's Department

of Justice Criminal History Section (CHS),[21] Ford was arrested
for an attack on a Garden Grove woman, reportedly a prostitute. In later years, details of this event would remain hazy. A
Los Angeles Times account, published in November of 1998,
asserted that "according to police records," Ford was accused
of raping, beating and robbing the woman. Some other published accounts held that Ford had robbed her of a package of
cigarettes. However, an official of the Garden Grove Police
Department, when contacted by the author, could find no record of any case on this supposed incident; neither could a
spokesperson for the Orange County District Attorney's Office. This is not to say the incident never took place; instead
it may have only been that no one in authority considered the
event serious enough to warrant prosecution, or even permanent record-keeping.

Sometime that same year, Ford obtained a job with a
Garden Grove–based furniture delivery service; and it was
there that he met the next woman who was to share his life,
Anaya. It also appears that by this time Wayne had abandoned
his first name, for his middle name, Adam. Whether this name
change was an outcome of his breakdown in the Marines, because of his arrest in Garden Grove, or for some other reason,
wasn't clear, at least in the records filed in support of his later
homicide arrest. But when he met Anaya, "Wayne" had been
swept into the dustbin of history, replaced by "Adam."

By her own account, Anaya was only 19 or 20 when she
met Ford. She worked in the delivery firm's office, and Ford's
job was assisting the delivery people. She recalled that he approached her for a date.

"I was dumb," Anaya said later.[22] "I don't know why I was
so stupid." She had thought "Adam" was going places; it took
her almost five years before she realized he wasn't.

---

21. State DOJ Ford history timeline, p. 12, prepared 12/17/1998, and included
in the materials supporting Ford's arrest on the homicide charges in San Bernardino County.
22. Interview with Anaya, by Humboldt County Detective Juan Freeman,
January 14, 1999, Humboldt County Sheriff's Case #97–7013.

Perhaps the most striking aspect of Anaya's description of her relationship with Ford is her insight into his character and personality. Taken together, her perceptions again appear as unbiased, uncoached, anecdotal evidence in support of the proposition that Ford had previously sustained brain damage.

Certainly, neither she nor her interviewer, Humboldt County Detective Juan Freeman, had, at the time of the interview, any idea that Ford's eventual defense might involve a claim of brain damage. That was still to come. Based on Anaya's words, all one had to do was consider some of Ford's bizarre actions (and reactions) during the time he was with Anaya, at least as she described them.

When Anaya first met Adam, he was working as an assistant for the furniture delivery people in Garden Grove. After a few months he took a new job delivering newspapers for *The Orange County Register*.

Based upon Anaya's account to Freeman, it doesn't sound as though she and Ford hit it off immediately in 1986. After an initial cup of coffee and a few dates, she and Ford argued. Ford, then living in Garden Grove, moved into a house with a married friend from the Marines in Dana Point.

After a few weeks, Ford had put aside his differences with Anaya, and she began to visit him at the Dana Point friend's house. Somewhere around this point, Ford left the furniture delivery service, and took the job delivering newspapers for the *Register*. Early the following year, Anaya moved in with Adam in a studio apartment in San Clemente. It appears, based on her interview with Detective Freeman, that Anaya knew nothing of Ford's arrest in connection with the assault on the prostitute in Garden Grove.

After moving in with Anaya, Ford appeared to have recovered, at least temporarily, some of his earlier ambition. He got a job as a car salesman in Irvine, and later one in San Clemente. It appears that Ford's sales skills left something to be desired, because by 1988, he'd taken a new job as a motorcycle mechanic in San Clemente.

Sometime in 1988, Ford's Marine friend in Dana Point broke up with his wife.

"And," Anaya told Freeman years later, "he [the friend] came to the door, and Adam ended up wanting to go live with him. And of course I should have . . . what a ding-dong." Anaya indicated to Freeman that she should have realized right then that "Adam" had no interest in maintaining a lifetime relationship with her. Anaya moved back in with her mother, while Ford and his Marine friend lived together.

Ford continued with the paper route, while he found a new job as a tow truck driver in San Clemente.

In early 1989, after some months more of her on-again, off-again relationship with Ford, Anaya left her mother's house to move in with him once more, again in San Clemente. Ford took a job with another towing company, and found additional work as a bus driver for the San Juan Capistrano School District. As Anaya remembered it, Ford had wanted to work with handicapped children. When he found out that his job was to drive the kids, not help them, he became unhappy, according to Anaya.

Eventually, Ford would find other jobs—as a lube and oil man at a San Clemente garage, and other similar work. According to Anaya, he attended community college classes, but remained unsatisfied.

From Anaya's perspective, Ford seemed to be congenitally unhappy.

"He was never challenged enough, I don't think," Anaya told Freeman. "He was very smart, and he went to school on and off through this time. And . . . he was too smart for his own good, I think. He'd get bored too quick. He's always depressed . . ."

Freeman suggested that Anaya might have been willing to pay for Ford's education if Ford had been able to do it.

"Oh," Anaya said, "I would have been willing to do . . . anything to make him happy . . . within certain boundaries, you know? I wanted to see him happy, because I believed in him. We had been engaged for a while . . . And it's so funny, I never really thought about a wedding. Now, how someone would stick around for that long, and never even think about a wedding, or kids . . . I think I was just waiting for him to make the right move in his life, but he never did it . . . So I got smart."

Judging from this description, here again is evidence of possible brain damage in Ford. As Lishwin suggested, raw intelligence of the brain-damaged person may be unaffected. But other aspects of character, such as long-term planning, goal discipline, attacks of ennui and depression, are frequent. Ford appeared to demonstrate all of these symptoms during his years with Anaya.

There is still more such evidence in Anaya's descriptions of Ford's sexual behavior—taken together, these seem to indicate a further coarsening of Ford's moral behavior, and again, a patent lack of concern as to others' feelings and judgments, which after all are the fundamental guideposts to socially acceptable behavior. Stripped to its essence, Ford's sexual behavior as described by Anaya seemed to indicate that Ford was a man increasingly obsessed by issues of control; while this may be a feature of a sociopath's personality, it may also be seen as the psychological orientation of a person obsessed with the prospect of losing someone important to him.

As a result, some personalities may continually subject their partners to tests—tests often involving pain.

As Leigh had noted, one of Ford's sexual peculiarities was his fascination for the female breast. The exercise with the holes in the sheets, the bondage, the wax impression, his suggestion to Bob that he help Wayne find a new woman with large breasts, all indicate a strong obsession on Ford's part. This continued in his relationship with Anaya.

"He wanted to put a safety pin in my nipple," Anaya told Detective Freeman. "I don't know why. I just wanted to please him. We had been together for quite a while, and I loved him a lot. And I thought, well, I'll try that. And it hurt. But he did that to me a couple of times.

"It didn't go all the way in. It just kind of pricked me. But I don't know why he did that."

The obsession with breasts also included biting, and being bitten. Once, in fact, Wayne came home, crying. When Anaya asked him what was wrong, Wayne didn't want to say. Anaya insisted.

Wayne told her he'd been walking on the sidewalk when he saw a woman, a stranger. Suddenly Wayne grabbed the woman's purse and threw it on the roof of a nearby building. And then he bit the woman's breast.

"It just didn't make any sense, someone grabbing a person and biting a girl's [breast], and then leaving," Anaya said. "I didn't believe him, I guess. I didn't understand the whole thing. But he told me that, and he was crying really bad."

This does indeed appear to be a clear instance of the loss of impulse control so often observed in people with brain damage. The striking image of Adam weeping about it seems to indicate that even he didn't understand what had come over him, and that he was at a loss as to how to control it.

In other areas of sexuality, Wayne continued to demonstrate a penchant for perversions. He tried to convince Anaya to have sex with another woman, or to agree to have sex with another man while he watched. Anaya refused. On several occasions Anaya discovered Wayne had a taste for voyeurism, and once Wayne deliberately exposed himself to a female houseguest.

For some reason, Wayne was more forthcoming about his family with Anaya than he had been with Leigh. Wayne told her that he'd been very close to his mother, and was devastated when she left.

"He was a very sensitive little boy, from what I understand," Anaya said. "And he was very close to his mom, and he said he used to hang on her dress when she was in the kitchen. And he just always wanted to be with her. And then one day, he said, she just looked at him and said, 'I don't want to be your mother anymore.' And she just left."

After his father remarried, Wayne told Anaya, he and his step-mother did not get along. Wayne told Anaya that his step-mother believed that he was trying to have sex with his step-sister.

"So his dad ended up putting him in a place like an apartment building, something he owned. And Adam would say how his dad would come by and give him money like once a week for food. It was the only way to keep peace [in the family]." This situation, if true, likely would have taken place around the time that Wayne would have broken into the store when he was 14 or 15. The antipathy toward his father's new wife might also explain some of Wayne's anger toward women, since the new wife had played a role in depriving Wayne of his father. Thus, in later striving to gain absolute control over the women in his life, Wayne may have been trying desperately to hold on to the "good" of his natural mother while at the same time punishing the "evil" of his hated step-mother.

In later years, once she was away from Adam, Anaya came to see that Wayne had no respect for women—that he found it impossible to relate to women as real people. Some of Wayne's co-workers noticed this as well, particularly at the family-owned towing company, where two of the bosses were women. Those former employees recalled that Wayne couldn't stand to be told what to do by a woman. It just tended to enrage him.

A similar observation was made by the wife of Scott, one of Wayne's best friends. Scott first met Wayne while working as a mechanic at the tow yard, and later helped Wayne get a job at a San Clemente auto repair place. Scott's wife, Linda, when interviewed by Juan Freeman in November of 1999, told Freeman that she'd never liked Wayne because she sensed from the night she first met him in a San Clemente bar, on her first date with Scott, that Wayne just didn't like women, and did not respect them. "He was a self-described male chauvinist pig," was the way Freeman reported Linda's remarks.[23]

Sometime around 1991, the relationship between Ford and Anaya began to cool off.

"It wasn't going anywhere," Anaya said. Wayne agreed that

23. Interview of Linda by Detective Freeman, November 18, 1999.

it was probably best if they parted, but as with Leigh, he didn't want to act precipitously.

"And so he said, 'Why don't we just break up slowly? It just seems like it would be easier for me.'" Anaya agreed. Each took a separate bedroom in the house they were renting in San Clemente.

Ford and Anaya thus lived as largely platonic housemates for the better part of a year. Finally Wayne decided to move out. He told Anaya that he'd found a place of his own. It turned out to be the house next door.

Anaya was angry. It seemed to her that Wayne wanted his freedom, but wasn't willing to give the same to her.

"And then I realized," Anaya said, "what kind of man he was." Wayne, in Anaya's mind, wanted to control her, or at least maintain some sort of dominant interest in her sex life. Anaya found another place to live. She had to leave her beloved dog behind with Wayne.

The dog, it appears, triggered the next incident that Wayne was to have with the police.

As noted, for several of the previous few years, Wayne had worked as a tow truck driver in San Clemente. The towing company had a yard directly behind Wayne's house, protected by a female retriever. One day near the end of the year, the retriever began trying to work her way through the fence to get into Wayne's yard. Wayne said later that he believed the dog was trying to attack Anaya's Samoyed. Wayne shot the tow yard dog with a shotgun. The dog didn't die immediately, but bled to death in the tow yard—though not before her piteous cries alerted the yard.

The towing people were furious. They called the police, and Wayne was arrested for animal cruelty. He pleaded guilty and was sentenced to a week in jail.

The incident seems to have ended Wayne's career as a tow truck driver. But by this time, Wayne was exploring the possibility of becoming a country–western singer. He soon found a new job as a singer and disc jockey in a fashionable San Clemente karaoke bar. It was while working in the bar that Wayne was to meet the next woman in his life.

9

Lucie

AS ANAYA HAD BEEN, AND LIKE LEIGH BEFORE HER, LUCIE was a very young woman—19 years old—when she first met the man she knew as Adam Ford in the spring of 1994. Lucie's father was a high-ranking police officer in Las Vegas, Nevada. Lucie had come to southern California to stay with her cousins in Mission Viejo, just a "sneeze," as Lucy put it, up the freeway from San Clemente.

Lucie first met Adam through Adam's friend Dave, the ex-Marine. Dave had taken her to the karaoke bar in San Clemente where Adam was working as a disc jockey. Adam soon began showering Lucie with flowers, and within a month Lucie had dropped Dave and had begun going out with Adam instead. By August they had moved in together. Adam dropped the karaoke job and took a new one with an auto repair service in San Clemente, where Scott also worked.

By October, Lucie and Adam decided to be married. Lucie also discovered that she was pregnant. She got an abortion. Then they went to Las Vegas and were married at the Tropicana Hotel.

At first, Lucie said later, life seemed normal. They spent time as a couple with Scott and his wife, Linda, and at least initially, it seemed ideal. "For a short period of time it was,"[24] Lucie said. "We would just go out and drink and play darts and have fun."

---

24. Interview of Lucie by Detective Juan Freeman, November 12, 1998.

Then Scott got a job in another county to the north, and Adam and Lucie helped them move; after that, Lucie had less support in dealing with Adam's increasingly bizarre whims.

"He wanted to like expand sexually," Lucie said. "He would want me to sleep with other men. While he was there in the room. And I would say, 'No, I don't really want to do that.' And he would get very depressed. He would just make my life hell. I can't even put this into words. He would just make my life so bad that I thought . . . if this will make him happy . . . it's stupid on my part."

Lucie eventually agreed to Adam's demands that she have sex with other men.

"I just thought, maybe [if she did] it would get back to normal. And so, I don't know the month [but] I got drunk, and we picked up a Marine from a bus stop. And we went back to the barracks . . . And so I was completely drunk. I didn't want to feel anything. And this happened three times. And I would tell him I just can't do that anymore. It's awful. I don't know why he would want to do that to me. And he said, 'Well, don't you want to make me happy?' And he'd get depressed, and I would say, just forget it . . ."

Even as she recounted this experience to Freeman, Lucie began to cry.

Adam often got into black moods, Lucie added, when she recovered her composure. He would sulk, she said, and be depressed. Often he would belittle her; and when he wasn't tearing her down, he was demanding that she cook for him— breakfast, lunch and dinner. Lucie did her best to comply with Adam's demands.

And Adam had a constant need for sleep, Lucie said, to the point where they could not even sleep together.

"If he did not get his eight hours of sleep he would just be so pissed off," she said, "and it was my fault. Almost for our entire marriage we didn't share the same bed, because I would toss and turn before I would go to sleep, and he just needed to be still. And so I mostly slept on the couch. 'Cause if he did not get his eight hours, he would threaten to not go to work, and [then] would lose his job." And if that happened, Lucie added, it would be all her fault.

In March of 1995, Lucie got pregnant once more. When she went in for an ultrasound examination and it was determined that the baby would be a boy, Adam was enthusiastic. If it had been a girl, Lucie guessed, Wayne would have wanted her to get another abortion.

Once Lucie became pregnant she absolutely refused to have sex with strange men, no matter how much Adam bugged her. The marriage staggered on, each seeking in the other something neither really had.

By August of that year, Lucie was in her fifth month of pregnancy. She and Adam planned to go to a classic car show in Pomona with Adam's brother Rod and Rod's wife. That morning, Lucie woke up hungry, and decided to make herself bacon and eggs for breakfast.

"I was sitting on our sofa with the TV tray in front of me, watching the TV and getting ready to eat, and he wakes up." Adam spotted the breakfast Lucie had cooked and wanted it for himself. Lucie told him to make his own breakfast.

Adam suddenly became enraged.

"So he just took control of me and he raped me," Lucie said. "It was bad. I didn't want anything to do with him. I just wanted him away from me . . . he took a belt and wrapped it around my neck and told me to suck his dick. And I wanted to bite it off, but I didn't want to get killed or anything. That was the only time I was really frightened of him."

Adam let her up, and Lucie ran out of the apartment, screaming. Adam tried to coax her back into the apartment, and eventually succeeded. Lucie went into the shower, and when Adam tried to get in with her, Lucie told him to get away from her. Afterward, Adam forced Lucie to have sex once more.

"He didn't understand why I was mad at him," Lucie said. "Like he really felt he had some right to do that. You know, I was his wife . . ."

Later that day they went to the car show with Rod and his wife; nothing more was said about the attack, and Lucie got the idea that Adam had already forgotten all about it.

The next week, Lucie left Adam and returned to stay with her mother in Las Vegas.

This, it turned out, was just the first of many separations and reconciliations between Adam and Lucie during the next year. This first time, Adam convinced Lucie to return. That December, Lucie gave birth to a boy. Lucie's father, the Las Vegas policeman, was overjoyed to be a grandfather. While visiting Lucie and Adam, Lucie's father tried to convince them to move to Las Vegas, saying that there would be plenty of job opportunities there for Adam, now that he had a child to support. Lucy thought that Adam and her father got on well.

Two months later, Adam, Lucie and their infant son moved to Las Vegas. Lucie's uncle pulled strings in the electricians' union to get Adam a job as an apprentice. At the time, the casino New York, New York was under construction, and the electrician's job paid very well. But Wayne was unhappy as an apprentice. He soon quit.

"I don't know why he didn't go on with it," Lucie said. "He had so many people wanting to help him . . . but Adam never asked for help, but then he kind of expected people to just hand him things, you know? Well, that didn't work out. My dad loved the guy, he could help out, but Adam never asked. We tried to get him a job driving trucks for Las Vegas Paving, and he never followed through with that . . .

"So one day he started driving cabs."

When they arrived in Las Vegas, Lucie had found an apartment in the same complex where her mother lived. This was convenient for Lucie, because her mother was available for help with the baby, as well as moral support. But some of the weirdness that had afflicted their marriage in San Clemente soon surfaced.

Adam soon began pressing Lucie to allow her breasts to be pierced with needles. Lucie did it, for awhile, but she didn't like it. Worse, Adam still wanted her to have sex with strange men, and this was definitely out, as far as Lucie was concerned. Adam kept trying to get her to tell him that she'd been a prostitute for some reason, and there didn't seem to be any way to convince Adam that it wasn't so.

Eventually Lucie obtained a job in Las Vegas, and was able to begin to put some sort of financial floor under her situation. She was able to get a car, and pay for the insurance. She put the baby in day care. Adam didn't like any of this. He didn't want Lucie to work, and he especially didn't want the baby to be in day care—"baby prison," he called it. But Lucie, as a mother, now had a great deal more life focus than Adam had anticipated.

Several times in the spring of 1996, Lucie took the baby and moved out of the apartment, taking refuge once more with her mother. Somehow Adam always managed to convince her to return. In late June she moved out yet again. As usual, Adam tried desperately to convince her to return; this time Lucie agreed to a two-week trial, on the condition that Adam had to change. For the first two days, Adam was amenable. But he soon reverted to his old ways, demanding service— food, sex on demand, obeisance, needles—all the bad stuff. Lucie decided, a few days after the Fourth of July of 1996, to cut her losses. She and the baby moved back in with her mother for good.

Wayne, or Adam—it's difficult to know what to call him at this point, because it seems clear that Ford himself wasn't exactly sure—now exhibited all of the ambivalence that he believed his own father had shown so many years before. On one hand he was thrilled to have a son, but on the other, he wanted Lucie to take virtually all of the responsibility. As Lucie remembered it later, even when the baby was born, while they were still living in Orange County, Adam had complained about having to go with her to the hospital for the birth.

Of course, one of the most interesting things about human psychology is how often we deny things that are desperately important to us. Lucie had no doubt that Adam was emotionally overjoyed to be a father, yet he appeared to have an enormous reluctance to take any responsibility for the life that he had helped to create—perhaps because of some debilitating doubt as to his own capacities as a parent, or because at some basic emotional level he recognized that parenthood would tie him to Lucie as he had never been tied before, which in turn would make him more emotionally vulnerable than he had ever been in his life.

In any event, Lucie had a terribly difficult time trying to enfold Adam into the life of his son, especially after the final break between the two in July of 1996. Lucie soon took up with another man, and she tried to conceal it from Adam. She tried to arrange for Adam to see the baby, but Adam just wasn't very effective as a caretaker; often he would spend five or ten minutes with the baby, then split. It seemed clear to Lucie that Adam desperately wanted them all to be together again, at least ostensibly, for the sake of the baby. But if it required the sort of demands Adam habitually made on her, Lucie simply couldn't do it.

Late that summer, Lucie and the baby finally left her mother's apartment and moved in with her father, the police officer. With Lucie now completely gone from the scene, and Lucie's father standing guard, Adam decided to leave Las Vegas. It appears, based on later police interviews with his brother Rod, that Adam tried to kill himself before leaving, although details of this are unclear.[25]

With the help of his brother, Adam returned to Eureka, and moved in with his grandmother. Some months later, he acquired an Airstream trailer from one of his aunts, and located a trailer-home space in Arcata. By the fall of 1997, Adam was working as a driver for an Arcata concrete company.

Lucie began divorce proceedings against Adam. As with Leigh more than a decade before, it would be a protracted affair. During the next year, Lucie was to recall, she was to

---

25. Interview of Rod Ford by Humboldt County Detective Juan Freeman, November 3, 1998. When discussing his brother's tempestuous relationship with Lucie, Rod Ford told Freeman, ". . . 'cause, you know, a couple of years ago, he tried to commit suicide. I went down to Las Vegas and pulled him out of that rat's nest."

have only two extended telephone conversations with Adam, and only two visits. One visit occurred in October of 1997, when Lucie arranged for Adam to see the baby at Scott and Linda's, who by then were living near the central California coast. Ford apparently drove down from Eureka in a 1985 El Camino truck he had been given by his father. Lucie and the baby came to Scott and Linda's so Adam could see his son. However, Lucie stayed the night in a nearby motel with her boyfriend, a fact she did not tell Adam, but which he nevertheless probably picked up on. Ford left Scott and Linda's on October 13, 1997, a date that would eventually have major significance for Freeman and the other investigators.

Several years later, when Lucie was to read that Adam had blamed his claimed killings on her supposed refusal to allow him to see his son, she was completely astounded. That had never happened, she said; never. The problem was, instead, that Adam simply couldn't be bothered. After all, she pointed out, it was Adam who had moved so far away; otherwise, he could have seen the baby any time he wanted to—and indeed, Lucie had encouraged him to see him far more often than he had. And from her perspective, it wasn't from lack of trying on her part; she eventually provided telephone records that she said showed numerous attempts on her part to call Adam to let him know how the baby was doing, but Adam could rarely be reached.

Adam's estrangement from Lucie seemed to do nothing to deter him from seeking women in the Eureka and Arcata area, however. Later, costomers of several drinking establishments in the Arcata area identified Adam as a frequent patron, one who appeared to be drinking to excess more and more often. Adam's growing capacity for alcohol apparently didn't deter very many women, who still seemed to see something in him that spoke of the enticing possibilities of both his vulnerability, and a hint of danger. To his trailer park neighbors, it seemed Adam frequently brought home overnight female guests, and on several occasions more than one.

One neighbor, Dan Ames, who lived in the trailer space

next to the one rented by Adam, found him a friendly if private person. Ames was well aware that Adam was cruising the local bars for pickups. When Adam asked Ames if he wanted to go drinking with him, Ames declined. He'd been in that lifestyle before, Ames explained later, and he never wanted to go back.

With the two trailers so near to each other, it was impossible for Ames not to know what Adam was up to. It seemed to Ames, in his later recollection, that there were two women in particular who stayed with Adam for several weeks in the summer or fall of 1997; one was the mother of a small boy. Ames formed the impression that the mother of the child was Adam's former wife, and the boy was his son. It was Ames' impression that the small boy irritated Adam with his childhood needs.

The second woman was a teenager, Ames recalled. He thought she might have been the older woman's younger sister, or related to her in some fashion. Then one day both the women were gone, and so was the boy; Ames could never figure out how the four had managed to live in the Airstream together for even a few weeks. It was so small, he figured, they had to be on top of each other all the time, and it couldn't have been very pleasant.

And there was one night when Ames woke up to hear an argument from Adam's Airstream. All he could hear was a woman's voice, apparently refusing something.

"Well," said the woman, "I'm not your wife, and I won't do it."

And after that, Ames heard nothing more.

After about a year driving for the concrete company, in the fall of 1997 Adam apparently sustained some sort of injury on the job, and obtained temporary disability compensation. When the injury healed, near February of the following year, Adam took a new job, this one driving a large, long-haul, Kenworth semi-tractor, painted black, which was usually coupled to a long flatbed trailer for hauling lumber products south from the Oregon mills to the central valley and to southern California; while returning north, the flatbed was often laden with other building materials, or sometimes empty.

According to the accounts of those who knew him in Eureka and Arcata, Adam liked the long-haul driving job much more than he did pushing the cement mixer. For one thing, he was largely on his own, without a supervisor constantly breathing down his neck. He picked up loads of lumber in Oregon and locations in north California, then drove south to unload at a variety of locations ranging from the Central Valley of California, to San Diego, and to Arizona and Las Vegas. Later, his truck logs—in many ways, haphazardly kept—revealed that Ford had made hundreds of trips up and down I-5, US 101, on I-10 through San Bernardino, on US 395, and frequently on Highway 58, the road through Buttonwillow into the Mojave Desert.

As it turned out, it was this job that would have the effect of putting Wayne Adam Ford on the road to serial murder.

IV
FREEMAN

1

The Torso

ON SUNDAY, OCTOBER 26, 1997, BOB POTTBERG, A EUREKA-area duck hunter, put his canoe into the water of Freshwater Slough, a broad, shallow tidal channel meandering through the lush green dairy pastures east of Eureka. It was Pottberg's intention to follow the slough all the way around the watery northern outskirts of the town to a small boat ramp on Humboldt Bay on the west side of the city, in effect Eureka's front-door to the world.

As one of the largest natural harbors on the Pacific Coast between San Francisco and Coos Bay to the north, people in Humboldt County once had great hopes that their area would turn into one of the major shipping destinations of the Pacific Coast. After all, Humboldt Bay—named in the 1950s by gold prospectors in honor of the then-famous European naturalist, Alexander von Humboldt—was more than 40 square miles of sheltered water, with nearly 175 miles of shoreline. But the problem the prospectors didn't anticipate was the terribly forbidding, mountainous terrain immediately behind the bay. It would prove to be virtually impossible to get a cost-effective rail line through to the port, and the gold mines in the Trinity Mountains behind the town never quite panned out. As a result, Eureka's fortunes were to be largely confined to fish and forest products for more than 150 years. There just wasn't an economic way to get manufactured goods over the mountains to the interior, or agricultural products out, so the port never realized the potential Eureka's founders had once envisioned.

Probably Eureka's most famous—or infamous—moment in history came in February of 1885, when, after a series of shootings between rival Chinese tongs enmeshed in a dispute over the town's vice trade, a city councilman was caught in a crossfire and accidentally shot dead. That same night, about 600 white men gathered in the streets of downtown Eureka, and talk soon began about wholesale lynchings. Instead, a committee of fifteen men was appointed to tell all the people of Chinese ancestry then in the city that they had twenty-four hours to get out of town. The next day, every single person of Chinese ancestry—men, women and children, including some who had lived most of their lives in the community— were shoved aboard two steamers in the harbor and unceremoniously deported to San Francisco. As a result, it is reported, no person of Chinese ancestry again resided in Eureka until after World War II. The population around Eureka and Arcata would remain overwhelmingly white for most of the twentieth century.[26]

As Pottberg came around a wide bend of the slough, passing under a rickety wooden cattle bridge, he saw what first appeared to be a large log on the muddy east bank. Pottberg paddled his canoe closer, and as he did so, decided that the log was actually a store mannequin, or at least what looked like a portion of one. Pottberg drew alongside the figure and poked it with his paddle. A swarm of flies immediately took to the air. That was when he realized the thing on the bank was no dummy; it had once been a human being. With a jolt of queasiness, Pottberg realized that the reason he hadn't at first recognized what he was looking at was that it hardly seemed human: the head was missing, as well as the arms and legs. It was, to put it quite starkly, stomach-turning in the extreme.

Pottberg had a cellular telephone with him. Backing away from his gruesome discovery, he placed a call to the Eureka

---

26. The story of the expulsion is told in Eureka historian Lynwood Carranco's book, *The Redwood Country*, published locally in Humboldt County in 1971.

police, and then paddled to a landing farther down the slough to await their arrival, even as the shock set in.

After meeting with Pottberg and checking their maps, the Eureka police soon realized that the human remains were actually just outside the city limits. That made it a case for the Humboldt County Sheriff's Department. Within a short time, deputies from that department arrived on the scene to take charge.

One of the first to take a close look was Humboldt County Sheriff's Lieutenant Frank Vulich. He noticed that, in addition to the missing head, arms and legs—cut off just below the buttocks—both breasts had been cut off as well, and that there was a long incision down the front of the body to the pelvic area. In effect, the torso had almost, but not quite been eviscerated. Because the tide was coming in, and there was about twenty feet of undisturbed mud between the body and the waterline, Vulich theorized that the torso had only recently floated to the mudbank, where it had stuck. That meant other body parts might be found in the vicinity. A California Highway Patrol aircraft was called in to overfly the slough. Based on the lack of "animal action" on the torso, it was believed that the remains had been in the water less than twenty-four hours.

Just after sundown, the remains were removed by a deputy coroner and taken to the morgue. Humboldt County's first and only Jane Doe of the year had been so badly chopped up that it would prove impossible to identify her.

The next morning, the case of Jane Doe was forwarded to the Humboldt County Sheriff Department's Criminal Investigation Division, where it wound up on the desk of Detective Juan Freeman. Without fingers to print, without a face to compare to a photo, without teeth to match to a dental chart, it was hard for Freeman to know where to begin.

At 51, Freeman had been a Humboldt County Sheriff's deputy since 1977—since 1975 if you counted the two years he had spent as a corrections officer in the county jail. He was somewhat unusual in that he did not go directly into law enforcement after growing up in Los Angeles. Not until he was nearly 30 years old did he find his calling, and only then after having owned first a leather goods business, and then a clock shop in the San Francisco Bay area. As Freeman later told it, he and his first wife had a dispute, and when it was over, so was the marriage. In a manner of speaking, the clocks had simply stopped striking.

On his arrival in Humboldt County, Freeman had taken a job as a school bus driver—something he would, ironically, have in common with Wayne Adam Ford. After a few lean years, Freeman decided he needed a better-paying job, so he joined the sheriff's department as a jailer. Apart from a few detours, as Freeman put it later, when the sheriff was forced to lay people off because of budget cutbacks, Freeman had been with the department in one job or another ever since.

While Humboldt County had its share of homicides—usually four or five a year, occasionally as many as twenty—nothing in Freeman's previous experience prepared him for the headless, armless, legless thing that had been Jane Doe.

Early the next morning, Freeman and two officials from the Humboldt County Coroner's Office took what was left of Jane Doe to Stockton, California, for an autopsy by an expert pathologist. Because of the lack of ordinary means of identification, an anthropologist also attended. The autopsy took over two hours, and when it was done, the pathologist, Dr. Bob Lawrence, said his best guess was that Jane Doe had once been about 5 feet 4 inches in height, had weighed about 120 pounds, was white with a possibility of some Hispanic blood, and had had either brown or auburn hair. Based on a low carbon content in her lung tissues, Dr. Lawrence theorized that she had never been a smoker, and in fact had probably lived in an area that had little or no air pollution. Dr. Lawrence also determined that while she was very young, she had previously given birth.

The portion of the remains that had been recovered showed a profusion of wounds, including twenty-seven stab wounds to the buttocks, one of them before death, and the rest after. Most of the post-mortem wounds were made by a small double-edged knife, but the wound made while the victim was still alive was caused by a larger single-edged blade.

The anthropologist, Dr. Butch Cecil, agreed with Lawrence's findings, and suggested that Jane Doe had been between the ages of 18 and 25.

Based on these findings, Freeman asked the state's Department of Justice for a computer run on young females reported missing between October 20 and October 26. Eventually the missing list would be expanded, and Freeman would check every single one, looking for the name of a young woman who matched Dr. Lawrence's description. It wasn't much to work with, but it was all Jane Doe had left to tell them.

Two days later, Freeman began a canvass of the area where the torso had been found. He encountered a man who operated a wood shop situated on the west bank of the slough. The man told Freeman that he'd noticed the torso floating in the slough several days before it was first reported, perhaps on October 22 or 23. He'd thought it was a piece of driftwood. It hadn't been until the following Sunday, after the police had come and gone, that the man learned that the object he'd seen had actually been a body. If this was true, it pushed the possible date of death back three or four days, if not longer.

The following day Freeman was back at the slough, this time with another deputy and a pair of dogs trained to sniff out cadavers. The dogs alerted at the place where the torso had been found, but nowhere else.

Later that afternoon, Freeman got a call from a detective in Calaveras County, in the Sierra Nevada foothills to the south and east. The detective told Freeman that he'd had a similar dismemberment case involving a prostitute from Sacramento, where the head, arms and legs had been removed. The case was never solved, but one of the suspects in the case had moved to Humboldt County, the detective told Freeman. Freeman opened a file on the man.

A few days later, Freeman was informed that someone had discovered a large amount of blood on the railroad trestle over the slough. Freeman sent two deputies to check it out. It turned out the blood was actually red paint.

Freeman contacted the Federal Bureau of Investigation in San Francisco, where a special unit organized to track serial killers was located. FBI Agent Candace DeLong, a member of the unit, told Freeman that it seemed likely that Jane Doe had been murdered by a "lust killer," that the person probably lived locally, and—more ominously—would probably kill again in the future.

The following week, Freeman distributed a nationwide description of Jane Doe, but kept back the details about the sexual nature of some of the wounds.

As October turned into November, he heard of still more possible suspects from the police old-boy network: a man in upstate New York, who had once lived in Humboldt County, was said to have penned a manuscript with graphic descriptions of sexual assault and dismemberment; two brothers, truck drivers from Oregon, were said to have committed murders up and down the West Coast (although no one had been able to prove it); a pathologist in Sacramento was said to have threatened his girlfriend with dismemberment; a man in eastern Oregon was thought to have dismembered a girl there seventeen years earlier; and still others. Freeman noted them all down, and even asked officers in these other parts of the country to see if there was any evidence that the suspect(s) had traveled to northern California during the month of October.

Using the state Department of Justice's computerized list of young females who had been reported missing, Freeman began the laborious task of contacting those police agencies to see if he could get a match to Jane Doe. By early January of 1998, he had eliminated forty of them; most of them had turned up safe and sound not long after being listed as missing on the computer.

At one point, a two-person team of criminal investigative profilers from the state Department of Justice came to Eureka to look over the area where Jane Doe's torso had been found. Agent Sharon Pagaling had been trained at the FBI's Behavioral Sciences Unit at Quantico, Virginia. Pagaling and her understudy, Richard Sinor, having already read Jane Doe's autopsy report, now walked over the scene at the slough and provided a preliminary assessment. Pagaling did not provide Freeman with a written report, but merely an oral briefing. Freeman's subsequent description of Pagaling's ideas about the torso, contained in his investigative file, differ in some significant respects from Pagaling's recollection of what she told Freeman.[27]

It was clear to Pagaling, who had reviewed a great many homicide cases in her work with the state's Department of Justice, that the killer had to be someone who was a local. It simply wasn't very likely that a stranger would have known enough about the backroads of Eureka to know where to put the torso into the slough without being observed. Likewise, Pagaling concluded that the killer was white—because of the overwhelming white demographic of the area. Pagaling guessed that the killer had a local job, that he'd done the deed at his home for privacy, and that he'd put the torso in the water while he was off from work, since it had been found on a Sunday, and apparently hadn't been in the water very long, if the coroner's report was accurate. Pagaling believed that the killer had dismembered the body in order to conceal its identity.

Although not mentioned by Pagaling to Freeman, a desire to conceal the identity of the victim suggested that the killer was aware that some other person might have seen him with the victim at some point prior to her death.

Pagaling and Sinor suggested that Freeman try to find out where the body had first been put into the slough, because other body parts might be found there; additionally, it might offer a hint of the route the killer had taken for the purpose of disposal, which could in turn suggest places where the killer

---

27. The author interviewed Pagaling in December of 2000, almost two years after Freeman's initial written summary of her remarks to him. Pagaling said she did not recall saying some of the things Freeman said she'd said, and was certain that at least some of Freeman's description of her remarks was in error. The synopsis provided here contains those surmises that occur in both accounts.

might live. They recommended that Freeman identify a day in which the tides were similar to the weekend of October 26; then, they said, Freeman should float inflatable objects from different starting points to see if any ended up on the mudbank. That way he might be able to locate the place where Jane Doe was first put into the water.

All of these were good, if general suggestions. But they didn't help Freeman very much with the other part of his problem: finding out who Jane Doe was. Barring the apprehension of someone caught in the act of committing the exact same sort of dismemberment crime in the area, knowing Jane Doe's true identity was the most important step in finding her killer, an outcome that was beginning to seem more remote with every passing day.

Then, late in January, Freeman was told that a human arm with hand attached had been found in the surf near Clam Beach, an area far to the north of the slough. He tried to have the hand fingerprinted, but it turned out that no usable prints could be raised.

Ten days later, just about out of options, Freeman decided to consult a psychic.

2

Visions

FREEMAN HAD CONSULTED KAY RHEA BEFORE; AS FAR AS he was concerned, Kay was the real deal: she'd provided accurate information in the past. He spoke with Rhea by telephone, and recorded her ideas.[28]

First Rhea asked Freeman to describe the location where Jane Doe was found. When Freeman did so, Rhea said the victim's hair was brown, not black.

"Kay also said right away that Jane Doe lived with the man who did this to her," Freeman reported.[29] "Kay said the killer is older and looks drawn. She said the victim traveled with him. She knew him. He lives in a wooded area and he may have worked with wood, like logs, not firewood. He wants to go east and north up into the woods. He crosses a county line which runs north and slopes to the east.

"Kay said she feels like he is hardened and has a beard on his face. He is at least 45 years of age. He has spent some time working with logs. He is living back up in the woods now. He would rather drink coffee and smoke than eat. He lives in a cabin or small house far up in the hills up a dirt road. He lives in a sheriff's jurisdiction, not city police. He

---

28. The transcript of this conversation was not provided in the recovered materials; as a result it's difficult to know whether Rhea's sometimes surprisingly accurate descriptions were unconsciously prompted by Freeman's own questions or responses.

29. From Freeman's third follow-up report, dated February 10, 1998.

has gray in a long untrimmed beard, at least 2 inches long.

"Kay went on to say he has had sex with the victim more than once. She said he owns a short pickup with a camper shell, and it rattles. It is possibly a Ford. There is evidence of dried blood in the camper or near this man. Kay said he waits for a monthly check to come in. It is for disability or veterans, but it is not retirement.

"Kay said this man has a lot of tattoos on his right arm. One is large and has to do with the Marines. It is from the elbow down. Kay said he drinks a lot and takes drugs. She said he killed her in a drunken rage. Kay said the man is not clear-headed a lot. He feels sorry for himself. She also said he lives in a marijuana growing area.

"Kay said the license plate to his truck is wired on the right side of the rear plate. His truck is an older compact truck about 15 years old. She said it is not well-maintained. She said he may know this area but does not live in Eureka.

"Kay said that he scattered the body parts. She said she is surprised that a leg has not shown up. Kay said she feels the legs are near Trinidad. She said she can see them on a blanket having sex. Kay described the victim as having an irregular nose. She had brown eyes, and an upper right tooth has metal in it, possibly gold. She is not tall. She knew him 2–3 months. Kay said there was not a lot of money. Kay said that he has a water barrel next to his house. She said that he whacked her a few times and she may have smoked marijuana with him. Kay said she is 19 or 20 years old. She may have Indian in her.

"Kay said he now regrets killing her. Sometimes he wishes she were back. Kay also said it is not like his conscience is bothering him, it is that he misses the things she did for him.

"Kay said he has bad teeth. They are yellow. Something happened to his ear. Kay said this man was beaten and deprived as a kid. She said he is originally from somewhere else. It starts with an M, like Missouri. She said not Montana. Somewhere where there are woods and backward people.

"Kay said this person is not a serial killer type guy. She said his ability to have sex is low because he has a small penis.

He gets very mad when somebody laughs at him about his size. Kay said the oriental [sic] girls laugh at him."

Rhea told Freeman that the man was a Viet Nam veteran who had worked with explosives. Then she said the reason the killer got so angry at Jane Doe was because she was going to leave him.

Kay remained convinced that Jane Doe's killer was a veteran who had been made deranged by the war. She envisioned a scene in which the killer and Jane Doe had a fight, and the killer struck her in a drunken or possibly drugged-out rage. While she was getting her things together to leave, the killer struck her in the head, killing her. He fell asleep, then awoke later and began cutting her body with a knife.

While parts of this were wildly off base, it would turn out that other parts were quite remarkably accurate, when arrayed against Wayne Adam Ford. There was, for example, Rhea's choice as the killer's truck—"possibly a Ford"[!] And it was true that Wayne often felt sorry for himself, and felt deprived as a child. He hated it when women dumped him. He had bad teeth, broken when he was hit by the car at Myford Road. He was in the Marines, and if he didn't handle explosives, he *was* trained in nuclear, biological and chemical warfare, which is pretty close. Wayne did regret his killings, to the point where he turned himself in. At the time of the torso's discovery, Wayne had been receiving a disability check for an injury he'd received while on the concrete driving job. And he did live in an Airstream trailer, which was somewhat similar to living in a cabin.

But while all of this was interesting—especially after Wayne's arrest—the trouble with the information was that it was both too specific and too general. What Freeman really needed was hard evidence, and of that, as the spring of 1998 came into view, he had precious little.

V

TINA GIBBS

1

Buttonwillow

ON THE EVENING OF JUNE 2, 1998, ABOUT TWO MILES WEST of the small cotton-growing town of Buttonwillow—itself about twenty-five miles west of Buck Owens country, Bakersfield, California—four members of a construction crew found themselves staring into the California Aqueduct, where they saw a naked woman in the water.

The Aqueduct, an engineering marvel that had been brought into existence nearly thirty years earlier by the vision of California Governor Pat Brown, father of current Oakland Mayor Jerry Brown, had transformed the landscape of Buttonwillow during the years of its existence. Indeed, hundreds of square miles of barren land had been made fertile by the concrete-lined channel that brought life-giving water from the north to the arid wastes of southern California's forgotten desert, the land north of the Tehachapie Mountains. Years before, Texans, Arkansans and Oklahomans of the Dust Bowl years had come in, riding their old flivvers as in *The Grapes of Wrath*. Now, thanks to the water, those immigrants' descendants were the backbone of a prosperous community of cotton farmers: COTTON CAPITAL, said the signs in Buttonwillow. And the evidence was everywhere—miles of fields, planted with green-growing plants that would soon bear the white fluff of which fabric is made.

The four construction workers stood at the fence that separated the public from the water, the one with the sign that warned in both English and Spanish that going into the canal was dangerous—"muy pelegroso." There in the middle of the fast-flowing man-made stream was the naked body of the woman. She wasn't moving, and it didn't take an Einstein to know that she was dead, hung up on the line of floats that stretched across the canal.

Shortly after 6 that evening, one of the workers called the police; in Buttonwillow, that meant the Kern County Sheriff's Department, which soon sent a patrol car to the scene, followed, a bit later, by detectives from the department's homicide squad.

The body in the water was just east of a bridge over the canal, an overcrossing that conveyed Highway 58 west from Bakersfield toward the nondescript Temblor Range of mountains almost due west, and the Caliente Range, a strange-looking series of rounded brown hillocks off in the far distance to the southwest. A line of gargantuan power line towers strode across the landscape in the middle distance, bearing electricity to places unseen. If followed to its logical conclusion, Highway 58 eventually tied in with U.S. 101 on the California Coast between Santa Barbara and San Luis Obispo. It was the same highway where James Dean had met his death in a blind intersection traffic accident some forty years before.

The woman in the aqueduct was young, it appeared. The sheriff's deputies launched a boat to approach the body. For some reason, by the time they got close enough to take photographs, the body had broken free of the buoyed line across the water, and had been washed up to a canal gate. As they saw it, the body was floating on its stomach, and had apparently been in the water for some time, as well as dead; the skin showed signs of decomposition, with various reddish patches that foretold imminent sloughing of the epidermis.

Eventually, after the photographs, the body was hooked, and brought to shore; there it was promptly placed in a blue plastic body bag and then taken to the Kern County Coroner's Office in Bakersfield for further examination.

The woman in the aqueduct had reddish-blonde hair, cropped fairly short; she was 5 feet 8 inches tall, and weighed approximately 145 pounds. On her left hand were five rings; on her right was a tattoo, the letters JJ, enclosed in a heart. There were no obvious signs of trauma—no stab wounds, no gunshots. Bruises on the face and neck seemed to indicate that the victim had been beaten and possibly strangled. After an autopsy, strangulation was confirmed by the presence of a fractured cartilage in the neck. A test for sexual assault indicated evidence of semen in the vaginal vault. A blood test was positive for both cocaine and alcohol. Based upon the amount of decomposition it appeared that the victim had been dead for several days.

Because the body had been immersed in water, it was difficult to obtain viable fingerprints. Eventually, the Kern County pathologist removed the victim's hands, and a somewhat blurry set of finger- and palm prints was recovered. An evidence technician then began trying to find a match to fingerprint sets that were on file.

Over the next month a number of possibilities for fingerprint matches were examined, but rejected. Finally, in mid-July, the evidence technician submitted the fingerprint set to the FBI and the state Department of Justice for assistance.

Thus, on July 29, 1998—almost two months after the victim had been found in the aqueduct—a match was finally made by a technician with the state Department of Justice. The dead woman was identified as Tina Renee Gibbs, 26 years old. She had a record of arrests in Washington State and in Reno, Nevada. Using records from those states, the Kern County Coroner's Office was able to locate Tina's father, Carlos, in Fayetteville, North Carolina.

Kern County Sheriff's Department Detective Gary Rhoades called Carlos Gibbs for background on Tina.

Carlos told Rhoades that he hadn't seen his daughter since she was very little. He said Tina's mother had left him and taken the child with her. It was not until 1990 that Carlos again had spoken with Tina, and since then, he'd only had sporadic contact with her. The last time, Carlos said, was on Christmas Day of 1997, when Tina called to say she was with her boyfriend, someone Carlos knew only as "Boo," in Las Vegas.

She gave Carlos a telephone number. Carlos said Tina told him that her mother, Mary, had died. Rhoades later discovered this wasn't true. He called Mary in Oklahoma, only to find that Mary hadn't seen her daughter since Christmas Eve in 1991. It appeared that Tina had spent most of her early teen years in Oregon.

When Rhoades checked the Las Vegas telephone number, he found out that it went to a Las Vegas motel on Boulder Highway.

"I contacted the Las Vegas Police Department homicide detail,"[30] Rhoades wrote, "and talked with Sergeant Rocky Alby. Sergeant Alby told me his department has several past contacts with Tina Gibbs and she is a known prostitute in their city. They have made several prostitution-related arrests of Tina Gibbs. He said his department last contacted and arrested Tina on 5-6-98, for obstructing a police officer. At that time, she was apparently living at a motel known for prostitution activity. . . . Sergeant Alby said all of her last addresses and locations where she was contacted are areas of the city and motels where prostitutes frequent and live. Sergeant Alby was not able to locate information about any people that would be helpful with this investigation. His department has forwarded various information about Tina Gibbs, which I have placed in the investigative file. I have no further information at this time."

And there the matter rested. Tina Gibbs was put down as a prostitute from Las Vegas. How she came to die, and how she wound up in the California Aqueduct hundreds of miles away from where she was last seen, went on the back burner of the Kern County Sheriff Department's stove. As far as most investigators were concerned, the likelihood of finding out who killed a prostitute from another city, months after the crime, was an extreme longshot. That was just the way it was:

---

30. Supplement report of Detective Gary Rhoades, Kern County Sheriff's Department, dated September 18, 1998, Case #98-00509.

getting murdered was an occupational hazard for people in the prostitution business, and Tina wasn't the first and certainly wouldn't be the last. Barring a surprise confession, it was unlikely that the crime would ever be solved.

2

Las Vegas

JUST FINDING OUT THIS MUCH ABOUT TINA GIBBS TOOK A lot of time. But had anyone made the effort, there *was* more information to be had. Whether that information would have led to Wayne Adam Ford can only be a matter of speculation. What is critical, however, in such investigations, is a determination of when a person was last seen. This can narrow the timeframe, which can be quite useful if and when a suspect is developed. As a general rule, however, doing this for people engaged in prostitution can be quite difficult, since their movements are rarely regular.

There was a possibility, however: Tina's last arrest in Las Vegas, on May 6, 1998, which was less than a month before she was found dead. When the Las Vegas sergeant indicated to Rhoades that his department was "not able to locate information about any people to contact who may have information that would be helpful with this investigation," that wasn't entirely accurate. Records held by the Las Vegas department indeed show a number of leads that might have been pursued, including the names of a number of people who knew Tina in Las Vegas, and who might have been helpful in pinpointing the last time she was seen, and where.

Las Vegas, of course, is a twenty-four-hour city. As more and more elaborate casinos have gone up spreading south out of the downtown area, the central core of the city has fallen on hard times. It was in this area where Tina Gibbs first became known to the officers of the Las Vegas Metropolitan Police, and out on Boulder Highway, to the east of the city. Both of these areas are as well-known for street prostitution as they are for seedy motels, some of them dating back to the construction of Boulder Dam more than sixty years earlier. Although regulated prostitution is legal in a few Nevada counties, it is illegal in Las Vegas' Clark County.

The first record of contact between the LVMPD and Tina dated back to a late Saturday night, on November 23, 1996. An undercover police officer posing as a customer picked her up in the 3000 block of Fremont, near the Showboat Hotel on the city's eastern edge.

"Upon entering my undercover vehicle,"[31] Vice Officer G. Canfora wrote, "Gibbs immediately asked me if I was a cop and I said no. I told her that I didn't have a lot of time and asked her if she had a place. Gibbs told me yes and told me to start driving. Gibbs told me that she had a 'date' a couple of days prior and that he had beat her up, choked her and hurt her windpipe. She went on to say that she had to be careful with her 'tricks' and wanted to go to a public parking lot. I told Gibbs that was no problem and she asked me what I wanted, and then followed it up and asked me if I wanted 'head,' which is a common term for oral sex, and I said yes. Gibbs asked me how much I wanted to spend and again followed it up with 'I charge twenty bucks.' I told Gibbs that was a great deal and gave a pre-arranged arrest signal."

About a month and a half later, Tina was again near the Showboat Hotel, when she was recognized by police officers who saw her making eye contact with passing drivers. Another undercover officer was sent to the scene.

Tina got in the officer's car, and again asked if he was a cop. This time the officer asked if *she* was a cop. When Tina said she wasn't, she offered to prove it to him. She raised her shirt to bare her breast. Then she told the officer to touch her, which he refused to do.

---

31. Report of Detective G. Canfora, November 24, 1996, #2009.

"Due to her comments,"[32] wrote Vice Officer D. Jacoby, "I then told her that she was making me nervous and that I didn't know if I wanted to get into trouble with the police. She stated, 'No, that's okay, it's just that police officers cannot touch me on my breast and they cannot touch other individuals.'

"At that time, unprovoked and without warning, Gibbs reached over with her right hand and grabbed in my crotch area and stated, 'See.' "

Eventually Jacoby struck a bargain with Tina, and Tina directed him to drive to an apartment parking lot in downtown Las Vegas. When they arrived, Tina was arrested once again.

The interesting thing about both of these arrests is what it shows about Tina Gibbs' state of mind at the time. In contrast to her later arrests in 1997 and 1998, Tina seems to have been alert, properly cautious, wary of a possible attack by a "trick," and concerned enough about being arrested to attempt to test the undercover officer. Her later encounters with the police showed a marked deterioration in her mental capacity, as the drug habit which had bedeviled her for so long grew worse and worse. Indeed, by the spring of 1998, she was barely co-herent in her encounters with the police, and desperate enough to do just about anything as long as she could get money for crack cocaine.

As a result of this second arrest, Tina was again booked at the Clark County Correctional Facility. This time she had to post bail of $1,100. And at this point a rather curious thing happened, something that might have provided the Kern County people with some possible leads had they followed up.

For one thing, Tina's bail was posted in the form of a ten percent bond, $111, by a retired Army man named Leo B. Hunt. Hunt, it turned out, was heavily involved in making pornographic films in the Las Vegas area; according to sources familiar with Hunt's operation, Hunt often bailed out young women arrested on prostitution charges in return for their working for him in his films. In filling out the bond applica-tion, Tina listed Hunt's residential address and telephone num-

---

32. Report of Detective D. Jacoby, December 9, 1996, #1866.

ber as her own. She noted that she'd previously been arrested on prostitution charges in Seattle and Tacoma, Washington. She noted that her mother was deceased, which of course, wasn't true. Then she listed a number of other references, and included telephone numbers, including her father Carlos in North Carolina, as well as four other Las Vegas acquaintances, among them the name of a man she said was her cousin. While it is true that some eighteen months later, it wasn't likely that all of these people might have still retained a connection with Tina, it is possible that some might have known who her current friends were when she was last seen.

And Leo Hunt certainly would have been interesting to talk to; even as Detective Rhoades was hearing that the LVMPD had no leads for him, Leo Hunt was about to be charged in a Las Vegas court with producing child pornography. Eventually, Hunt would be convicted, and face a term of up to forty years in prison. In May of 2000, the 62-year-old Hunt killed himself with a gun.[33]

But in September 1998, when investigators were making what now appear to be half-hearted efforts to identify Tina's killer, Leo Hunt was still in circulation, and even under investigation. He would have been someone important to talk to, particularly since, after having bailed Tina out, he apparently revoked his bond three days after posting it, which caused Tina to be re-arrested. Just why Hunt would revoke the bond only three days later remains obscure, but it seems likely that he and Tina may have had some sort of dispute. Her revocation paper is stamped "flight risk," which hardly seems a significant worry on a $111 bond. But Hunt is no longer around to explain just what any of this meant.

Eventually Tina got out of jail again, and returned to prostitution. Her next arrest, June 14, 1997, was out in the sprawling southeastern strip area, near Desert Inn Road and Boulder Highway. Tina went through the same crotch-grabbing ploy as the last time. She told undercover officer G. Shannon that the police didn't like her because she was hard to catch. She

33. LVMPD report #000515-0460, May 15, 2000.

told him that on the street her name was "Big Mama." She said that she got most of the dates in that particular stretch of the highway. Her fee was now $50. The officer agreed to the price, and pulled off on the shoulder of the highway and arrested her.

A little more than two months later, Tina was downtown in Las Vegas in a man's car. This time patrol officers stopped the car for being a "suspicious vehicle," which probably meant they had seen Tina pick up a trick. When they searched Tina they found a crack pipe in her jacket pocket. Tina was arrested once more for possession of narcotics paraphernalia.

Later in September of 1997, Tina was arrested once more for prostitution. This time she didn't bother to go through any of the "trick tests," which seems to indicate that her previous alertness was beginning to fail, and her desperation to get money was growing. From this point forward, also, the frequency of contacts with the police was also beginning to increase.

Just a month later, Tina was again arrested for possession of a crack pipe, this time in front of an older apartment building in the run-down part of old Las Vegas.

A month after this, in November, Tina was found passed out behind the wheel of a 1991 Ford Ranger truck on the city's industrialized north side. The truck had all its tires blown out and was "parked horizontally in the travel lanes" of East Searles Street. This time Tina was arrested for obstructing traffic, having no driver's license, and no proof of insurance. Where Tina had come into possession of the truck was a mystery.

Still, this is evidence that Tina's drug problem was becoming unmanageable. Passing out in the middle of the street while behind the wheel was a sure sign that she was losing the capacity to take care of herself.

The following month, Tina was again arrested for prostitution in downtown Las Vegas. This time she offered to do whatever the undercover officer wanted for $100 an hour, an offer that tends to show the state of her desperation.

At this point there seems to have been a break in the pattern. Rather than a monthly arrest, as had been the case throughout the fall of 1997, there were no new arrests well into the spring of 1998. The chances are that Tina spent much of this time in the Clark County Correctional Facility, due to her many arrests and probation violations. While being in jail is certainly no picnic, at least it has the effect of detoxifying someone grievously addicted to drugs.

But the reality of street prostitution in a major American city like Las Vegas—or Reno, or Seattle, or San Francisco, or any other metropolitan area one cares to mention—is that the entire practice is seen as a game: by the prostitutes, who play hide from the cops; by the cops, who play seek for the prostitutes; by the courts, who run them through the legal machinery and tax them in the form of fines; by the bail bonds people, who make their living on their clients' misfortunes; and by the "tricks," some of whom see the people they hire as utterly disposable.

And, of course there was the other reality: that there was much more to the life of Tina Gibbs than this sad progression of drugs, tricks, arrests and obvious desperation; and it was the need to understand this about the people Ford had victimized that had so exercised *San Jose Mercury News* columnist Sue Hutchison.

It's too bad, therefore, that Hutchison didn't act on her own impulse at the time she wrote her column excoriating the news media for treating Ford "like a rock star," and ignoring the victims. If she had tried, for example, to locate Tina's family in a small town in Oklahoma—whose name and location she could have discerned with a minimal amount of digging—she would have learned that until she was 16 or so, Tina was a normal, middle-class teenager who had lived much of her life in the rather pleasant small towns of Richland, Washington, and Beaverton and Seaside, Oregon.

I eventually contacted Tina's mother in Oklahoma, and was startled to learn that in all the years since the discovery of her only child's body in the aqueduct on June 2, 1998, she'd had only *one* official telephone call—that of Gary Rhoades—and that only in the immediate aftermath of Tina's identification.

I was likewise shocked to discover that no one from the authorities had ever explained to Tina's mother how Tina had come to be murdered, or what her life had been like in the years before she was killed.

It might be argued, of course, that this was a kindness to Tina's mother—sparing her the dreadful details of the events that had taken place before Tina's death, and the events of the murder itself. But I don't think so. Instead of sparing Mary, the authorities had in fact spared themselves—from the pain of having to tell Mary the truth. By the time I talked to her, Mary only wanted to know what had happened, and that with an intensity that was unrelenting: until she knew these details—exactly—she couldn't really come to grips with the fact that her child was dead, or why.

As we have seen, Tina's mother had left Carlos Gibbs when Tina was very young. According to Mary, Carlos worked mainly in carnivals at the time Tina was born, April 27, 1972. The two had disputes, according to Mary, over Carlos' work and his drinking. A second marriage followed in Georgia, which also failed. Mary recalled the early years of Tina's childhood as being hard; Mary said that she herself had endured abuse as a young girl, and so was quite protective of Tina.

Eventually Mary met Ron, who was in military service in Georgia. After they were married, Ron and Mary moved to Ron's old hometown in eastern Washington State, where they lived for several years, before Ron took a job as a police officer in Oregon.

"She always thought of Ron as her daddy," Mary said, "not Carlos." Just why Tina would list her mother as "deceased" on her bail application is a mystery; it may be that she didn't want anyone calling her mother, pestering her while they were searching for Tina, given Tina's eventual occupation and addiction.

In Mary's recollection, as of that of her husband, Ron, and Mary's sister Dottie—Tina's aunt—Tina had always been a sweet child, a better than average student, and someone who had looked forward to being a wife and a mother as she was growing up.

"She was never boy crazy," said her Aunt Dottie, and she took pride in being clean and well-dressed.

But around the age of 16 or 17, Tina had fallen in with some boys who used drugs. Some drug use led to more drug use, and eventually Tina left home to live on her own. Ultimately, Tina became addicted to crack. Occasionally she would call her mother to talk, but eventually, even that came to an end. As Mary had told Rhoades, she hadn't heard from Tina since that Christmas of 1991.

Why, then, had she called Carlos at Christmas of 1997, and not her mother?

At this point it's impossible to say for sure. It may be that Tina simply didn't want her mother to know what kind of life she was living, that she wanted to spare her the pain, or possibly, recriminations. It may have been that Tina saw in her father Carlos, the one-time carnival worker, a kindred free spirit, someone who might understand better what her life was like.

Whatever the relationship Tina had or no longer had with her family, one other thing remains clear: no matter how bad things got, no matter what she did to herself, Tina Renee Gibbs did not deserve to die.

It is tragic that a young woman as pretty as Tina, and as bright, should have fallen into such terrible circumstances; what is even worse is that we, as a society, don't seem to care enough to help such people out of such trouble when they get into it. This was nowhere more true than it was in a place like Las Vegas, Nevada, where everything—even a ride with a trucker—is a game of chance.

Tina's final encounter with the Las Vegas police came on May 6, 1998. Two Las Vegas officers, searching for a Los Angeles juvenile gang member on a murder charge, heard that the juvenile was possibly staying with a group of adults in a motel out on the Boulder Highway strip. Because of the possibility of gunplay, five detectives put on their distinctive yellow jackets, hung their badges around their necks, and armed themselves with exterior gunbelts. They went to the motel in two separate teams, one to cover the rear of the establishment, and another in front.

As two of the detectives drove into the motel's front parking area, Tina spotted them. She went into one of the motel rooms, Number 8.

"Seconds later," wrote Detective A. Chavez, "Hispanic subjects started running out of room #8. As the subjects were running out of the room, they were looking at us." Chavez and his partner yelled "Stop!," but the males kept on running. At this point Chavez saw Tina and two other men run into another room, Number 10, where they apparently locked the door, because when still another man attempted to get into that room, he couldn't. Chavez' partner arrested that one, and then Chavez kicked down the door to room #10, where he found two black males and one black female. With his gun drawn, Chavez ordered the trio to lie on the floor. They complied. One of the two Hispanics broke a window in the motel room's kitchen area and tried to escape, while Tina and the second man hid in the bedroom. Chavez placed everyone under arrest, including Tina for obstruction of justice. The juvenile they had been seeking wasn't caught.

As a result of this encounter, it is clear that up until three weeks before she was last seen, Tina was in contact with people she obviously trusted. Moreover, all of those she had been with had been arrested, and presumably they had been identified. A little work on tracking some of those people down to see where and when they had last seen Tina would likely have borne fruit for a stubborn investigator.

There is one other aspect to Tina's sad final years in Las Vegas that needs to be remarked upon.

It is clear from the record of Tina's numerous prostitution arrests that she worked the streets exclusively. That was where she encountered her customers, whom she serviced for as little as $20. In other words, Tina Gibbs was not a high-priced call girl operating out of some protected environment, such as a high-rise hotel or even a massage parlor. Tina was doing a volume business. That in turn meant that time was money. In order for her to pay for her drug habit, Tina had to turn a lot of tricks.

As a result, it is highly unlikely—indeed, almost impossible—that Tina Gibbs was killed anywhere inside the state of California. The idea of Tina voluntarily going across the state border with any trick is completely out of the question. After all, as soon as she was done with one customer, she needed to find another. She never would have left the streets to ride nearly an hour to the state line, for the simple reason that she could make far more money staying in Las Vegas and continuing her volume business.

It is possible, of course, that Tina was kidnapped in Las Vegas, and taken by force over the state line; but if Wayne Adam Ford was telling the truth when he claimed that he was the one who killed her, that scenario is likewise highly unlikely, because it is clear that Ford's killings took place during the sexual encounter, and Ford himself said this encounter with Tina Gibbs had taken place off Tropicana Boulevard in Las Vegas in late May 1998, at a time when he was in Las Vegas in the hope of seeing Lucie and his son.

As Ford put it later, he called Lucie several times when he was in Las Vegas on May 30, 1998, but no one answered the telephone.

Wayne in his Marine dress uniform with his new bride, Leigh, at the couple's wedding reception in June of 1981. The marriage would founder within two years, primarily because of Wayne's controlling behavior toward his wife. USED WITH PERMISSION

Ocean Grove Lodge and its cocktail lounge in Trinidad, California. Wayne tried to drink his conscience under the table here on the night of November 2, 1998, but the conscience won. The next day, Wayne turned himself in to deputies of the Humboldt County Sheriff's Department. CARLTON SMITH

The small cabin at the Ocean Grove where Wayne sat on the bed waiting for his brother Rod before deciding to turn himself in. CARLTON SMITH

California's Mojave Desert, where Wayne often traveled in his big rig, and where he is said to have dumped two of his victims.
CARLTON SMITH

The mud bank on Ryan's Slough, just east of Eureka, California. Here, the eviscerated, headless, armless, legless torso of an unknown woman was found in October 1997. Wayne is said to have confessed to killing the woman and dismembering her body. To this day, she remains unidentified.
CARLTON SMITH

The Las Vegas
Metropolitan Police
booking photo for
Tina Renee Gibbs.
LAS VEGAS
METROPOLITAN
POLICE

Tina Gibbs in happier times.
MARY GIBBS

The California Aqueduct west of Buttonwillow. The nude body of Tina Renee Gibbs—who was last seen alive in Las Vegas, Nevada—was found hung up on the float line across the fast-moving waters in June 1998. CARLTON SMITH

The California Aqueduct is dangerous and difficult to access. This sign near Buttonwillow has been shot by gun-toting vandals. CARLTON SMITH

Lanett White.
STATE OF CALIFORNIA
DEPARTMENT OF
MOTOR VEHICLES

An irrigation ditch near Lodi, California, where the body of Lanett White was discovered near the base of a large tree in September, 1998. Some witnesses say they had seen a woman resembling Lanett at a truck stop not far from this location, but Wayne allegedly claimed that he actually picked up Lanett several days earlier at a truck stop farther to the south, in Ontario, California.
CARLTON SMITH

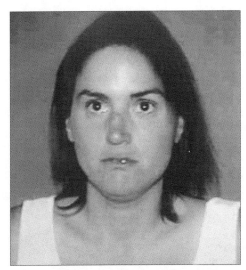

Patricia Tamez.
SAN BERNARDINO
COUNTY SHERIFF'S
DEPARTMENT

A gate at the California Aqueduct near Hesperia, leading to a tunnel under I-15, the main highway connecting Southern California with Las Vegas. The partially dismembered body of Patricia Tamez was found wedged against the gate's concrete façade in October 1998. By the time experts arrived to retrieve it, it had slipped under the façade and into a debris trap between the gate and tunnel. Had the body entered the tunnel, it would have remained trapped for weeks, or even months. CARLTON SMITH

Humboldt County Detective Juan Freeman.
JUAN FREEMAN

Wayne Adam Ford at his arraignment. November, 1998.
SAN FRANCISCO CHRONICLE

VI

SONOMA INTERLUDE

1

The Man in the Truck

IT WAS LATE ON A SUNDAY NIGHT, NEARLY MIDNIGHT, IN the small city of Santa Rosa, about an hour north of San Francisco on U.S. Highway 101. Near the south end of town, not far from where the main drag, Santa Rosa Avenue, exited the freeway, a young woman from San Pablo, California, found herself walking near the ample parking lot of a large home improvement emporium, which had hours earlier closed its doors for the night. Sometime around 11 p.m., the 22-year-old woman with light brown hair, a slight build and a skimpy skirt accepted a "date" from a tall, muscular man driving a large black semi-tractor rig hauling a long flatbed trailer.

The young woman had apparently been working the prostitution "stroll" of Santa Rosa Avenue for some time. As she entered the trucker's rig, she had about $400 in her possession, apparently her earnings from the evening's work.

Everything seemed to go according to plan at first. She and the trucker had sex, presumably after the man had given her some money; it was an inviolate rule for those engaging in prostitution to get the money up front; the service was, of course, fungible. The trucker told her his name was Adam.

Before she knew what was happening, the trucker became belligerent. The young woman found herself bound with ropes and bungee cords; the trucker began hitting her face, breasts and back with his fists and with a belt, and said if she didn't do what he wanted, he would kill her. He poked her with a narrow, hidden object, and told her it was a gun.

With the woman immobilized in the sleeper portion of the big rig, the trucker started his machine and headed north on 101. Some miles later, not far from the small town of Cloverdale, he pulled into a turnout off the highway and shut off the truck. Then he returned to the sleeper area and proceeded to repeatedly rape, sodomize and force the young woman to orally copulate him; he tied a necktie around her neck as if it was a leash, and another around her hands.

The trucker seemed crazed. He'd already ripped her blouse to shreds. As the vicious attack proceeded, the young woman realized that her very life was hanging in the balance. Her survival might depend on keeping the man from going completely off his rocker. That meant trying to appear as compliant as possible. Any resistence only seemed to egg him on.

When she begged to be let go, this only appeared to make him angrier.

"You're not listening," he told her. "You're not doing what I say. You're not cooperating."

At one point, because of the pressure of the tie around her neck, the young woman passed out. When she regained consciousness, the man who called himself Adam told her that she'd fainted, and that he'd had to perform cardiopulmonary resuscitation to revive her.

At length, after the attack was over and "Adam" appeared to be sated, his demeanor changed once more. He seemed quite a bit calmer. He allowed her to put the remnants of her clothes on, but not before taking the $400 from her.

"I fantasized about doing this to someone," he told her, now seeming reflective. "[But] I was turned off afterward. It wasn't as good as I thought it would be."

With that, the man dragged the young woman from the truck. He pulled her to a darkened cliff on the far side of the turnout, and gave her a shove that sent her rolling over the side. Then he drove off.

Not long after the man in the black semi drove off, another driver heading northbound on Highway 101, Art Holquin of Santa Maria, California, saw what at first appeared to be a crazy person in the turnout, waving her arms hysterically. Holquin didn't know what to make of this, at first. He saw that the woman appeared to be half-naked, with blood all over her upper torso. Holquin drew his Peterbilt truck to a stop in the turnout, and grabbed his tire iron. He wasn't sure if this might not be some sort of weird set-up.[34]

But it wasn't. The woman, Holquin soon realized, was in a state of near complete shock.

"Help me! Help me!" she screamed, and Holquin agreed to do just that. He noticed that the woman was bruised and bloody all over her upper body, and her upper arms and chest were filled with stickers that had impaled themselves on her body as she'd rolled over and over down the hidden hillside into the blackness. A necktie was still around her neck and one wrist.

Shakily, the young woman told Holquin that a trucker had picked her up in Santa Rosa and had raped and sodomized her. Now she was trusting yet another trucker to get her to safety. Holquin gave the young woman his jacket, and they set out for the nearest telephone, which turned out to be about fifteen miles farther north. As they drove, the young woman told Holquin the whole story; he soon realized that the truck that had picked up the young woman was a Kenworth, whose sleeper portion was designed differently from Holquin's own Peterbilt.

At length, they came to an exit, and found a telephone, where Holquin called the police for help. After the usual jurisdictional confusion, two Sonoma County sheriff's deputies, accompanied by a female deputy, finally arrived, and took the young woman to the hospital. Meanwhile, Holquin gave the deputies his story; one thing was sure, he thought: whoever had done this to the woman had to be sick.

One of the responding deputies, identified only as C. Bone, filled out the initial report. Although Deputy Bone listed the young woman's injuries as "minor," she was nevertheless listed in "fair" condition. As was obvious to Holquin, her en-

---

34. Interview of witness Art Holquin by the author, November 20, 2000.

counter with the man in the black truck had traumatized her severely. Later, Holquin said he would never forget the night as long as he lived: the young woman, half-naked, running toward his truck, screaming; what was worse, Holquin said, was that the woman had tried to stop other motorists, only to see them rush on past, unwilling to get involved.

Bone would eventually file a seven-page report on the attack, although only a single page, and that somewhat censored, would be released by the Sonoma County Sheriff's Department. There was one curious aspect of the report, however. Although the attack had commenced at about 11 p.m. on August 23, 1998, and lasted until almost 2:30 a.m. early the following morning, Bone's written report wasn't completed until just after midnight on August 25, 1998—nearly a full day later.

Because of the Sonoma County authorities' decision to withhold the last six pages of Bone's report, it isn't possible to say just what the Sonoma County Sheriff's Department did with the information provided to them by the young woman (whose name and address were withheld from the public, as is required in law enforcement reports about victims of sex crimes in California). It wasn't clear, for example, whether the young woman gave deputies a description of the vehicle, or its license plate, or of the assailant who had given his name as Adam,[35] or whether anyone did anything to find out who the man had been.

---

35. Details of this incident were suppressed by officers of the Sonoma County Sheriff's Department, who at first declined to provide any information whatsoever, citing the "gag" order that was eventually issued in the Ford case in Humboldt County, and pointing out that the case involved a "serial murder," as if that somehow exempted the department from laws governing public disclosure. Sonoma County officials eventually elected not to prosecute Ford at all for the Sonoma attack, even though they claimed Ford eventually confessed to it, and that the victim had identified him as the attacker. Thus, the Sonoma officials in effect "convicted" Ford by press release, and then refused to provide any evidence to back up their claims, and more importantly, what they did (or didn't do) to try to solve the crime.

The sketchy details provided here were gleaned from a one-page "inci-

There were at least three things that were significant about this encounter with the trucker and the unnamed young woman, however.

The first, of course, is the obsessive need for control demonstrated by the attacker: the binding of the victim, followed by the death threats, then the assaults (again with the breasts), and of course, the use of one necktie as "a leash," as a psychological profiler put it afterward, which itself was reminiscent of the belt around Lucie's neck in 1996. Here, if anything, was a mode of attack in which the killing was not the primary objective, but the control over the victim; and even when the victim lost consciousness, the attacker claimed to have attempted to revive her.

Second, had the attacker truly had murder on his mind, the woman would have been dead. After all, if the attacker *was* Ford, and if he had already killed twice, why take a chance on a third victim living to identify him? True, the attacker *did* shove his victim off a darkened cliff, but this was far short of the dismemberment in the case of Jane Doe, or even the strangulation of Tina Gibbs. This appears to be strong evidence that Ford's primary motive was not to murder, but to sexually dominate his victims—that, as Ford was later to contend, the murders were never intended but were the result of domination sex that went beyond Ford's control.

And if it was true—as would be alleged later that fall—that Ford had treated at least five other prostitutes from east Bakersfield in much the same fashion during this period of time, that would be yet further evidence that *murder* was never

---

dent" report filed by the Sonoma department, obtained under a California Public Records Act request filed by the author in May of 2000. Additional details emerged as a result of expert testimony before the San Bernardino County Grand Jury by criminal profiler John Yarbrough on July 27, 2000, as well as the author's interview of witness Holquin. The six pages of material held back by the Sonoma authorities, however, would show how much effort they invested in trying to find the assailant.

Arguably, had Wayne Adam Ford been quickly arrested on the allegations made by the young woman in Sonoma County, at least two lives might have been saved over the next two months.

Ford's intention. The logic is quite simple: if Ford had wanted to kill the Sonoma woman, he could easily have done so.

The final aspect of the encounter that bears thinking about is the change in the trucker's demeanor as the encounter unfolded: first, willing "trick," offering money for sex; then "belligerence," as described in the reports of Deputy Bone and profiler Yarbrough; after satiation, a calmness and reflectiveness demonstrated by the attacker; followed in turn by the violent shove over the brambled cliff. This could be reflective of someone whose moods are easily changeable, again a symptom of someone suffering from brain damage, as Dr. Lishman has held.

In any event, in the early morning hours of August 24, 1998, the big semi with its trailer pulled off into the darkness, leaving a terrified 22-year-old behind, to be rescued by the 52-year-old Holquin. That this woman would become critical evidence for both sides in the future now seems obvious—for the prosecution, in terms of aggravation, that is, to show Ford's violent, callous nature; for the defense, to show that he had never actually intended to kill, but only that he'd lost control during a violent sexual encounter. But by the time Wayne Adam Ford came forward with his confession in November, the 22-year-old woman could no longer be found by either side. That was the nature of the business of prostitution; as poor Tina Gibbs had discovered, living or dying was often simply the luck of the draw.

VII
LANETT WHITE

1

Fontana Farewell

LATE ON THE EVENING OF SUNDAY, SEPTEMBER 20, A 25-year-old Fontana, California, woman named Lanett Deyon White changed into yellow panties and a bra, a pair of faded blue jeans, a light blue, patterned tank-top with buttons down the front, a brown plaid, long-sleeved shirt, and a pair of thick-soled open-toed high-heeled sandals. She told her cousin Sharon Bailey that she was going to the store just around the corner; one of the small children in the house had wanted some milk, and there was none to be had.

Sharon thought Lanett seemed upset; she was sniffling, as if she'd been crying. When Sharon asked Lanett what was wrong, Lanett wouldn't say. A few minutes later, Lanett left the house she shared with Sharon, another cousin, Charlotte, and Lanett's two small children. Around 10 p.m., Lanett walked into the night, and was never again seen alive by anyone who knew her. Or at least, that would be the official version of the story for some time to come.

For someone as young as she was, Lanett had already had her own full share of trouble. Already the mother of four children—ages 9, 8, 3, and nine months—Lanett had recently been involved in a dispute with her own mother and father, who themselves were barely making ends meet in a low-rent apartment in nearby Ontario, California. Late in August, after some sort of disagreement, Lanett's mother and father had asked her to move. Lanett took the two youngest children and settled in with her cousins a few miles away in working class Fontana, just an exhaust plume away from the frequently traffic-jammed San Bernardino Freeway.

That Lanett was sexually precocious seems beyond dispute; her first child, a daughter, was born the day after Lanett's sixteenth birthday; another child, a son with a different father, was born just a little over ten months later. The third child, also a boy, was born to a third father five years after that, and a fourth son, of a fourth father, arrived in early January of 1998.

Judging from Lanett's records in the courts of San Bernardino County, she appears to have had both limited education and job skills; she soon fell in with a crowd that skirted the edge of the law. Most of Lanett's earlier troubles took place in the small city of Chino, a former agricultural community wedged in between eastern Los Angeles County and southwestern San Bernardino County. At one time, Chino was well-known for growing hay and alfalfa for the area's dairy farms; but by the 1990s, and with the construction of a state prison and its attendant employment, Chino had grown into a mini-city of nearly 60,000 people, many of them middle-class homeowners and apartment dwellers who commuted to jobs in Los Angeles, Riverside, Orange and San Bernardino Counties.

The first adult record of Lanett's malefactions dates back to September of 1994, when she would have been almost 22, and the mother of two children.[36] In the company of another woman, Lanett was arrested and charged with forgery. Based upon the report of a Chino Police Department officer who identified himself as R. Planas, Lanett and the second woman attempted to cash a forged personal check for $500 at a Chino bank. When Officer Planas asked Lanett where she had gotten the check, Lanett told him it had been given to her by a woman for whom she had done some work.

The problem had come when Lanett asked her companion to cash the check, since she had no identification herself. The companion presented the check, and the teller then compared

---

36. Report of Chino Police Officer R. Planas, #94-09-0920, Sept. 28, 1994.

the signature on the check to the account holder's signature card, which was that of a man. The teller's supervisor then called the man's wife at home, and the wife said she didn't believe that her husband had written such a check. The wife then called her husband at work, and the husband denied writing the check. The wife then called the bank back and told the teller that her husband had lost his checkbook about seven weeks before, and had never bothered to notify anyone.

Whatever the merits of this story—it should be noted that it is not unusual for men to pay for illicit services with checks, and then to deny they wrote them, often adding the explanation that their checkbook was "lost" or "stolen"—Lanett and her companion were promptly arrested on the forgery charges. Lanett now claimed that she'd gotten the check from a third party, someone she knew as Robin, as partial payment of a debt. But Lanett couldn't remember "Robin" 's last name; she added that Robin lived in a motel in the city of Ontario. When she got the check, Lanett added, it was already signed by the husband, but the amount was blank. Lanett filled in the amount, and wrote in the words, "loan payment."

Officer Planas clearly wasn't buying much, if any, of this story. He took Lanett and her companion to jail.

"As I spoke with White," he wrote, "I noticed that she displayed pronounced symptoms of methamphetamine influence. White's pupils were dilated, her mouth was dry, and her tongue had a build-up of white caking substance on the top portion of same. I also conducted a pupil examination. Based upon all the symptoms displayed I formed the opinion that she was under the influence of methamphetamine. White submitted a urine sample and was issued a citation for same."

The urine test proved positive for methamphetamine, and Lanett was booked for felony forgery and misdemeanor methamphetamine use. In her booking sheet, Lanett claimed she was pregnant.

This, unfortunately, was not the end of the forgery episode. Less than a month later, Lanett was back in hot water, this time over still more checks from the same account. This time she was charged with burglary.

The circumstances of how Lanett and her friend had come into possession of the disputed checks remained murky; for one thing, "Robin" couldn't be located. As a result, the case of the checks was assigned to an investigator in early October of 1994—coincidentally, just about the time that Ford and Lucie were preparing to be married in Las Vegas. At the time, of course, Ford wouldn't have known Lanett in the least.

About two weeks into the investigation, the officer assigned to the check case was confronted by the wife of the man on whose account the checks were written; the woman told the investigator that she'd found two more checks that had the forged signatures of her husband. Both of these checks had been cashed for a total of $816.

The investigator now tracked down an address for the payee on the checks; but, apparently guessing that the payee was a dupe of Lanett, the investigator called Lanett first. Lanett admitted that she knew the payee, but said she was a friend of a friend, and that she wasn't sure she knew how to contact her.

"Based on my conversation with Lanett," the investigator wrote,[37] "I did not believe I would receive any additional help." The investigator then sent a letter to the check payee, asking her to contact the police.

Subsequently the payee came in to the police station and readily identified the checks. She said she'd gotten them from Lanett, who had been her brother's girlfriend for four years. According to the payee, the boyfriend and Lanett had been evicted from the apartment they shared, and as a result, the boyfriend was about $2,000 in debt. He wanted Lanett to pay some of the costs from the eviction, and Lanett agreed, saying she would soon be receiving checks from her job, and that she would give some of the money to the boyfriend. Because Lanett didn't have any identification, she wanted her boyfriend to give the blank check to his sister so she could cash it. A few days later, the trio went through the same process.

---

37. Report of Chino Police Department Detective D. Devey, Case #94-12-475.

The whole setup seemed suspicious to the investigator, particularly since Lanett did not appear to have a job, and therefore, no legitimate access to any checks.

"Based on the same checks being cashed by Lanett during her [earlier] arrest and the same checks being given to [the payee], and the identification of Lanett as the person who gave her the checks, I formed the opinion that Lanett was the person who was responsible . . ." the investigator wrote.

All of this took several months to unravel. Finally, in early February 1995, the investigator went to an address in Chino where Lanett was thought to be staying; it turned out that it was the apartment of Lanett's mother and father. Lanett's parents had no idea where she was, or when she would be back.

A week later, the investigator put out a wanted bulletin for Lanett. On February 7, Lanett was taken into custody by a Chino patrol officer, and taken to police headquarters for questioning.

Lanett continued to insist that she'd gotten the questionable checks from "Robin." She said she'd sold her car to Robin, and Robin was making payments. But before all the payments had been made, Robin stopped giving her checks, so Lanett had kept both the checks as well as the car.

"Lanett insisted she was given the checks by Robin, and did not know the checks were not good and should not have been cashed," the investigator wrote. "Lanett told me she did not know Robin's last name." But Lanett told the investigator that Robin lived in a motel that was located near an Ontario striptease joint.

The investigator then went to the motel, where she found that indeed Robin did exist, but that she had moved to an unknown new address. Without Robin to contradict her story, there was no definitive evidence against Lanett; nevertheless, when the case was called for trial, Lanett failed to appear, and warrants were issued for her arrest.[38]

---

38. Report of San Bernardino County Sheriff's Department booking, file #95-10-429, October 13, 1995, based upon arrest of Chino Police Department in citation #C 013358, October 13, 1995.

Taken as a whole, the bogus checks episode sheds some light on the quality of Lanett White's existence in the years before her death. For one thing, she was quite young—21, and already the mother of two small children, as well as being pregnant with a third. She had a boyfriend—Lanett told the investigator that he was her "husband"—who seems to have been less than successful as a breadwinner, in that the family was evicted. Nor did Lanett appear to have a job, or even any identification, if the tales of the check "dupes" could be believed.

The checks episode also shows that when she was in trouble, Lanett turned to her mother and father for support, although neither of them had much to spare. It also shows that even at 21, Lanett had already developed a habit for methamphetamine, a viciously addictive drug that robs people of both judgment and will. And it likely shows that Lanett was at least in contact with people who frequented strip clubs, as "Robin's" last known address indicated; thus, it is entirely possible that the checkbook—missing for seven weeks, and never reported lost by the husband until an attempt was made to cash one of the checks—was lifted by "Robin" or one of her associates at the strip joint, and passed on to Lanett, who in turn used associates of her boyfriend as "cut-outs" to cash the checks.

This is an all-too-common variant of the ancient badger game; it relies upon the loser of the checkbook being too embarrassed to report the original theft; and what it indicates is that even at the age of 21, Lanett White was enmeshed in a loose-knit gang of pickpockets, drug dealers and con-artists who gathered around the striptease joint as their working turf.

Hanging out in such company can not only bring a person to potential legal grief, as Lanett discovered, it usually has an even more deleterious side effect—drug addiction.

Ten months after having been involved in the bogus check imbroglio, Lanett was again arrested for use of methamphetamine, this time after having been involved in a car wreck involving a friend's borrowed Camaro. Apparently the car was involved in a hit-and-run accident near Chino, and the car involved had been seen near Lanett's apartment.

A Chino patrol officer spotted the black Camaro in a carport at Lanett's apartment. He could see that the car had recent front-end damage, and could smell the odors of burnt oil and leaking antifreeze. It seemed clear that this was the suspect car. The officer ran the license plate, and while he was waiting for the results, a man in the complex approached him to admit that the car was his, but that he had loaned it to a girlfriend. The man then took another officer to Lanett's apartment. When he returned, the second officer had Lanett with him. Lanett admitted that she'd been driving the Camaro.

While talking with Lanett, the officer noticed once again that her pupils were dilated; he also noticed that while she spoke quite rapidly, her words were slurred; Lanett seemed quite nervous and "fidgety," as the officer put it.

At that point the police dispatcher radioed back with the word that there were two bench warrants out on Lanett, from the bad check charges and the earlier methamphetamine arrest. Together, the bail on the outstanding warrants totaled $30,000. Lanett was taken into custody, where she was made to give another urine test for methamphetamine.[39]

Six months later, the 23-year-old Lanett was in trouble once again; this time she was arrested by Chino police for being drunk in public. In this April 5, 1996, incident, Lanett seems to have gotten involved in a dispute with a man, apparently a new boyfriend, in a Chino-area bar.[40] The argument broke out on the dance floor, and the bar's bouncer tossed both Lanett and the man out of the establishment. But the bouncer soon let the man back in, while refusing admittance to Lanett, claiming she was too intoxicated.

This seems to have infuriated Lanett. She went into the

---

39. The final disposition of these charges was not apparent in the Chino court records, although two of the four cases lodged against her in that court show that she was listed as a fugitive, and that warrants were still outstanding for her arrest, more than two years after she had been found dead.
40. Report of Chino Police Officer Sergeant L. Tomicic, Jr., Case #96-04-130, April 6, 1996.

parking lot and located the car of the bouncer, who also apparently doubled as the club's disc jockey. According to a witness, Lanett went to the dj's car and broke off the antenna. She then began whacking the windshield with the broken metal rod. Apparently still unsatisfied with the damage she'd done, Lanett then got on the hood of the car "and started walking on same" with her high-heeled shoes, according to the officer's report. Afterward, Lanett went back to the front door of the bar and sat on a stool outside waiting for her boyfriend to come out.

By that time, the police had been called. They found Lanett, none too steady in equilibrium, still sitting on the bar stool.

"It appeared," wrote patrol officer R. Crolen, "as if White was having a hard time sitting on the stool. She continually slipped off the stool and had to catch herself so she would not fall to the ground."

When Officer Crolen asked Lanett what the matter was, she burst into tears.

"White could only tell me her name and nothing else without starting to cry."

Crolen talked with White's boyfriend, who told him they'd had an argument earlier in the evening, and that Lanett had taken a swing at him. Apparently that was when the dj had given her the heave-ho. Crolen tried to convince the boyfriend to take Lanett home. But on the way to the car, she started arguing with the boyfriend again, and this time got so mad she began to chase him through the parking lot. At that point, Officer Crolen decided to arrest Lanett on the theory that she was so intoxicated she was no longer capable of taking care of herself.

It is doubtful whether there is a police officer anywhere in America who hasn't encountered a similar situation. And while the basic details were dutifully recorded—a lovers' spat, a bouncer's exclusionary decision, an act of retaliatory vandalism, too much to drink, an attempted reconciliation gone awry—nothing in the officers' reports [subsequently, the vandalism was discovered, and the dj insisted on pressing charges against Lanett for the damages, which he later estimated at about $1,700] indicates just why Lanett was so drunk and unhappy that night. But then, the ordinary traumas of ordinary people simply aren't sufficiently unusual to make it into the body of an arresting officer's report, even though they eventually become threads in the seldom-seen tapestry of a future murder victim's life. It was so ordinary that no one paid any attention, certainly not the news media; and it was the tragedy of Lanett White's poor, impoverished existence that no one really cared about her until she was dead, and then only as the victim of a bizarre murder that could have happened to almost anyone, given the same sort of circumstances.

Even after Lanett was dead, the county's welfare department persisted in suing her for failure to comply with child support orders. At least, when he learned in July 2000 of the bench warrants for the dead Lanett's arrest, Judge Smith ordered them quashed.

2

Lodi

JUST AFTER NOON ON SEPTEMBER 25, 1998, THREE MEN driving a truck hauling a cattle trailer on the way to Vallejo, California, pulled into a large gravel turnout off State Highway 12, not far from Interstate 5 near Lodi, midway between Stockton and Sacramento in California's broad central valley. The truck's engine had been misfiring, and the three men decided to replace one of the spark plug wires.

The turnout itself appeared to be a frequent stop-off for trucks headed from the nearby I-5 freeway toward the communities of north San Francisco Bay; it was well littered with the usual sorts of roadside trash: paper cups, ruptured fan belts, beer cans, broken bottles, fast-food wrappers, pieces of old tire tread and empty motor oil cans. There was a large black walnut tree shading part of the turnout, and beyond the tree, an irrigation ditch perhaps twenty feet across at its widest. Beyond the ditch, a vineyard extended off into the distance as far as the eye could see. On the south side of the highway, a gray multi-story agricultural elevator, a complex of hoppers and conveyor belts and steel latticework, towered over the landscape.

With about 60,000 residents, the small city of Lodi considered itself "the Winegrape Capital of the World," and indeed, ranked first in production of grapes for zinfandel, cabernet, sauvignon, chardonnay and merlot wines. Strategically located between the state's two major north-south arteries, I-5 and Highway 99, just ninety miles east of San Francisco and thirty-five miles south of Sacramento, fifteen miles away from a deep water port at Stockton, and with excellent rail access, Lodi was ideally situated as an agricultural community.

It was, of course, a rather bucolic community—the sort of place where high school kids bent on having a wild night might get inebriated and steal into an isolated pasture by moonlight to engage in the sport of "cow tipping," as they called it: sneaking up on an unsuspecting and snoozing cow and shoving her over to everyone's great merriment. Except, of course, the cow's.

As the three men brought their misfiring truck to a stop in the turnout, across the highway from the gigantic elevator—once used to store flower seeds—one of the men, Rinaldo Lorenzo, glanced down into the irrigation ditch and noticed the naked and quite dead body of a young woman. He called to one of the other men, John Ware, and within a minute or two Ware had crossed Highway 12 to rouse a man at the gigantic elevator, telling him that there was a dead woman in the ditch across the road, and that he should call the cops.

As it happened, elevator manager John Hoff and his assistant, Greg Moreno, had no telephone; they did, however, have access to a two-way radio, which they used to contact the elevator's business operation office not far away. The office women, in turn, called the San Joaquin County Sheriff's Department. Before the deputies could arrive, however, Ware, Lorenzo and their companion fixed their truck and drove off. It would be several months before anyone would learn who they had been, but by then, it wouldn't make any difference.

The first to arrive was the fire department rescue squad; but the firemen knew there was nothing they could do: it was obvious that the woman had been dead for quite some time.

Next to arrive were two sheriff's deputies, who cordoned off the scene, and made sure that the fire truck left the exact way it had come: no one wanted to mess up any possible suspect tire tracks. And a few minutes after that, three homicide detectives from the San Joaquin County Sheriff's Department came, and with their arrival, the official investigation into just how the unknown woman met her grisly end began.

The whole proceeding was committed to video tape and still cameras as it went forward.

The woman lying in the bottom of the ditch, just under the large walnut tree on the bank, was fairly large: at least 5 feet 10 inches tall, and over 150 pounds. She was on her back, with her knees up, and slightly bent; the bulk of her body was lying in just over a foot of slow-running irrigation water. Both arms were thrown out; it appeared that someone had simply pitched her body into the ditch from the turnout near the walnut tree, and then fled. Her face and chest were already black from decomposition; that in turn suggested that she had been dead for several days at least.

The case was assigned to Detective Mike Jones. Two other detectives began scouring the ditch and the surrounding turnout area for evidence, taking photographs as they went. The detectives found a number of items in the turnout that seemed significant, including several articles of clothing—a plaid, dark-blue-and-beige long-sleeved shirt, one brown leather glove, and a blue plastic tarp, with blood stains, found near the body in the trickle of water in the ditch. There was a cloth bracelet on the victim's wrist, a ring on the index finger, and a yellow metal necklace around the neck. It appeared that the victim had several tattoos.

The canvass of the area around the turnout yielded several other items of interest: one was a white plastic bag, with a possible blood stain; this sack bore a logo from a nationwide chain of truck stops called "Flying J." Not far from the body, the detectives found several leaves bearing possible blood stains, a bloody paper towel, a saw blade, a plastic water bottle, a small lipstick container, a disposable lighter, a plastic sack that once contained paper plates, and some additional samples of hair. All of these items suggested possible links to the victim.

Later that afternoon, just before 5 p.m., the body was removed from the ditch and taken to the San Joaquin County Coroner's facility near French Camp, just south of Stockton.

There, a pathologist, Dr. Diane Vertes, performed an examination.

The first thing Vertes noted in her subsequent report was "a puncture mark lateral to the right breast," not a large wound, but one about a quarter-inch across. The absence of hemorrhage in the surrounding tissue seemed to suggest that it had been inflicted after death.

It was clear to Vertes that the body had been decomposing for at least several days. The skin slippage and erosion of the epidermis was accompanied by the loss of much of the victim's hair; and the discoloration of the tissues indicated that decomposition was fairly advanced—at least two to five days, it appeared. The tattoos, at least, were still discernible: on the right breast the words, "Mi Madre Debi"; on the left breast, "Ignacio"; on the right rear shoulder, a heart with a ribbon; and on the right exterior ankle in cursive writing, letters that appeared to read "My Mac."

But despite the thoroughgoing examination, Dr. Vertes could find no obvious cause of the woman's death: no broken bones, no clear neck bruising from possible strangulation, no gunshot holes—in short, nothing, except for the single small stab wound to the area of the right breast, which apparently had taken place after death. All that Vertes could find were some slight markings on the neck that appeared to be consistent with the pattern of the necklace; but internal examination of the neck structures showed none of the hemorrhaging one would expect to see with a manual strangulation. Vertes also noted some red marks on the back of the head, but whether they were pre- or post-mortem was impossible to determine.

What did any of this mean? No one could say for sure; one possibility was a fatal overdose, while another was a form of murderous suffocation that the substantial decomposition had made impossible to verify.

Still, one thing was for sure: the woman had hardly gone out to the irrigation ditch in the middle of nowhere, stripped off her clothes, lay down on a blue tarp to bleed, died, and then stabbed herself with a narrow pointed object after she was already dead. There was one other item of possible interest: a chemical analysis showed a measurable amount of meth-amphetamine in the victim's blood at the time of her death—enough to get high on, but not nearly enough to kill her. There were no other drugs found in the victim's system. Now, given the circumstances, even if the exact cause of death wasn't clear, the manner was obvious: it was almost certainly a case of murder.

At this point, in contrast to their counterparts in Kern County two months earlier, the San Joaquin investigators were granted some good fortune: the hands of their victim yielded useable prints for identification purposes. By late afternoon on the day the body had been pulled from the ditch, the state's computerized system had provided a match: Lanett Deyon White, aged 25, formerly of Chino, California, who had gone out on the night of Sunday, September 20, to buy some milk for her baby, and had never come back.

Lanett's fingerprints were in the state's computer system, of course, because of her prior encounters with the Chino Police Department; those records in turn led Detective Jones to Lanett's father in Ontario, California, the city next to Chino. That same evening, Jones called Lanett's father in Ontario and notified him that his daughter was dead.

Lanett's father told Jones he had no idea how or why Lanett had wound up in northern California. The last he and Lanett's mother had seen her, he said, was approximately a month before, when she had moved in with her cousin, Charlotte, in Fontana, another small city next to Ontario. Lanett's father gave Jones Charlotte's address.

All of these events had taken place on Friday afternoon, September 25, 1998; by early Monday morning, Jones and his partner, Detective David Claypool, were on their way to Ontario to meet with Lanett's mother, Debra—"Mi Madre Debi," as the tattoo had so lovingly described.

Debra decided to meet with the two detectives at her sister's house. Debra said that Lanett and her children had moved out of the apartment they had shared with Debra and her husband in early September after a dispute. Debra said they'd had to "kick her out." Subsequently, Lanett had gone to live with her cousin Charlotte at the Fontana apartment. The last time she'd seen Lanett, Debra said, was on Wednesday, September 16, 1998; but she'd received a call from her sister, Lanett's Aunt Judy, on September 22, saying that Lanett had gone to a restaurant in Fontana to pick up a check. But after leaving to go to the restaurant, Lanett had never turned up again, according to Debra. She added that Debra had four children, and gave their ages.

Later that same evening, Jones and Claypool tracked down Lanett's cousin Charlotte to get her version of when Lanett was last seen.

Charlotte was 24. She lived in a Fontana apartment not far from Interstate 10, the main route between Los Angeles, San Bernardino, and Phoenix, Arizona, with her 21-year-old sister Sharon, her cousin Lanett, and seven children, two of whom were Lanett's youngest.

Charlotte told the detectives that Lanett had been living with them for about three weeks before she disappeared. The last time she'd seen Lanett was about 6 p.m. on Sunday night, September 20, when she'd gone to the corner store. Since they had no telephone in the house, the three women used the nearby pay phone at the store. Charlotte thought Lanett had gone to call a friend, someone named Mario. When Lanett had come back, she had a bottle of wine cooler with her. Charlotte admitted to the detectives that she, Lanett and a neighborhood friend had smoked some methamphetamine ("crank") earlier in the afternoon. Shortly after Lanett had come back from the store, Charlotte said, she'd seen Lanett talking outside the house to a man in a white pickup truck with a blue stripe. Then she herself had gone to bed.

Several hours later, when she woke up, Charlotte saw Lanett getting dressed in a brown-and-black dress. Lanett again went to the store, and returned with more wine cooler. By this time, Lanett's friend Mario had arrived at the apartment. Charlotte returned to bed once more.

Still later the same night, Charlotte said, she was awakened by the crying of Lanett's three-month-old baby. When she asked where Lanett was, Mario told her that she had gone to a nearby restaurant "to pick up a check." Charlotte said she'd told Mario that Lanett had met someone at the store the night before, and had arranged to "make some money."

When Lanett didn't come back that Sunday night, Charlotte said, she'd gone back to bed, while Mario slept on the living room couch. By the following afternoon, when she still hadn't returned, Mario and Ignacio—one of Mario's friends, and the father of Lanett's baby—went to the corner store themselves to see what had become of Lanett.

"I asked Charlotte what Lanett was wearing when she last left," Jones wrote in his follow-up report, "and she said she was wearing a pair of faded jeans, a pair of black and white tennis shoe style sandals that are open-toed and very high-heeled, a tank top, and a brownish, plaid shirt.

"Charlotte said," Jones added, "that it was not like her [Lanett] to leave her baby with Charlotte for any extended period of time."

3

Dead Ends

NONE OF THIS WAS PARTICULARLY HELPFUL TO JONES AND Claypool, because it shed no light on the central mystery: how had Lanett gotten all the way from Fontana on Sunday night, September 20, to Lodi, more than 400 miles to the north, by at most the following Friday, September 25, when she was found dead in the ditch? Since it was obvious from the decomposition that Lanett had been dead several days before she was found, the question was: What happened to Lanett when she'd gone to the store Sunday night?

The next afternoon, Jones and Claypool went to the corner store to look for more information about Lanett. The store was directly across the street from the restaurant where Lanett had intended to "pick up a check," as her mother had told the detectives.

The owner of the store told the detectives that while the store had a video surveillance camera, the tapes for September 20 had been re-used; therefore it would be impossible to see whether Lanett had ever arrived on the night she went out. The owner provided the detectives with the name and address of the clerk who normally was on duty at night.

An hour or so later, Jones and Claypool contacted the night clerk. He said Lanett had been at the store three times on Sunday, September 20, and had made three different calls from the pay phone. The last time he'd seen her had been just after 9:30 p.m. He also said that Lanett told him that she would come back at 11 p.m. to talk with him. But a few minutes after 11, the clerk and his assistant closed the store, without seeing her.

The following morning, Jones and Claypool followed up on a tip from someone in the neighborhood, who had reported seeing a particular vehicle occasionally stopped by the residence to talk to Lanett. This tip led them to a 52-year-old gray-haired man, slightly over six feet and weighing nearly 280 pounds; it appears that the man was identified through his license plate.

The big gray-haired man readily admitted to having met Lanett on numerous occasions. In fact, he said, he had just heard that she had been found dead. The last time he saw her, the big man said, was possibly on Wednesday, September 23, or Thursday, September 24, 1998. This, of course, was at least three days later than Lanett's cousins had seen her as she was on her way to the store.

But the big man admitted he wasn't entirely sure of his dates. He didn't have a steady job, he explained, and sometimes he became confused as to his days and dates. The big man admitted that he was a crank user, about a quarter of a gram a day, which had the effect of further discounting the accuracy of his recollection. He said he couldn't remember what he'd been doing, or even where he'd been on Sunday, September 20. Jones and Claypool searched the big man's truck, but found nothing.

Later that morning, Jones and Claypool finally made contact with Ignacio, the father of Lanett's youngest child.

Ignacio told the detectives that the last time *he*'d seen Lanett was on Saturday morning, September 19. On the following day he went to Victorville to visit with his sister's family, and returned to his own apartment late on Sunday night. The next morning he went to see Lanett at the apartment she shared with Charlotte, Sharon and the seven children; that was when he learned that Lanett had left late Sunday night and had never come back. Ignacio said he waited all day at Charlotte's apartment for Lanett to return, with no results. Mario, who'd spent Sunday night on Charlotte's couch waiting for Lanett to come back, was still there. Ignacio said that around 5 P.M. on Monday afternoon, the twenty-first, he and Mario had gone to the store to see what had happened to Lanett, but couldn't find out anything.

At that point, Detectives Jones and Claypool had almost run out of leads. About the only thing anyone could say for sure was that Lanett had headed around the corner to the liquor store, where at least one of the clerks had been expecting her, but that she had never arrived. Given the fact that the walk from the apartment to the liquor store was less than 600 feet, it began to seem increasingly likely that either something had happened to Lanett on the way to the store, or that at least one of the people Jones and Claypool had interviewed so far wasn't telling the entire truth.

After the interviews with Ignacio, Mario, Charlotte and the store clerks, Jones and Claypool were down to what seemed to be their last hope: Charlotte's younger sister Sharon, also Lanett's cousin. In talking with Sharon, the detectives for the first time began to get a better handle on the sequence of events that had unfolded on the night when Lanett was last seen.

As far as Sharon could remember, Lanett had been to the liquor store on two different occasions on Saturday, the night before she was last seen. The first time had been around 5:30 p.m. Lanett had returned from the store with $30 in cash. Lanett had previously told Sharon that she was going to get $30 from the man at the store.

"I'm just going to let him touch me," Sharon remembered Lanett telling her. As far as Sharon could tell, the man at the store willing to pay Lanett $30 was the night clerk, who had already been interviewed by Jones and Claypool.

Sharon's next recollection was that Lanett returned to the store once more about 9:30 p.m. on the same night. When she came back this time, Lanett told her that she was supposed to go back about 11:30 to meet the night clerk and another man. They were all going to have a drink, Lanett told Sharon, and she'd get $70 this time. But something happened, Lanett told

Sharon, and the $70 meeting was postponed to the following night, Sunday, September 20.

As Sharon recalled the events of Sunday, Lanett had gone to the liquor store around 7:30 p.m. to call Mario; Sharon herself had never met Mario [who, police later discovered, was also known as "Armando"], and so knew almost nothing about him. Around 9 p.m. on Sunday, Mario had arrived at Charlotte's apartment. As far as Sharon could tell, Lanett spent most of this time sitting on Mario's lap in a chair in the front yard, kissing him.

About 9:30 or so, Sharon said, she'd gone inside to lie down; around 10 p.m., she was awakened by the hall light being turned on. She saw that Lanett had come inside and was changing her clothes.

"Sharon said Lanett appeared to be upset," Detective Claypool wrote in his follow-up report.[41] "She said that she was sniffling like she had been crying. Sharon asked Lanett what was wrong; however, she wouldn't answer her."

Claypool asked Sharon what Lanett had been wearing after she'd changed her clothes. Sharon described the yellow bra and panties, the light blue jeans, the tank-top, the long-sleeved shirt, and the high-heeled, open-toed sandals.

"Sharon also advised that while she was talking to Lanett in the hallway, one of the children woke up wanting some milk. Sharon said she told the child they didn't have any milk and they would have to wait until morning. She said at that point Lanett offered to go down to the liquor store and get some milk." This was the last time Sharon saw her cousin.

When Lanett left, Sharon continued, Mario [Armando] stayed behind; then, "sometime after 11 o'clock . . . Mario knocked on the door and woke them up. She [Sharon] stated that he was a little worried because Lanett had not returned from the liquor store."

This is one indication that the stories provided to the San Joaquin detectives by those closest to Lanett were less than

41. Supplemental Report of Detective Dave Claypool, September 30, 1998, San Joaquin County Sheriff's Department Case #98-21038.

complete. On one hand, Sharon asserted that Mario stayed behind when Lanett went to the liquor store; but in the next breath, she described Mario as knocking on the door and waking everyone up "sometime after 11" to say he was worried because Lanett hadn't returned. So where was Mario [Armando] between the time Lanett left for the store and "sometime after 11" when he knocked on the door and woke everyone up? Clearly he wasn't asleep on the couch, and he wasn't even inside the house.

Around 2 or 3 a.m., Mario walked to the store to see if he could find Lanett; she was nowhere to be found, according to Sharon. At that point Mario returned to the couch for the rest of the night; the next afternoon, as Charlotte had already described, he went with Ignacio to the liquor store one more time, again without finding Lanett.

Much later, a spokesman for the San Joaquin County Sheriff's Department acknowledged the deficiencies in the statements of Mario [Armando] with regard to Lanett's disappearance; given her manner of dress, her habit of accosting men driving near the Fontana apartment, her arrangements with the liquor store clerk, her statements about going to the restaurant to "pick up a check," the probabilities are that Lanett had been for some time engaged in prostitution, and most likely with the knowledge and assistance of Mario.

These facts, coupled with information later developed, to the effect that Lanett had actually gone that Sunday night to a Fontana truck stop near the intersection of Cherry and Slover Avenues—a place known for its prostitution activity, about three miles from the liquor store—was strong evidence that Lanett had started "working," as the parlance had it. How she got from Charlotte's house to the truck stop would remain a matter of educated conjecture on the part of Jones and Claypool, although they had their suspicions.

Thus, the picture of Lanett White that emerges during her final days is one of a woman who was scuffling—someone trying all sorts of different scams in an effort to make ends meet; impoverished, trying to take care of her small children, someone who had fallen into the company of those who similarly eked out marginal existences with minor frauds and petty crime, while using methamphetamine to take the uglier edges off of life: not a pretty picture, and certainly not the sort of "pristine victim" that usually attracted the rabid interest of the news media, as *San Jose Mercury News* columnist Sue Hutchison had made clear in the aftermath of Wayne Adam Ford's arrest.

Still, in late September, without the information that Lanett had actually gone to the truck stop instead of the liquor store, San Joaquin detectives Jones and Claypool were temporarily stumped. From the facts they had gathered, it seemed likely that Lanett had gone hooking, all right; the question was where? And again: how did she get from Fontana to Lodi, so far away?

On October 1, 1998, having temporarily given up on his inquiries in the Fontana area, Detective Jones decided to try the puzzle from the other end: he went to the intersection of Highway 12 and Interstate 5 in Lodi, where there was a truck stop sometimes frequented by prostitutes. There he encountered a clerk at a Texaco station, one Elinor Torres. Jones showed Torres a photograph of Lanett and asked her if she recognized the woman in the picture; Elinor said she did.

"She said she last saw her on Wednesday or Thursday of the previous week, this would be the week of September 23rd or 24th. I asked her if she could tell me what the victim was wearing and she said she was wearing a washed out or faded jeans, a tank top that buttoned up the middle, and some high sandaled shoes."

Elinor's description of Lanett's clothing was so spot-on that it later was to create a puzzle: either Lanett, alive and well, had actually been at the Texaco station in Lodi on the twenty-third or twenty-fourth, or Detective Jones inadvertently coached her on what to say. The description, coupled with the fact that Jones provided Elinor with a photograph of Lanett, rather than a more common array of photos, suggests that he was initially convinced that Lanett had been alive in Lodi at least three days after last being seen in Fontana, and was making a good-faith effort to move the focus of his investigation closer to the scene of the crime, that is, the irrigation ditch near the vineyard.

In support of this notion, Jones had the drug-addled recollection of the big man in Fontana to fall back on, who'd said he thought he'd possibly last seen Lanett on the twenty-third or twenty-fourth, which was three or four days after the supposed walk to the store.

Elinor Torres now told Jones that the woman she'd identified as Lanett had been present at the station with two men, both with ponytails, one Anglo and the other Hispanic, as well as one other woman. To Jones, this suggested the possibility that Lanett had somehow been taken from Fontana to northern California to work as a prostitute in the days immediately following Sunday, September 20.

Then, in a reversal of the usual procedure, Elinor was asked to come into the sheriff's department to help prepare an identikit drawing of the people she saw. This took place on the following day; this time Elinor said the woman she'd identified as Lanett was about 5 feet 4 inches tall, and weighed about 125 pounds, with reddish-blonde hair. This description clearly was dissimilar to Lanett, who was 5' 10", and weighed close to 160 pounds before her death. Jones' putative sighting of a living Lanett near Lodi began to look like a chimera.

Elinor next provided identikit descriptions of the two men she thought she'd seen with Lanett; but both descriptions were so general that they could have fit nearly anyone; as a result, Detectives Jones and Claypool realized that their leads to the murderer of Lanett White, who'd supposedly gone out to buy milk in Fontana, but who'd wound up dead in a ditch 400 miles away from home, were dwindling into nothingness.

VIII
PATTY TAMEZ

1

Victorville

JUST AS BAKERSFIELD BECAME FAMOUS AS THE HOME OF country music star Buck Owens, the area near Victorville, California, has its own show business past. This was the retirement home of Roy Rogers and Dale Evans, who made the high desert land north of the San Bernardino Mountains famous—at least in the minds of legions of televised real estate pitchmen who praised its dry, empty land for its wide open spaces, clean air and good country living. Just the presence of the retired singing cowboy and his stylish wife helped promote the development of thousands of acres of desert wasteland into several growing communities, including Adelanto, Hesperia, and Apple Valley, bedroom communities all, nestled cheek by jowl beneath the north-facing shadow of the craggy San Bernardinos to the south. Best of all, the cheap lots were just an hour's drive away from the Los Angeles basin.

But Roy, who in retirement eventually became the star attraction of his own museum, first in Apple Valley, then in Victorville, before his death in July of 1998, was only one of a number of relatively recent immigrants to the High Desert over the previous 120 years. Victorville itself had been there for a half-century before Roy Rogers ever sang a note or fired a single bullet or hopped into the saddle of his ever-patient horse Trigger, or shot a single scene; and as the years passed after Roy's retirement, there were those in the burgeoning desert sprawl who said that no matter what the land developers

liked to claim, in the real-life High Desert there were far too
few happy trails to go around.

This land north of the San Bernardino Mountains is as stark
as it is beautiful in its own way. In the distance, to all points
of the compass, huge rocky peaks thrust up unexpectedly from
the dusty plains—sudden, ancient volcanic islands seemingly
bare of the slightest form of foliage, eternally eroding in long
taluses of sand and gravel, white rocks shimmering in the
dancing heat. Between these scattered rocky outcrops lay miles
upon miles of emptiness, an ocean of sand, marked in nearly
uniform patterns by creosote brush and other sparse desert
plants, occasionally broken by patches of crooked Joshua
trees, thrusting their spiky limbs skyward as if in supplication
for the merest drop of rain. The flat spaces, and their rocky
mountainous eruptions, invite the imagination to wonder: who
lives here, and how the hell can they make a living? And yet
this desert has sustained a population, sparse though it may
be, for thousands of years: first Native Americans, followed
by pick-and-shovel miners in search of the one big strike; then
the Saints, as the Mormons were called, spreading southwest-
ward from their Deseret of Utah, over the dry lands of the
Mojave, and eventually down into the town of San Bernardino
itself as the nineteenth century unfolded.

The emptiness of the vast land can be deceiving; portions
of the apparently flat plain remain dangerous to this day for
the unwary off-roader: one false turn on an all-terrain vehicle
or motorcycle and you can find yourself hurtling down a hidden mine shaft, a fatal plunge if there ever was one.

Victorville's history really began with the California Southern Railroad, later known as the Atchison, Topeka and Santa
Fe, which arrived in the area in the early 1880s. A brush and
tree-choked riverbed, the Mojave, swollen in the spring,
largely dry in the summer, flows north out of the San Bernardino Mountains into the barren land, where it eventually evap-
orates or perhaps goes partially underground; the water, at
least near Victorville, was enough to replenish the steam trains
on their voyage through the desert, and in 1886, the town that
grew up around the train station was named after Jacob Nash

Victor, the railroad's construction superintendent at the time. Within a few years, farms were established on the bottom land near the river, and eventually substantial limestone deposits were located nearby, which formed the basis of the area's cement industry, which remains today as the most important business of the area.

By 1926, a federal highway, the famous Route 66, came through the town, linking the area for the first time to the rest of the country by automobile. One of those who arrived in this manner was the young Roy Rogers, who went on to form his own singing group, the Sons of the Pioneers; the old flivver that brought Roy to fame and fortune remains one of the featured attractions of the museum that now bears his name.

Eventually several new highways arrived, as well; one, U.S. 395, ran south from Reno, Nevada, along the eastern escarpment of the Sierra Nevada Mountains, through the water-rich Owens Valley north of the desert, and then through the high desert itself, eventually to tie in with Route 66 near Victorville. In later years, still more highways were built, connecting Victorville to Palmdale and Lancaster, north of the San Gabriel Mountains from Los Angeles; I-15 to Las Vegas; and I-40 to the Colorado River border with Arizona.

Eventually, former Governor Pat Brown's California Aqueduct arrived, too, turning much of the bone-dry desert land around the old town into a potential subdivision bonanza that was eagerly boosted by the television pitchmen, even if it never quite boomed the way its backers had first intended.

In the years after the arrival of the aqueduct and its water, the several towns around Victorville did start to grow; one of them, Hesperia (now known as "Despairia" to the same wits who call Apple Valley "Crapple Valley"), is almost the equal of Victorville in size—both around 60,000 residents, although Hesperia tends to be a bit more sprawling in its growth than the older town.

Thus, by the late 1990s, the Victorville area had become something of a transportation hub, as its various appendages continued to edge, tract by tract, into what used to be homes for coyotes, jack rabbits, rattlesnakes, owls and mice.

Today, if a driver takes U.S. 395 north from Victorville for some 42 miles, he or she will eventually come to a small hamlet called Four Corners, which is actually a collection of gas stations and a few eateries, along with what appears to be some sort of power transmission station, whose gargantuan size dwarfs the rest of the buildings at the isolated intersection. From Four Corners, one can proceed east by State Highway 58 to Barstow, yet another old railroad town some 33 miles distant, where the road forks once more—east and north by U.S. Interstate 15, which runs over a series of spectacularly rocky, ever-higher ridges, then sharply downhill to the state line at Nevada, and thence eventually to Las Vegas; or more directly due east, on Interstate 40, generally paralleling the old Santa Fe railroad tracks through the desert to the town of Needles, pitched on the banks above the Colorado River; once across the water, a driver is into northern Arizona, heading toward the small cities of Flagstaff and Kingman.

But if one instead turns west at Four Corners on Highway 58, he or she will cross another flat plain of desert brush, broken by the broad white surface of Edwards Dry Lake, the Air Force test-flight facility once made famous by Right Stuff heroes like Chuck Yeager, who broke the sound barrier high above those same barren salt flats, or Scott Crossfield, who flew the X-15, America's first true manned space vehicle; even today, large crowds often gather at Edwards to watch the occasional landings of the Space Shuttle, returning to Earth in the world's most elegant if heaviest glide.

Still farther west from Edwards on Highway 58 is the town of Mojave—probably more motels and eateries in one square mile than any other place on earth, with the possible exception of Las Vegas. The town of Mojave is also famous as the storage depot for the world's largest collection of unused jet airliners: Boeing 737s, 747s, 727s, along with McDonnell–Douglas models of every type, all parked, idle, spared from accelerated deterioration by the dry desert air, and all in all, the world's largest junkyard of airplane spare parts.

Shortly after leaving the town of Mojave, the driver in his car begins to climb once more, this time through a twisting canyon that leads to the summit of the spectacular oak-and-pine-studded Tehachapi Mountains, high enough above the High Desert to get regular snowfalls in winter. The old town atop the grade, once a major railroad watering stop over the mountains, remains one of California's best-kept secrets as a place to live, with a near year-round temperate climate, virtually no air pollution, and plenty of jobs: it also happens to be the location of one of California's largest prison institutions.

Still following Highway 58 west from Tehachapi, going downhill now, and past more unusual rock formations, a driver will eventually bottom out in the flat farmlands of the lower Central Valley of California, and soon enough will arrive in Buck Owens country, Bakersfield, the land of oil and cotton, although not necessarily in that order. Through the city of Bakersfield, Highway 58 stretches still farther west, as we have seen, past the cotton field hamlet of Buttonwillow, where the southern arm of the California aqueduct rushes by on its way southeast toward Victorville, and its ultimate final crossing of the San Bernardino Mountains into the city founded more than a hundred years ago by the Saints. This, then, is the High Desert, the upper Mojave, and the scene of many of Wayne Adam Ford's travels, and several of his alleged depredations.

It was in Old Victorville, where the famous Route 66 once came through (long before the freeway to Las Vegas that replaced it) that on October 22, 1998, a 45-year-old railroad conductor named Larry Halverson was sitting in his small Burlington Northern Santa Fe office at the corner of 6th and D Streets, laid out a hundred years earlier next to the rail lines and the old train station. Halverson's job was conducting the Victorville Local, a train that services industries in and around Victorville. Once the local had made its pickups and deliveries, Halverson and the rest of the train crew would park their locomotive in the yard across D Street, and he would repair to the office to finish up his paperwork early in the afternoon.

Sometime between 1 and 2 p.m. on October 22, 1998, as

he worked on his records, Halverson glanced out his office window. A large, black semi-tractor truck with writing on the side door had pulled up in front of the railroad's office, facing northbound on 6th Street—long known in local lore as the town's red-light district. As Halverson watched, he saw a familiar young woman whom he knew to be named Patricia Tamez, walk over to the truck, and strike up a conversation with the driver, whose face was visible to Halverson in profile. About a minute later, the young woman walked around the front of the truck, climbed in the passenger side door, and the truck drove off.

None of this surprised Halverson. Patty had been hanging out around the intersection of 6th and D Streets for some months, and was a familiar sight to almost everyone in the area. Occasionally, in fact, Patty came into Halverson's office and cadged food, water or cigarettes. Halverson and the others who worked in the office knew Patty was as a prostitute, and that the corner of 6th and D was one of her regular spots for soliciting clients. Over the months, Halverson and others had often seen Patty make deals with drivers as they came by the intersection.

On this particular afternoon, as he watched Patty enter the large black truck, the face of the man behind the wheel stuck in Halverson's mind.[42] The truck driver was white, in his middle 30s, with several days' growth of beard.

Patty was wearing her a maroon-colored jacket tied around her waist, a light-colored, loose-fitting top, blue shorts, and white tennis shoes without socks. The truck began pulling away even before Patty had fully entered. Halverson was to recall seeing the tail of Patty's maroon jacket flapping outside the truck's window, and Patty pulling it back inside.

The big black truck then turned the corner onto D Street, which was Old Route 66, and headed east, where the street soon branched into a divided highway, State Route 18, the "Happy Trails Highway," as it was called, that headed into

---

42. Report of San Bernardino County sheriff's Detective Jeff Staggs, December 11, 1998, Case #19906853.

Apple Valley. After leaving Apple Valley, the Happy Trails Highway threaded its way into nearby Lucerne Valley, where one of the state's largest cement plants, owned by the Mitsubishi Cement Corporation, was located. The truck's departure toward Apple Valley seemed odd to Halverson, because he knew that Patty didn't like going too far out of her regular area. That's one reason that the incident stuck in his mind.

Most of the people who had businesses or shops at the intersection of 6th and D Streets were quite familiar with Patty. Many felt compassion for the sweet, if sometimes a bit addle-brained girl, who was often hungry and ill-clad. Those who knew her best knew that she had suffered for years from a debilitating addiction to methamphetamine; and in fact, had spent considerable time at a San Bernardino–area state hospital being treated for mental illness that stemmed from her addiction.

As we have seen, of all of the victims said to have been murdered by Wayne Adam Ford, none was the "pristine victim" spoken of by *San Jose Mercury News* columnist Sue Hutchison. The last days of Tina Gibbs' life in Las Vegas must have been a horror; and Lanett White's desperate effort to cope with her own addiction even while trying to take care of her babies is likewise an essay in tragedy. But Patty Tamez' final days were, if anything, even worse; and what makes Patty's situation even sadder is the fact that it was all so unnecessary.

Patty was born in Texas on April 25, 1969. Her father was just 18 years old, and her mother, Anna, younger than that. Patty's mother and father divorced, and her mother moved to Michigan. At one point, her father remarried, although the marriage would be annulled in 1998. Later, there would be little information publicly released about Patty's early years,[43] although several newspapers were able to make contact with some people who had known her, once her death was linked to Wayne Adam Ford. One old friend, identified by *Las Vegas*

---

43. Efforts by the author to contact Patty's father, still living in the Victorville area, were unsuccessful.

Review-Journal reporter Glen Puit as Deborah Reck, recalled Patty as an upper-middle-class college student who dropped out of school because "she was really into crystal meth."[44] So there it was again—methamphetamine, the same substance that had turned Lanett White's life upside down, just as crack cocaine had ruined Tina Gibbs'. But while Tina and Lanett's habits may have been debilitating, Patty's was mind-blowing.

By most accounts in the aftermath of her death, Patty was both beautiful and smart as a teenager, and as a young woman. She attended West Valley College. Judging from some of her school work that was seized during one of her subsequent arrests, Patty was a better than average student; certainly she evidenced excellent writing and thinking skills, along with well-formed, consistent handwriting. But the court records of San Bernardino County show that by the early 1990s, when Patty was in her early twenties, things began to change. At some point, Patty apparently became pregnant and had a baby; it appears that the baby was taken from her as a result of her growing drug problem.

Based on the records, it seems that Patty's full-scale plunge down the methamphetamine mine shaft began, at the latest, near the end of 1992. On New Year's Day of 1993, around 7 p.m. in the evening, Patty and a 28-year-old man named Listerman, driving Patty's sixteen-year-old brown Cadillac sedan, pulled into the parking lot of a Hesperia motel not far from 1-15. A pair of patrol deputies from the San Bernardino County Sheriff's Department, each in separate units, noticed them. The deputies decided to check out the old car's occupants; they later claimed that they believed the tags on the car were invalid, which wasn't actually the case.

As the deputies approached the car, Patty got out to talk to them. She seemed nervous. As she began to talk, both deputies noticed a blue vinyl zippered bag in the back seat of the old Cadillac. If the deputies' report is to be believed, the bag was open, and a triple beam scale, usually used for weighing gram amounts of drugs, was plainly visible; one of the deputies also

---

claimed that he observed "a white powdery substance in the bag."[45] The deputies immediately arrested both Patty and Listerman, who by this time had also exited the car.

The deputies then separated Patty and Listerman, putting each in the back of their respective patrol cars. They then began to search the Cadillac, and soon discovered "large quantities of what appeared to be drug lab paraphernalia," along with an unloaded assault rifle in the back seat. A search of the trunk yielded several taped boxes that also appeared to contain drug lab materials, including glassware and chemicals. The deputies then called in the department's narcotics investigation team to take over.

Patty first admitted that the Cadillac belonged to her, then said it didn't; nor did any of the drug materials or the gun found in the car belong to her, she insisted. She claimed that she'd parked the car at the motel the night before, and when she woke up on New Year's morning, it was gone. Just how it got back to the motel, and why Patty was sitting in it that next night was unresolved, because Patty now refused to answer any more questions.

The old Cadillac was indeed filled with equipment used in the manufacture of methamphetamine, as the narcotics detectives easily determined, so Patty and Listerman were taken to jail.

*   *   *

45. Report of San Bernardino County Sheriff's Deputies Johnston and Bloomingdale, DR#199300021, January 1, 1993. The deputies' report formed the basis of probable cause for the subsequent search of the old Cadillac, and the arrests; by stating that he could observe the scale and the "white powdery substance" in the zipped blue bag, Deputy Johnson appeared to be making the case that he was entitled to make the arrest and conduct the search because the items were in "plain view," an exception to the Fourth Amendment's ban on unwarranted searches and seizures. Just why two deputies were in the parking lot in separate vehicles is unclear, but it suggests that they may have in fact expected Listerman and Patty to make an appearance, possibly as a result of a tip from an informant. In all candor, many police officers will admit, when not under oath, that when they have information from an informant, "plain view" can sometimes approximate x-ray vision, sometimes even through zippered blue vinyl bags.

Three months later, Patty and Listerman were at it again, this time at a motel in Ontario. A member of the Ontario Police narcotics squad obtained information from an informant asserting that Patty was staying at an Ontario motel, and selling meth from the motel room.[46]

The narcotics officer notified his department's patrol section, which sent two officers to the motel room. Shortly before 10:30 p.m., the two uniformed officers knocked on the motel room door. Patty answered. The two officers explained that they'd had complaints that Patty was selling drugs, and wanted to come inside. Patty said she hadn't actually rented the room, and didn't think she had the authority to admit them. She then tried to leave the room, closing the door after her. But the two officers smelled "a very strong chemical odor" coming from the room, so they prevented Patty from shutting the door, and entered anyway. Both officers were pretty sure someone was cooking methamphetamine, and because they knew the chemicals used to make the drug were volatile and potentially explosive, decided to act immediately without a warrant. One of the officers found Listerman inside near a stash of glassware and chemicals used to make methamphetamine. Both Listerman and Patty were taken to jail. Another search of Patty's car out in the motel parking lot turned up further evidence.

At the Ontario police station, Listerman and Patty separated; this time Patty said the meth cooking was all Listerman's idea, and that she had nothing to do with it.

"I just want to let you know," Patty told the officers, "that even though I was involved in the last meth case I had nothing to do with this. Jim [Listerman] was the one driving my car and had probably picked up all this stuff from his friend . . ." and here Patty named one of Listerman's acquaintances.

For his part, Listerman denied having any knowledge of any of the drug manufacturing supplies.

Following these two arrests, both of the methamphetamine

---

46. Report 93-3-1456, by Officer M. Rohn, Ontario Police Department, March 16, 1993.

cases against Patty began making their laborious way through the San Bernardino County court system. It appears that at one point the two cases were consolidated, but making sense of the court records today remains difficult, in part because so many of the papers filed in both cases were only partially completed by the clerks. Indeed, the overall impression of the court's written record is one of a gigantic paper mill, churning out ream upon ream of cursorily completed forms, as legions of common miscreants were processed as quickly as possible through the spinning doors of the justice system, day in, day out, month after month and year after year.

From the court records, it appears that Patty agreed to plead guilty to a single count of possession of methamphetamine precursors, the illegal chemical substances used to make meth. Listerman entered a guilty plea on three similar counts, including possession of methamphetamine for sale. For her plea, Patty agreed to the time she'd served in jail from the March arrest, approximately two months, five years' probation, and enrollment in a drug recovery program. The sentence was made to do double duty by standing as punishment for the March arrest as well.[47]

At first, the system seemed to be working: in an interoffice memo dated in late December of 1993, Patty's probation officer reported that she had successfully completed a two-month in-patient drug treatment program by the end of July 1993. A month later, Patty was given permission to go to Arlington, Virginia, to look for a job. This apparently didn't work out; three weeks later, in late September of 1993, she returned to Hesperia and re-enrolled in college. Upon her return, she was put in a drug suppression program, and was required to be tested twice a week. She was clean throughout November; the probation officer went on vacation for the first two weeks of the following month.

On December 14, the probation officer reported satisfaction with Patty's progress.

"The defendant has thus far complied with her terms of

---

47. San Bernardino County Superior Court file, FVI00299 and FWV00651.

probation," wrote Probation Officer Leo Stager.[48] "She is young, impulsive and a drug abuser since the age of 13. She has not however been regularly drug tested until her recent assignment to the drug suppression unit.

"After January 1, 1994, it is expected that she will be under much closer supervision and any use of drugs quickly noted. The agreement was that she complete a drug program in order for jail time to be expunged. It is recommended that she has met that requirement and the stay [of additional jail time] become permanent."

But the stricter testing regimen quickly proved Patty's undoing. By late March of 1994, Patty had failed seven such tests. The probation officer gave her one more chance to enroll at an in-patient treatment clinic if she wanted to stay out of jail. Patty called him to say she'd signed up for a bed; subsequently, the officer discovered that she had never shown up. At that point, the officer asked that her probation be revoked. It appears that Patty contested the revocation. The court record is unclear as to whether she eventually returned to drug rehabilitation in 1994, or whether she was returned to jail for the probation violations for an unknown period of time.

The following year, 1995, seems to have been a better one for Patty; at least the court records show no arrests or probation violations. But by November of 1996, Patty began having problems again.

In a rather strange incident that took place on October 21, 1996, Patty was observed at St. Mary's Hospital in Apple Valley. Shortly before 6 p.m., a hospital security officer was notified that someone had gotten into the hospital's medical records office and was busily scattering files around the nearby parking lot. By the time the officer arrived, the person was gone. The guard then entered the hospital's emergency room to see if anyone was there. As he entered a hallway near the radiation section, he saw Patty pulling a linen cart down the hall.

---

48. Interoffice memo, Stager to Judge J. Lewis Liesch, San Bernardino Superior Court, December 14, 1993.

As soon as she saw the security guard, Patty bolted for the nearest exit. The guard gave chase, finally catching her by the tail of her sweatshirt. Patty began fighting with the guard, who put a headlock on Patty. Patty punched him in the groin and face. Another hospital staffer arrived and helped him handcuff Patty.

When the sheriff's deputy arrived, he asked Patty what had happened.[49] Patty told the deputy that she'd been in the hospital near the radiation section because she'd decided to do some volunteer work for the hospital. Noticing that the linen cart was unattended in the hallway, she decided to move it out of the way. The deputy checked: Patty had never before volunteered to do anything at the hospital. "I needed something to keep me busy," Patty told him.

A check of the cart showed that it had more than just the usual soiled linens. It also included several sets of clean surgical scrubs, some food trays, and a mop wringer. It appeared that Patty had been the one who'd scattered the medical records; she said she'd been looking for one to bring to a friend who worked in the radiation section.

Further questioning by the deputy brought out the fact that Patty had recently been committed for mental observation at the hospital, and that her original intent was to seek out the psychiatrist who had treated her, to request that he release her from the commitment. She wandered around the hospital for a while and then got lost; that was when she saw the linen cart. She took the cart into a staff break room, and began cleaning up; she thought she'd do this to "pass the time and keep herself busy," the deputy reported.

When the deputy confronted Patty about inconsistencies in her statements, she told him she didn't want anything she said to be official, since it would find its way to the judge and the probation department if it was put down on paper; Patty kept mentioning that the authorities thought she was mentally in-

---

49. San Bernardino County Sheriff's Department report 189607024, October 22, 1996.

competent, and she didn't want to give them any new reasons to believe that was really the case.

The deputy arrested Patty and charged her with grand theft; once again her probation officer asked that her probation be revoked. And indeed, at this point, it appears that things began to go even more seriously wrong for Patty: the court records show that three additional criminal complaints were filed against her over the next seven months, even as her mental status became an ever-larger issue in the court proceedings against her.

While waiting for her next probation revocation hearing, Patty was again arrested by the sheriff's department on January 20, 1997; this time she was charged with shoplifting a pair of blue jeans from a Sears store, then taking the jeans to a nearby Mervyn's, and exchanging them for a $19.38 credit voucher.[50] After buying a pair of panties, Patty shoplifted a second pair of jeans from Mervyn's, valued at $40, and attempted to leave the store. Security guards from both stores accosted her outside, and a short struggle ensued.

When the sheriff's deputy arrived, Patty was matter-of-fact about the shoplifting. She said that when the security guards accosted her, she panicked and began to fight with them.

"I asked Tamez if she had intended on stealing the blue jeans prior to entering the store," wrote Deputy M. Dyson in his report, "which she indicated yes. She stated she needed money for food." Patty was jailed this time in Rancho Cucamonga, miles away from her family in Hesperia.

Two months later, while the original revocation hearing was still pending, along with the new shoplifting charges, Patty endured a serious mental breakdown, one that almost certainly was the result of severe methamphetamine addiction.

On the morning of Thursday, March 6, 1997, personnel assigned to the Army National Guard Armory building in Apple Valley arrived at work to find a light blue suitcase perched

---

50. San Bernardino County Sheriff's Department report 179700654, January 20, 1997.

atop a trash can that had been placed against the building's front door. One of the guardsmen noticed that the suitcase had a name tag on it bearing the name "Tony Rogers." The name was familiar because Patty for some time had been pestering one of the recruiters who worked at the Armory; apparently she was under the impression (or delusion) that the recruiter was involved in some sort of clandestine work with "Tony Rogers." It turned out that Patty had been dating a man by that name, who was then in state prison.

Having recognized the name, and realizing that Patty probably had something to do with leaving the suitcase at the Armory's front door, the guardsmen guessed that the suitcase might contain some sort of bomb. They called the San Bernardino County Sheriff's Department bomb squad, which evacuated all the surrounding buildings, including several medical offices, and blockaded all the roadways near the Armory, including the "Happy Trails Highway." The bomb squad rendered the suitcase harmless, and then opened it.

"The suitcase was found to contain an assortment of Bibles and other books," wrote the investigating officer, identified as H. Howell.[51] "There was a red plastic folder with handwritten notes on secret codes. There was a book about 'Top Secret Data Encryption Techniques.' "

In later interviews with the guardsmen, it appeared that Patty first began appearing at the Armory several weeks earlier with the seeming intention of enlisting in the Army.

"She seemed normal at first," Deputy Howell recounted in his report, "but as their conversation continued she became irrational and irate with him [the recruiter] so he asked her to leave. She visited the Armory several times after that. On one occasion she pinned an envelope to his board in his office. The envelope was addressed to her and came from a Tony Rogers, stamped State Prison Generated Mail. She mailed another piece of correspondence to him for Tony Rogers, care of him at the Armory's address. The envelope contained four

---

51. Report of San Bernardino County Sheriff's Deputy H. Howell, Case #189701485, March 6, 1997.

written pages of government conspiracies and cover-ups, of illegal specimen testing on people, of church involvement, names of people she wanted him to 'take out,' etc.

"Then she made four calls to the Armory, leaving threatening messages on his recorder. Each time she called she was more upset, yelling and cussing on the phone. One call she stated that 'you're going to get it, I'm not fucking with you anymore, you can be eliminated.' All the calls came at earlier morning hours, approximately 2 a.m. Then the calls stopped and she hadn't come by the Armory for a while."

Further checking of the suitcase showed there were actually four tags, all of them Victor Valley Hospital visitors' passes. Two were marked "Tony Rogers, Department of Defense"; the other two were marked "CIA C/O Tamez."

For some reason, Patty had concluded that she was a secret agent, and that the Army recruiter was her contact with her control, who was the Tony Rogers who had been her boyfriend. What seems entirely evident from this incident was that Patty had entered the throes of the sort of extreme paranoia that often develops among prolonged methamphetamine users, as the drug habit progresses, and users eat less, get less sleep, and actually sustain organic brain damage.

The sheriff's department set off on a search for Patty. Deputies from the Hesperia substation went to Patty's parents' house, but her step-mother said that Patty hadn't been home all night. She wasn't surprised about the "bomb": she said Patty had done the same thing the year before at the Child Protective Services offices in Victorville.

Not much later, the deputies got another call from the Armory: Patty had returned, "retrieving items," whatever that meant. The deputies caught up with Patty at a nearby bus stop. They arrested her and put her in double handcuffs, transporting her once again to the jail at Rancho Cucamonga. Patty was charged with maliciously planting a false bomb "with the intent to cause another to fear for his or her personal safety," which could result in up to a year in prison if convicted.

During a subsequent interview of the recruiter, the deputies learned that Patty had claimed that she'd already joined the

Army; she was frustrated that no one had bothered to contact her. She said she'd joined the Army through "the Pelican Brief Program."

"She explained [to the recruiter]," Howell continued in his report, "that when she was in the Barstow jail she was watching the Pelican Brief movie and at the end [there were] secret messages for her to help her country and join the reserves. She waited for them to contact her and after a while she decided to contact them herself; she was tired of waiting. When he noticed that she was not talking coherently, he asked her to leave." That was the encounter that led to Patty's feud with the National Guard that ended with the false bomb threat.

Patty eventually was released from jail to await trial on the false bomb charge, the grand theft from the hospital, the blue jean shoplifting incidents, and her probation revocation hearings. All of this took time to organize, get placed on the calendar, sort out conflicting dates, and other minutiae that form such a large part of the justice system. Thus, Patty was still free, and still doing drugs on June 17, 1997, when she was again arrested for shoplifting. This time the pinch came in the middle of the afternoon at a Victorville supermarket. A security guard at the market spotted Patty stowing one package of a frozen cheese lasagna dinner and one package of tampons, worth a grand total of $5.98. The store wanted Patty arrested.

The sheriff's deputy who responded found Patty indifferent to her arrest. She'd been hungry, she told Deputy K. Bodiford,[52] so she decided to help herself to the package of frozen food; she needed tampons, so she took a package. When the deputy asked if she'd any intention of paying for the articles, Patty said no.

"It is important to note," wrote Deputy Bodiford, "that while speaking with Tamez she was continually talking to herself and stating that God was with her and that she would soon be going to see God."

*   *   *

52. San Bernardino County Sheriff's Department report 179705520, June 17, 1997.

By this point, Patty's probation officer, the prosecutor's office, the judges, and certainly the police were all aware that Patty's mind had slipped its moorings. In August of 1997 she was recommended for a mental evaluation. It was clear to everyone that Patty was incompetent to assist in her own defense, and all of her pending criminal cases were put on hold. In November of 1997 Patty was committed to Patton State Hospital, a secure facility specializing in treatment of mentally disordered offenders. Frequently, the treatment involves use of therapy with psychotropic drugs such as Haldol or Thorazine—ironically, the same stuff that had been used on Wayne when he'd gone nuts in the Marines. But where the Marines had simply wanted to keep Wayne from assaulting other people, the objective of the hospital's therapy for Patty was to break the cycle of addiction to the illicit substance, and stabilize her cognitive and emotional functions.

By February of 1998, Patty was well enough to be released from the hospital. She returned to court, where the judge found her competent, and she admitted her violations. The next-to-last entry in her court file indicates that she was released on her own recognizance to await sentencing on April 17, 1998, and that she intended to live with her father and step-mother in Hesperia. But when April 17 arrived, Patty was a no-show, and a new bench warrant was issued for her arrest.

Given the state of disorganization of many of Patty's court files, it's not possible to say with absolute certainty that she was not picked up at some point on the bench warrant; but there does not seem to be any record of it, if it did occur. Given the fact that Patty was a well-known figure around the intersection of 6th and D Streets in Victorville in the summer of 1998, and that she was obviously involved in prostitution, it can only be concluded that no one in authority seemed to care very much what happened to her. It was an indifference that would cost her very life.

2

Gate 64

ON THE NIGHT OF OCTOBER 23, 1997, A 19-YEAR-OLD MAN named Bryan Stankiewicz was proceeding westbound on a little-used road that paralleled the rushing waters of former Governor Brown's dream, the California Aqueduct. Stankiewicz was a private security guard, hired by the water authority to keep an eye on the water in its concrete channel as it rushed southeastward toward its final reservoir, Silverwood Lake, before beginning its final climb over the San Bernardino Mountains to the Los Angeles basin on the other side.

Stankiewicz began his patrol shift at Silverwood Lake about 5 p.m. that day. It was for the most part, boring work: just making sure someone or something was kept out of the water, and that nothing seemed to be going wrong with the automated machinery that kept the broad stream flowing. It was Stankiewicz's routine to meet his fellow security guard, 61-year-old Leland Myers, whose job it was to cover the aqueduct from the west. The two usually met where the water crossed under the I-15 freeway in Hesperia between 9 and 9:30 every night at Gate Number 64. Once they met, they were under orders to call the security office to check in.

Shortly after 9 p.m. on this night, Myers met Stankiewicz as usual, and the pair unlocked the gate to the chainlink fence around the pump house, the mechanism that propelled the water under the freeway to the higher ground on the other side. As Myers and Stankiewicz made their way on either side of the pump house, they checked the water by the gate. Often things got trapped in the gate just before the pumps.

As Stankiewicz shined his flashlight into the roiling water below, he called out sharply to Myers. "We got a body here," he said.

Myers went immediately to Stankiewicz's position and looked for himself. Sure enough, there appeared to be the body of a woman, face up, being battered against the concrete abutment that separated the water into two streams before it passed into the pumps. Myers and Stankiewicz returned immediately to the pump house and phoned their office and asked their dispatcher to call the California Highway Patrol. They waited at the pump house until the first CHP unit arrived. They took the officer down to the gate, but the body was gone.

Stankiewicz and Myers led the CHP officer farther down the channel to a spot where the water pooled before entering the pumping mechanism. There they found the body floating in the pool. Myers and Stankiewicz called the aqueduct controllers to request that the gates be closed to prevent the body from flowing any farther away.

Shortly after 9:30 p.m., the California Highway Patrol notified the San Bernardino County Sheriff's Department about the body in the aqueduct. Simultaneously, the CHP directed its area helicopter—usually used to spot speeders on their way to Las Vegas—to overfly the area near I-15 and Armagosa Road, which fronted the pump house of Gate 64. CHP officers Mike Adams and Dale Levin overflew the gate area and channel, but saw nothing other than the CHP's ground units, and the two security guards. Adams and Levin flew farther upstream to the west for about two miles, but saw no other bodies, or anything unusual from the air.

By about 9:50 p.m., the first road-based CHP officer arrived; also arriving was a man in civilian clothing who identified himself as a San Bernardino County reserve sheriff's deputy, and began taking photographs; just how *he* had come to the scene wasn't immediately clear. Just before 10 p.m. the CHP officer and the two security guards showed CHP Sergeant T. S. Harbert the body in the water.

"I looked," Harbert wrote later in his report,[53] "and observed the totally nude body of a WFA [white female adult], estimated to be approximately in her early 20s, face up in the water. I noticed that one of the young woman's breasts appeared to have been severed completely off, and it appeared to have been accomplished with a sharp instrument. The missing breast was not seen in the area. Due to the lighting conditions (night), the distance of the body from the upper ground surface (estimated at approximately 15–20 feet away) and the surrounding water, no other trauma was readily apparent. However, the woman certainly appeared to be the victim of a homicide."

At this point, regular San Bernardino County sheriff's deputies began arriving at the scene. CHP Sergeant Harbert decided to turn the investigation over to the county, since it was clear that the woman had been murdered, a crime that was out of his purview. Shortly thereafter, San Bernardino County sheriff's homicide sergeant Mike Lenihan arrived to take control; he was soon joined by his detectives, Frank Gonzales, Mike Gillam and Jeff Staggs.

A team of divers was called to the scene to remove the body. After placing it in a blue plastic bag, they pulled it ashore just before 1 a.m. At that point, Detective Gonzales and San Bernardino County Coroner's Investigator Steve Foster made a closer inspection of the body.

"I saw that the female had a scar across her stomach," Gonzales wrote, "below her right rib cage, and her left breast had been cut away by a sharp instrument. I also saw marks that were around her wrists and ankles. It appeared the female was bound in some fashion."[54] Foster was able to lift fingerprints from the victim at the scene. He gave the fingerprint card to Detective Gillam, who rushed the print to the department's crime lab in San Bernardino. Shortly after 2:30 a.m., forensic technician Sharon McHenry identified the prints. Patty Tamez's short, sad life was over.

53. CHP incident report of Sergeant. T. S. Harbert, October 25, 1998, Case #1998-06-853.
54. Report of Detective Frank Gonzales, San Bernardino County Sheriff's Department, Case 1999806853, dated October 29, 1998.

3

Search for a Killer

THE NEXT MORNING, ONCE THE SUN WAS UP, THE SHERIFF'S department began a thorough search of the area near the aqueduct.

A bit before 9 a.m., a short distance up the aqueduct, Lenihan and his team noticed that the wire fence protecting the aqueduct channel had been pried up, leaving a gap that would have permitted access to the water. Next to the gap they also noticed tire impressions and what appeared to be shoe prints. Lenihan called for a crime scene specialist to come to examine the area and take photographs. Gonzales himself discovered a blue-and-white plaid shirt off the frontage road on the east side of the freeway. An even more extensive search was planned for the following day.

Meanwhile, Patty's extensive records in the files of the sheriff's department were the obvious place for the detectives to start. It was clear to Lenihan and the rest of his team that Patty had a well-documented history of mental illness, and that she had been involved in both drugs and prostitution (although she had apparently never been arrested for the latter crime).

The likeliest place begin finding out what had happened to Patty was to start with her known associates, available from the department's records. One man, Michael,[55] who had been an acquaintance of Patty's for years (whose name Patty had used in renting the Ontario motel room, and who had originally sold her

---

55. Michael's last name is omitted here to protect his privacy.

the old brown Cadillac, both noted by police in connection with the earlier methamphetamine arrests) was contacted by Detective Gonzales almost first thing the following morning. Gonzales played it subtle. He told Michael he was there to investigate a missing persons report on Patty, not telling him that he knew she had been found dead the night before.

Michael displayed no discernible reaction to Gonzales' ploy. Michael worked the night shift at the hospital where Patty had earlier been arrested for grand theft (the charge was eventually reduced to trespassing after all of Patty's mental troubles were taken into account). He said he'd known Patty for about six years, which dated the relationship back to 1992. The last time he'd seen her, Michael told Gonzales, was late on Tuesday or Wednesday night when she'd jumped over his locked gate and knocked on his front door. Michael said he knew it was Patty; he didn't bother to get up. Eventually, however, he relented and let her sleep in his car. Later that night he had to go to work at the hospital, so he dropped her at another friend's house, but not before giving her some blankets. He'd been trying to get Patty off drugs for years, Michael added, but had been unsuccessful. He denied that he and Patty had a sexual relationship.

Michael asked Gonzales whether he'd contacted Patty's father; Gonzales said he hadn't. Michael gave Gonzales Patty's father's address, as well as the address of the other friend's house where he had left Patty several nights earlier.

A bit more than an hour later, Gonzales contacted Patty's father; it was Gonzales' unhappy task to tell him that his daughter had been found dead. Gonzales' report did not record Patty's father's reaction to the news.

The last time he'd seen Patty, her father told Gonzales, was about one week earlier. He knew that his daughter had drug and mental problems, he said, and he occasionally provided her with a place to sleep. Most recently, he added, Patty had been staying at a motel in Victorville. He also directed Gonzales to see the same friend whom Michael had mentioned. Gonzales noted down the name; he intended to see the man at the first available opportunity.

*   *   *

The following morning, Sunday, October 25, Lenihan's group
was out in force, this time combing the area around the aqueduct for clues. Nine volunteers from the county's search and
rescue team assisted. Two teams tramped by foot on both sides
of the aqueduct west from I-15 to Gate 53, the gate immediately to the west several miles away. Three other teams in all-
terrain vehicles went even farther west along both sides of the
aqueduct. The north side of the waterway had a small paved
road which permitted access to foot and bicycle traffic, while
the south side had only a dirt road, which was not accessible
to the public.

The search lasted until almost 5 p.m. The only thing found
was a pair of women's sunglasses, and some dark stains on
an overcrossing; the stains turned out not to be blood.

While the search was proceeding, Gonzales had returned to
Patty's father's house to show him the blue-and-white plaid
shirt. Patty's father said it looked like something Patty had
worn in the recent past.

Next Gonzales paid a visit to Spivy,[56] the man Patty's father and Michael had both suggested that he see. Spivy was
44, and a self-employed mechanic. He said he'd last seen Patty
on Thursday, October 22, around 8 a.m., when she'd left his
house after being left there by Michael.

Spivy told Gonzales that he knew Patty was a drug user
and a space case, but he felt sorry for her. That's why he
sometimes let her stay at his house, Spivy said. He thought
Patty had been stealing things from him—small things, really,
but enough so that Spivy didn't entirely trust her.

When he last saw her, Spivy added, she was wearing white
sweatpants, a white tee-shirt, a burgundy long-sleeved jacket
he had just given her, and black-and-white tennis shoes. Patty
told him she was going to "work" at Value Best, a thrift store
at 7th and C Streets, down in Old Victorville near the railyard.

Spivy admitted that he knew Patty was working as a prostitute; and at this point, he gave Gonzales a valuable lead:

---

56. Spivy's last name is omitted here to protect his privacy.

usually when Patty picked up dates, Spivy said, she did so near 7th and D Streets in Old Victorville, and usually she took her dates into the desert near the dead end of Jupiter Avenue, an isolated industrial area just over the Mojave River wash, and on the north side of I-15.

A check of that area apparently turned up nothing of evidentiary value, because there is no note of anything found there in the sheriff's reports.

But this is how it is with most homicide investigations: interviews, checking, verifying; interviews, checking, verifying. It could get tedious—but only for the living.

Despite the lack of useful leads, Gonzales and other detectives ploughed forward, attempting to interview as many people as possible who had known or possibly seen Patty within the past few days. A woman who had seen Patty's picture after the news of her death was broadcast on television called to say she had seen Patty at a Victorville motel with at least one other woman about 3 p.m. on Friday, October 23. This, of course, was the afternoon of the night that Patty had been found dead. About a week before, the woman told Gonzales, Patty told her that she had been beaten up by a truck driver near Barstow, because she'd tried to take his wallet.

In retrospect, it's difficult to evaluate the accuracy of this recollection. While it's fair to say that the woman who spoke to Gonzales was well-meaning, and probably was pretty sure about when she last saw Patty, she might have been in error. According to the woman, Patty had been wearing a white top with light-colored shorts or a skirt. And it seems unlikely that Patty would go all the way to Barstow for a "trick," when most who knew her agreed that she rarely left her downtown Victorville haunt.

At this point, Gonzales knew nothing of railroad conductor Larry Halverson's sighting of Patty, because Halverson had not yet come forward. By the time he was interviewed, November 6, 1998, three days after Ford's arrest in Eureka, Halverson described Patty as wearing blue shorts, and a "maroon" jacket— the same jacket that Spivy had already told Gonzales that he had given Patty the night before Halverson saw her. Halverson was to tell Gonzales he was certain about the date because of the papers he had been working on at the time, which, of course, contained the date. Most importantly, Halverson described the truck driven by the man who had picked Patty up, and even gave a general description of the driver. The truck's description perfectly matched the one that Ford was driving, and Halverson's description of the driver was close as well.

At least three other witnesses also reported seeing Patty in the area of 6th and D Streets in the afternoon, but none of the three was sure if they had seen her on Thursday or Friday. All three witnesses agreed that Patty had gotten into a pickup truck with tinted windows, which headed into Apple Valley; two of the witnesses thought this took place around 5 or 6 p.m. Obviously this could not have been Ford, who wasn't driving anything like a pickup truck.

Based upon other actions taken by Ford on October 22 and 23, however, it appears that Patty's last day alive was that Thursday afternoon, October 22, because yet another witness would have ample reason to recall seeing Ford about fifteen miles farther east later the same afternoon, and at exactly 3:51 p.m. Other evidence would eventually put Ford hundreds of miles away from the Victorville area the morning of the following day. The question that still hangs over Patty Tamez' last day is: had Ford already killed her by 3:51 p.m. on Thursday, or was she still alive that evening? Was she tied up and immobilized in Ford's truck when he was seen at 3:51, and thus, susceptible to possible rescue?

Absent public accessibility to Ford's own statements—limited, as we have seen, by Judge Smith's effort to protect Ford's rights against self-incrimination—it's impossible to tell with certainty whether there was a slim possibility that Patty might have been rescued from Ford's truck that fatal Thursday afternoon.

At 10 a.m. on Wednesday, October 28, the San Bernardino County Coroner's forensic pathologist, Deputy Medical Examiner Dr. Steven Trenkle, began the post-mortem on Patty.

This is always grisly work, the business of taking apart a human body to find out what happened to it, and who might be responsible. The pathologist who can't look at his work as a scientific endeavor is probably well-advised to find another kind of employment.

The severing of the left breast was gruesome enough, but Trenkle soon found other significant trauma. It appeared that Patty had been tied hand and foot; marks from the bindings were still apparent. There were a number of bruises to her face and the back of her head, the latter suggesting that she had been hit with a blunt object; there was ample evidence of hemorrhage within the neck, lungs, mouth, face, eyes and brain, evidence that she had been strangled. And Trenkle discovered that Patty's back had been broken, higher up on her spinal cord. The fractures would have caused her to have been paralyzed from the chest down. It was possible, Trenkle added, that she had been alive when her breast was removed, when she was shoved in the water. Trenkle listed drowning as a possible cause of death, but added that he believed Patty was dead before the immersion took place. Swabs from the vaginal vault yielded traces of sperm, and several fibers were recovered from the body as well.

Trenkle also noted a number of other illnesses and injuries to Patty that had preceded the attack. Her arms, he noted, showed evidence of needle tracks; it was apparent that Patty had been injecting herself with drugs over a substantial period of time. There was a scar on one wrist that appeared to be evidence of a possible suicide attempt. Patty's gall bladder showed signs of disorder, as did her liver and bile ducts. And Patty's heart was enlarged, which sometimes is a result of prolonged methamphetamine use. In all, Patty was in poor health for someone of her age; in some way, perhaps, she had known what she was talking about when, the year before, she'd told the sheriff's deputy that she would soon be going to see God.

Over the next several days, both searches and interviews continued. A pornographic magazine found in a portable toilet was seized; a pink ball-point pen; a black blouse with apparent blood stains; on November 1, yet another wide-ranging search was conducted, this one of an empty field about half a mile west of I-15, and several miles north of the aqueduct. Additionally, a search team on horseback combed a dry gulch, Oro Grande Wash, that paralleled the freeway all the way to the aqueduct. This search netted a number of artifacts: a pair of light blue women's pants, a white tank top, an open container of lubricating gel, a stained white towel, and a .22 caliber air pistol. It seemed possible that this was the area where the attack on Patty had occurred, if indeed the recovered clothing had belonged to her.

But as October edged into November of 1998, Lenihan and his detectives were no closer to identifying the person who had killed Patty Tamez than they had been on the night her body was discovered in the aqueduct.

Then, at 9:09 a.m. on the morning of November 4, the San Bernardino Sheriff's Department received a teletype message from the Humboldt County Sheriff's Department.

```
Homicide Subject in Custody
We have subject in custody for homicide.
[MATERIAL DELETED]. The most recent victim
within the last two weeks came from Lucerne
Valley. One female from Las Vegas. Both of
them white. The third female, a Mexican or In-
dian, came from the Ontario, Ca area.
```

The teletype then listed additional details of the crimes, including the places where Wayne had told Freeman that he believed he had disposed of the victims. All of this material was likewise deleted under Judge Smith's order. The teletype continued:

```
Subject: Ford, Wayne Adam. Goes by Adam. WMA
6'2" 200 Haz Bro DOB 120361
Truck driver
Refer/Det. Juan Freeman/Humboldt Co SO
```

IX

ADAM
NOVEMBER 1998

1

Rodney

THE EVENING AT OCEAN GROVE LODGE IN TRINIDAD, CAL-ifornia, would stand out in owner Marco Ibarra's mind for years afterward. It wasn't only that within a matter of days he and his establishment were overrun by news media shock troops, wanting to know all about the serial killer who had just turned himself in after spending the night at Marco's motel. Even before the onslaught—indeed, going back to the very moment he had rented Wayne Adam Ford the one-room cabin—Ibarra had had a growing sense that something unusual was about to happen.

Ford had arrived at the bar around noon, as Ibarra said later, and began drinking almost at once. At one point Ford had asked Ibarra for coins to buy newspapers; it appeared to Ibarra that he was combing the news pages for something specific, but didn't seem to find what he was looking for.

By the evening, when Ford had rented the room, Ibarra was sure something was up. Despite all the alcohol he had consumed, Ford didn't seem drunk at all. The man's idle talk—about either getting drunk or blowing his brains out—loomed ever larger in Ibarra's mind as he observed Ford staring out the window. Ibarra wondered whether the man was actually going to do it—pull out a gun and blow his brains out, and in the motel room Marco had just rented to him.

But Wayne Adam Ford was waiting for his brother Rod to come to help him decide what to do.

*   *   *

Rod had taken the call from his brother about 7 p.m. on November 2, a Monday night. Rod lived in the Vallejo area, about 260 miles to the south, and with the twists and turns of Highway 101, at least a five-hour drive away.

Rod arrived about 1 a.m., to find Wayne waiting for him, watching television. Later, Rod described this encounter in an interview with Juan Freeman. As the transcript of the interview was substantially redacted because of Judge Smith's ruling, it's not possible to know exactly what transpired. It appears, however, that Wayne was in a highly emotional state, and possibly threatening suicide.[57] As Rod put it to Freeman, Wayne had suffered for years from various emotional problems; usually when he felt desperate, he called on his older brother for help. Apparently, during this encounter, Wayne said something dire to Rod almost immediately. "As soon as he opened the door . . ." Rod told Freeman—but the subsequent phrase was deleted.

"And we talked for about an hour-and-a-half, two hours . . . [Additional material deleted.] And I told him that I loved him," Rod continued, "and that's why I was there, to help him." Rod apparently pressed Wayne to say what was agitating him, but Wayne was reticent. Finally Rod said he was tired from driving so far; he suggested that they both get some sleep, get up in the morning, get some breakfast, and sort things out.

The next morning, they got up around 7:30 or so, and drove into Eureka. They had breakfast at a Denny's. Rod kept trying to find out what was bothering Wayne, but Wayne wouldn't be specific.

"I tried to find out what was bugging him," Rod told Freeman, "some of the problems. [Material deleted.] And I asked him, 'What do you mean, hurt some people?' [Material deleted]."

"And that's all he would say?" Freeman asked.

"Yeah," Rod said.

---

57. Interview of Rod Ford by Humboldt County Detective Juan Freeman, about 7:30 p.m., Tuesday, November 3, 1998.

He and Wayne had further discussions, with Rod evidently trying to get his brother to be more specific. Whatever Wayne told Rod was likewise deleted, but apparently again was not specific. "And at that point," Rod continued to Freeman, "I couldn't really get anything out of him."

The brothers continued talking after breakfast, with Wayne still despondent and Rod still trying to find out what the real problem was. They went to the Eureka Zoo, where they had spent time as boys when visiting their grandmother; talking about various family members, recalling old experiences in Eureka and other places, and finally going to a movie.

At one point, Wayne apparently told Rod that he didn't expect to ever see his son again.

"I kept asking," Rod told Freeman, " 'Why do you think you're not going to see your son?' And I remember, he [wouldn't] elaborate on anything. He just kept saying [material deleted, apparently a reference to Wayne's earlier statement that he had hurt some people].

"And I said, 'Well, what did you do, I mean, did you just beat somebody up, or break a guy's arm, or—you know?' And he said [material deleted.]"

"He doesn't want to tell you?" Freeman asked.

"He didn't want to tell me," Rod said. "And I told him, 'I can't really, if you don't tell me something I can't help you.' [Material deleted.]"

Wayne apparently now said something about Lucie and his son, and made some sort of statement that alarmed Rod.

"And I told him, 'You shouldn't be talking that way, it's not right.' "

The brothers drove around Eureka for a while, and continued talking. Wayne was still feeling very bad. Rod asked him again what he had done, and again Wayne gave a non-specific response.

"And I said," Rod continued, " 'Well, if you feel this way, or you feel that bad, then we need to go [to the police], we need to go right now.' " Apparently, at one point Wayne actually placed a telephone call to the sheriff's department, saying that he was coming in because he had "hurt a lot of people."[58] But on the way to the sheriff's department Wayne began to have second thoughts.

"And that was at the point where he like tried to delay coming over here. And I just told him, you know, you've done something, and you need help, [material deleted], then we gotta do it now. And I said . . . none of this waiting stuff, we're not going to go do something else. And God. He said [material deleted]. So we parked my truck at my grandmother's house . . . and we walked over here. And on the way he basically just cried most of the way. [Material deleted.] I told him that he was my brother and I love him and that I was gonna help him any way I could."

Rod and Wayne walked into the visitors' lobby of the Humboldt County Sheriff's Department. Rod picked up the intercom telephone and told a woman behind the desk that he wanted to turn his brother in. He still wasn't sure exactly what Wayne had done.

Shortly after 6:30 p.m., two sheriff's deputies emerged from behind the locked door separating the public area from the department's inner offices. Based on Wayne's earlier telephone call, they had apparently been expecting him. Exactly what happened next remains unclear; either Wayne made a statement to the effect that he had "done something bad," and then voluntarily produced the Ziploc bag with a human breast from his jacket pocket, or the deputies for some reason decided to search him. The police were later to claim that Wayne was not in custody when the severed breast was discovered. Nevertheless, the Ziploc bag was produced, along with its grisly evidence. Rod later told Freeman that what actually happened was that the two deputies came out, and Wayne made some sort of statement to the effect that he wanted to turn himself in, and that he wanted to speak to an attorney. "And they said, 'Well, if you want an attorney then we really can't, you know, listen to anything you tell us.' And he [Wayne] said, [material deleted]. And that's when they, they pulled that [the severed breast] out."

"So he had that in his pocket the whole day and you just didn't know it?" Freeman asked.

"I guess so," Rod said. "He was wearing the jacket all day. And he never said anything to me. And, you know, that's it. And here we are."

2

"You Have the Right to an Attorney . . ."

FREEMAN WAS AT HOME AT 6:30 P.M. ON TUESDAY EVENING when Wayne and Rod first appeared at the sheriff's department. According to the department's night watch commander, two deputies had come out to talk to Wayne, and Wayne made some sort of inculpatory statement, which was later deleted from the publicly accessible record.

Exactly what was said and why the two deputies did what they did remains unclear, at least based on the available records. What is clear is that the watch commander "looked in the subject's pocket and saw a plastic bag containing what looked like human flesh. [The watch commander] removed the bag and found it to contain the breast of a human female with nipple attached."[59] It remains the police position that even at this point Wayne was not in custody.

Apparently Wayne then made some additional statements that were deleted. At that point Wayne *was* placed under arrest, and Detective Freeman was notified by the watch commander to come to the sheriff's department.

As Freeman was driving in, the jail personnel began processing Wayne for booking. A jail memorandum dictated

---

59. Affidavit in support of search by Humboldt County Deputy District Attorney Jim Dawson, Humboldt County Superior Court Search Warrant #4134, November 3, 1998.

shortly thereafter by the night shift supervisor Robert Ross indicates the following:[60]

"You might want to videotape this," the booking sergeant told Ross, as he and two other deputies prepped Wayne for entry into the jail. Ross started the videotape camera, and recorded Ford making a variety of "spontaneous statements."

Ross' report continued: "At one point Deputy [Mike] Gainey said to Ford, 'Earlier you told us you wanted an attorney present when [you] talked to us. Have you changed your mind?'

"Ford said [material deleted].

"Ford continued to make spontaneous statements."

By the time the booking was completed, Freeman had arrived to try to question Wayne, and this is where the complications became even greater.

As indicated earlier, the decision by Judge Smith in San Bernardino County to order the deletions of all statements made by Ford to all police officers subsequent to his arrest on November 3 was a double-edged sword. While it protected Ford's right against self-incrimination (before the legal admissibility of the statements was determined by the court), it also had the effect of concealing the statements made by the police themselves as they endeavored to obtain information. As a result, when the constitutionality of much of the evidence that would later be presented against Ford was brought into question, it wasn't immediately possible to know whether the statements had in fact been illegally obtained.

But if justice grinds slowly, it does actually turn; eventually, at least some of the details of what transpired between Freeman and Ford on that fateful night rose into the sunshine of public access in the form of a motion to dismiss all the charges against Ford by his San Bernardino County public defender, Joseph Canty.

In his motion, filed with the San Bernardino Superior Court

---

60. Incident report of Humboldt County Correctional Facility, 1830 hours, 11/3/1998, submitted by HCCF Officer Robert Ross.

on October 27, 2000, Canty shed light for the first time on what actually happened when Ford made his confession.[61]

In this motion—which was effectively seeking to have all the charges against Ford thrown out because of Canty's contention that Freeman and others of the Humboldt County Sheriff's Department had deliberately violated Ford's right to speak to a lawyer before answering any questions—Canty contended that Freeman essentially ignored Ford's repeated requests to talk to a lawyer before answering any questions, and that he actually attempted to coerce Ford into cooperating with him by unfair and perhaps unconstitutional means.

After recounting the circumstances of Rod and Wayne's appearance in the sheriff's department lobby about 6:30 p.m., Canty contended that Ford almost immediately asked to be allowed to speak to a lawyer.

"He did so in the lobby when he first came in," Canty contended. "He did so after being handcuffed and taken into the jail; and he did so when detectives who had been summoned requested that he submit to an interview. His requests for an attorney were met by the detectives with suggestions that, if he wanted to 'clear something up,' this would be incompatible with having an attorney present."

Canty contended that once he'd asked to talk to a lawyer before talking to the police, Ford was told that his desire to do so wasn't in keeping with his expressed desire to atone for his actions; that, if he had a lawyer, there would be "no way for you to clear your conscience." In other words, if Ford really wanted to help people, he had to talk without a lawyer. At no point, Canty contended, was Ford ever read his right to have an attorney present, as contemplated in the now-famous

---

61. Motion to Dismiss pursuant to Penal Code Section 995, Wayne Adam Ford, San Bernardino County Superior Court, filed October 27, 2000. Canty's motion was based upon some of the material that Judge Smith had earlier ordered be withheld from public access; as Ford's lawyer, Canty was entitled to release the material at the proper time, which came when he asked the court to dismiss the charges against Ford; this was how the statements finally came to light.

Miranda decision. Still, said Canty, Ford persisted in his desire to speak to a lawyer.[62]

Freeman then left the interview room, according to Canty, and proceeded to talk instead to Rod; portions of that conversation were outlined in the preceding chapter.

It should be noted that as a widely applied rule under the Constitution, police officers are required to arrange for prisoners to speak to lawyers when they request to be allowed to do so; moreover, Section 825(b) of the California Penal Code allows a prisoner to request a visit by an attorney, and adds that "any officer having charge of the prisoner who willfully refuses or neglects to allow that attorney to visit a prisoner is guilty of a misdemeanor." The law also permits prisoners to be allowed to consult with relatives. That, in essence, is what Freeman did; rather than contact a lawyer on Ford's behalf, he chose to intercede with Rod Ford in a possible effort to induce Rod to convince Wayne to start answering questions.

In his conversation with Freeman,[63] Rod told the detective that it had always been his advice to his brother, " 'Well, make sure that you get an attorney.' I mean, if you've done something you need an attorney, you need to get an attorney. I've always told him that and I told him that again today. I, you know, don't just walk in and . . ."

"Well," said Freeman, "that's not helping us."

"Well, I'm sorry it's not helping," Rod said.

"We're not going to solve anything if he doesn't talk to us," Freeman said.

Rod explained that when he advised Wayne to talk to a lawyer, he'd no idea of what Wayne had really meant when he'd said he'd been "hurting people."

---

62. Detective Freeman, who had been provided with a copy of Canty's motions with their allegations, declined the author's request for comment on the issues raised by Canty, contending that a "gag" order issued by Humboldt County Judge Bruce Watson in November of 1998 prevented him from making any statements about the Ford case.

63. The interview between Freeman and Rod Ford was recorded by Freeman at about 7:40 p.m. on November 3, 1998, portions of which were referred to in the preceding chapter.

"Well," said Freeman, "it certainly didn't help, 'cause now we're stuck. And now that he wants an attorney, we can't talk to him any more. So we can't find out what happened."

According to the interview transcript, Freeman now asked Rod Ford a series of questions designed to elicit information on places where Ford might have been living; this was necessary preparation to obtain a search warrant, although Freeman didn't let Rod know that was what his purpose was. At some point during this conversation, which Freeman's transcript indicates ended at 8:06 p.m., either Rod asked to visit Wayne, or Freeman suggested that he visit him; the records aren't entirely clear,[64] although the jail supervisor's written report seems to show that it was Rod who wanted to speak to Wayne:[65]

At about 2015 [8:15 p.m.], Ford's brother Calvin [Rod] Ford requested a visit. Detective Freeman called and asked if I could approve the visit. I authorized Calvin Ford to visit with his brother inmate Wayne Ford in North Facility Visiting Booth Number 11. I went to N325 [apparently a jail control room] and connected audio cassette recorder Number 2 to North Visiting Booth Number 11.

In other words, the jail officials now bugged the conversation between Rod and Wayne.

In this conversation, Rod told Wayne that the police "were kind of mad that I told you to get an attorney."[66]

"They got mad at you?" Wayne asked Rod.

"It's okay," Rod told Wayne.

Wayne was angry at the jailers for putting pressure on Rod.

---

64. Freeman's investigation file notes that "Rod asked me if I wanted him to talk to his brother. I told him no, I couldn't ask him to do that. He asked if he could visit his brother. I told him that if he wants to talk to his brother, I could arrange a visit at the jail. I did arrange a visit and Rod went to the jail to see his brother."

65. Continuation of report of jail supervisor Robert Ross, November 3, 1998, referred to in the preceding chapter.

66. Canty's motion to dismiss, October 27, 2000.

But Rod now suggested that if there were people out there who needed help—if Wayne knew where others might be, who might be hurting, he should tell the police. Rod suggested to Wayne that despite his earlier advice, maybe getting an attorney wasn't such a hot idea, because once a lawyer got involved, maybe the police would never be able to help any of the people Wayne had hurt. Rod told Wayne he intended to go back to the police to tell them to try talking to Wayne again.

"Okay," Wayne said.

"Because people have to know why," Rod said. "I mean, there's families."

Subsequent to the brothers' surreptitiously monitored conversation, Rod Ford returned to Freeman, and told him that Wayne now wanted to talk. About 9:15 Freeman went back in to see Wayne. The contents of this conversation, the second between Wayne Ford and Freeman and their first substantive exchange, was one of those withheld from the public by Judge Smith in his June 2000 ruling.

However, in his October 27, 2000, motion to dismiss, Canty reported that, based upon the audio tape of this interview between Freeman and Ford, the following exchange took place:

> "Okay," Freeman told Wayne, "what happens is, because you've indicated that you need an attorney, I can't ask you what happened. Is that okay with you?"
> "Yeah," Ford said.

Freeman continued nevertheless, although Canty's contention was that this was yet another perfectly clear request by Wayne Ford to be allowed a chance to talk to a lawyer before answering any questions from the police. It appears from his remarks that Freeman had decided to play on Ford's conscience—certainly an unusual strategy for a typical serial killer, who almost by definition has no conscience, as experts like Mike Rustigan and Jack Levin have repeatedly asserted. But Freeman's interaction with Rod, along with the secretly monitored conversation between the brothers, may have given him the idea that Wayne might be susceptible to an appeal to conscience.

"You," Freeman told Ford, "you would rather not straighten some things out because, I mean, obviously there's a woman out there missing a breast. Or maybe more?" Freeman was doubtless thinking about his still-unsolved Torso Case as he asked his questions.

"And you know," Freeman continued, "if you don't want to tell us what happened, we may not be able to straighten anything out. Because we don't know who that belongs to. We don't know what else you might have done. You know, what other families you might have hurt."

According to Canty's motion, Freeman continued to play on Ford's emotions, and suggested that if he got a lawyer, he could never clear his conscience.

"And if you have," Freeman told Ford, "if you need an attorney, there is no way you're going to be able to clear your conscience, so I mean, that's okay. That's your right. But, you know, if you need to get something off your chest, and clear your conscience and maybe try to help some families and some people that you've hurt, then you need to decide that you don't want an attorney, and you want to talk to me.

"I'm not gonna, I'm certainly not gonna try and twist your arm," Freeman continued. "So what I'm saying is if you would like to clear some things up, and maybe help some families out there, or a family at least, then you know, you need to talk to me.

"But if you, if you still feel like you need an attorney, then we'll stop everything right now, and just go from there. So, it's up to you, Wayne."

So Freeman, after talking with Rod and explaining the problem to him, and then helping him explain the problem to Wayne, now laid the choice before Wayne: he could talk and clear his conscience, maybe help some people (and maybe even himself), or not, it's all up to him; but if he asks for a lawyer, he'll never be able to clear his conscience; or at least, so Freeman implied.

"I need an attorney," Wayne told Freeman.

* * *

This first substantive conversation between Wayne and Freeman began at 9:15 p.m., and would last until about 10:45 p.m. According to Canty's motion, which was based upon the audio tape and transcripts of the interview, Wayne was crying almost throughout the conversation. When Freeman told Wayne that the jail staff had said that Wayne was ready to talk, Wayne responded, "My brother told me I should talk to you." Freeman asked Wayne if he agreed with his brother. "Well," Wayne said, "he said I should talk."

Wayne began to cry once more, and now, for the first time, Freeman read Wayne his rights under *Miranda*, which, as almost every American now knows from interminable television police dramas, includes the right to remain silent and the right to an attorney—a court-appointed attorney if the person cannot afford one. Freeman asked if Ford understood his rights, and Ford said he did. Freeman now asked if Wayne still wanted to talk about the crimes. Wayne said he did. But Freeman never asked if Wayne had formally waived his right to a lawyer, according to Canty. It would be Canty's position that since Wayne's repeated earlier requests to speak to a lawyer had been ignored, his agreement to begin talking at that point was invalid without a formal waiver. Wayne might want to talk, but he wanted to do it with a lawyer present. Freeman wanted Wayne to talk, but he believed that once a lawyer got involved, Wayne would be told to clam up. Thus there was a frustrating impasse for both sides.

"Detective Freeman then interrogates Mr. Ford for several minutes," Canty contended. "Sometimes during this conversation, Mr. Ford is crying and emotional. They discuss matters concerning the San Bernardino County victim [Patty Tamez] and the Humboldt County victim [the Torso Case]. At times he [Ford] says there are things he would rather not talk about. At times he says he is having trouble thinking."

Some minutes into this conversation, according to Canty, Ford again said he wanted to talk to a lawyer. At another point, when Freeman asked where certain items of evidence might be located, and whether Ford might be willing to show him,

Ford asked Freeman whether he would be willing to let a defense lawyer accompany them if they went to look.

"Can't we just get an attorney and do all this too?" Ford asked Freeman. Freeman then indicated that things didn't work that way. Once a lawyer was in the mix, Freeman told Ford, everything would stop, "because what will happen is that the attorney will tell you not to talk to me anymore."

Canty was later to complain that the audio tape of the interview was of such poor quality that it was difficult to make out a number of statements by either Ford or Freeman, and that the written transcript of the interview was filled with mistransliterations, and even Freeman in his investigative report agrees. "The quality of the recording is poor due to the unfavorable acoustics and echoes in the interview room," Freeman's report noted.

Ford continued to cry throughout the encounter, and at one point admitted that there might be "two others," meaning murder victims. At least once, and maybe more than once, Wayne told Freeman that he wanted to kill himself, although Wayne later denied that he said anything of the kind.[67] Canty said the transcript, as prepared by the authorities, leaves the impression that Ford "at some point . . . responded affirmatively to a willingness to give up an attorney." But, said Canty, the entire transcript is filled with so many passages marked "inaudible" that it was difficult to reach the conclusion that Ford ever willingly or expressly gave up his right to speak to a lawyer. And if Freeman and the rest of the Humboldt County officials had deliberately prevented Ford from talking to a lawyer after he had so frequently requested one, that meant that everything Ford said from the time he first entered the sheriff's department lobby had to be thrown out, because it could never be used against him in a court of law.

---

67. In his interview with *Los Angeles Times* reporter James Rainey, in October 1999, Wayne specifically denied ever saying he wanted to kill himself during his interview with Freeman.

3

Searches and Confessions

WHILE ROD WAS HAVING HIS TAPED CONVERSATION WITH Wayne, Freeman was also busy. He called Humboldt County Deputy District Attorney Jim Dawson, and filled him in; Dawson had already obtained a description of Wayne's Airstream trailer in Arcata. Dawson said he'd write a warrant to search the trailer for evidence that night.

It appears that during his second interview, Freeman learned from Wayne that in addition to his trailer, he had a makeshift campsite not far from the Ocean Grove Lodge in Trinidad. It likewise appears that Ford told Freeman that he had at first kept some parts of the torso of Jane Doe in a freezer in his Arcata trailer, and had only recently taken them to his campsite near Trinidad to bury them there.

As the time was now nearing 11 p.m., Freeman decided to send deputies to the area of the campsite to secure it until the next day.

Meanwhile, the search warrant for Wayne's trailer was granted by a Humboldt County judge at 10:20 p.m.; it was not, however, immediately executed. Dawson had already called the Arcata Police and asked them to stand guard over the trailer until the search could take place. Arcata officers asked some of the neighbors about the last time they had seen Ford; several said he hadn't been around the trailer for as long as a week. Meanwhile, Freeman had Ford placed under a suicide watch in the jail; the jail's log states, "while being interviewed by detectives, [Ford] repeatedly said he was going to kill himself." The jail guards made checks of Wayne in his cell every fifteen minutes the rest of that night and all the next day. After that, Wayne was placed in "administrative segregation"—solitary—because his new notoriety put him at risk of being killed by the other jail inmates.

The following morning, after Freeman had sent his western states' teletype advising all police agencies of Ford's arrest—thereby setting off the rush to Eureka by the detectives from San Bernardino, San Joaquin and Kern Counties—Freeman made arrangements to meet with California Department of Justice experts at Ford's campsite near Trinidad. If Ford's statements from the night before were to be believed, some portions of the Torso Case victim might be found there.

The campsite was located in the woods, a little over 100 feet east of the Seawood Drive off-ramp from 101; the off-ramp was less than a mile from the Ocean Grove Lodge. The deputies Freeman had sent out the night before had readily located the place; there was still a tent pitched under a grove of trees.

At least one of the deputies present when Freeman arrived told him that when he first got to the scene, he'd smelled something nearby; but nobody had yet been able to find anything. There were two tire tracks not far away, and these were photographed for comparison with Ford's own vehicle, a Jeep which had been found parked at the Arcata trailer site. The tent itself did not immediately appear to yield any useful evidence, although it was seized for a subsequent close inspection for possible trace evidence. At length, Freeman decided to go back to Eureka to talk to Wayne once more to see where the body parts were.

About 2 p.m., Freeman and Deputy District Attorney Dawson began the second substantive interview with Wayne; this one was also recorded. Virtually all of the contents of this interview remained sealed by Judge Smith, but it appears that on this occasion Wayne told the authorities where to find the remains he said he had taken to the campsite. It appears, from Freeman's investigation report, that the decision was made to take Ford to the site so he could help them locate the body parts.

Shortly before 4 p.m. on November 4—about when *Times-Standard* reporter Rhonda Parker was assembling her story on the truck driver with the breast in his jacket pocket—several of the body parts were located. A call was made to the Humboldt County Coroner's Office, as well as to a forensic pathologist, to have them come to the campsite to process the remains.

Deputy Coroner Charles Van Buskirk, who had assisted in the recovery of the torso from the slough more than a year earlier, wrote what happened next:[68]

"We were directed to a hole," Van Buskirk wrote, "at the bottom of a tree about 25 feet from the area where the tent was reported to have been located. The hole was 2 by 3 feet and 12 to 18 inches deep. The hole had irregular sides and some rather deep pockets extending away from the hole . . . [I]mmediately visible in the hole was some thin white plastic sheeting, appearing to be kitchen garbage bag. I observed what appeared to be the end of a transversely cut limb. The bone, surrounding musculature and skin were somewhat obscured by adherent forest material."

As Van Buskirk and fellow Deputy Coroner Roy Horton went ahead, they were eventually to uncover two human thighs and several other pieces of human tissue, possibly human breasts.

The forensic pathologist now examined the recovered body parts, and noticed that they seemed quite fresh; the lack of post-mortem decomposition indicated that they had somehow been preserved for some time. The pathologist was then told that Ford had said that he had kept the thighs frozen in his trailer freezer for about a year.

The deputy coroners then took the body parts back to the morgue in Eureka. Over the next several days, a number of examinations were conducted by Department of Justice experts

---

68. Report of Humboldt County Deputy Coroner Charles L. Van Buskirk, November 4, 1998.

and others, both for DNA typing and other comparison purposes. Eventually, nearly a month later, the experts agreed: the thighs, at least, had come from Jane Doe.

So what really happened to Jane Doe? Where was she from, how did she come to die, and why did Ford cut her body into pieces?

The answers to all these questions are, of course, contained in the statements Ford gave to Freeman and Dawson on November 3 and 4, 1998. The sealing of the statements, however, prevents the public from knowing just what happened—at least until, or if, the statements are ever allowed into evidence.

Still, based upon partial accounts published before Ford's first defense lawyer, Kevin Robinson, obtained his gag order, and by comparing those accounts with documents eventually filed by San Bernardino County prosecutors in the following year, some sort of approximation of the events that led the investigators to the small hole near Trinidad can be assembled.

If one believes some of the initial published reports—obtained by news reporters in the immediate aftermath of Ford's surrender, but before the gag order was issued—Ford claimed to have barely known Jane Doe before he killed her; he said he couldn't remember her name. He recalled that he had first contacted her as a hitchhiker on October 14, the day after he had visited Lucie and his son at Scott and Linda's.

Either he had picked her up in downtown Eureka, or out by the Bayshore Mall, Eureka's newest commercial site. Ford had noticed her because of her large breasts, he told Freeman.[69] He'd invited Jane Doe back to his trailer, where they had sex, during which he had choked her to death with his hands. Wayne claimed that this had been an "accident," and that afterward he had attempted to resuscitate her, to no avail. Afterward, Ford put Jane Doe's body in the bathtub of his trailer, and cut it apart with a saw, a razor blade and some knives, in part to make it easier to conceal.

---

69. People's Response to Demurrer, San Bernardino County, December 2, 1999.

"I had to make her smaller," Ford told Freeman during his interviews. "I had to get rid of them [the body parts]." Ford also placed the severed breasts in a pot on his stove and boiled them, and retained the rendered substance in a coffee can in his trailer.[70]

Subsequently—and again based on initial public accounts before the gag order—Ford had taken the head and arms of Jane Doe and buried them in a gravel bank of the Mad River not far from his Arcata trailer.

However, this account of the murder as an unforeseen "accident" ignored some important facts: based upon the number of post-mortem stab wounds to the torso, observed during the initial autopsy in October of 1997, it appeared that Ford's dismemberment efforts were also caused by some sort of frenzied rage at the victim.

This left the unresolved question: where was the head? Without it, it might never be possible to give Jane Doe her true name.

After leaving the Trinidad campsite, Freeman had Ford taken to the Mad River area in the hope that Ford could lead searchers to the place where he had buried Jane Doe's head.

But the search was fruitless.

"The area," Freeman wrote in his later report, "was clean and there was no sign of anything. Knowing that there was very high water the previous winter, we assumed that everything had been washed away." Freeman also assumed that the arm which was recovered near Clam Beach near the end of January 1999 had been one of the parts buried by Ford, along with a piece of skull that the public had never been told about.

Freeman's report, at least as redacted by Judge Smith's order, now includes a large blank section; presumably this represents additional discussion between Freeman and Ford that was kept back from public disclosure.

Freeman's report then continues:

---

70. People's Response to Demurrer, San Bernardino County, December 2, 1999.

"We left the Mad River area at 1640 hours [4:40 p.m.]. We transported Adam back to Eureka and we stopped and bought him a Whopper and iced tea." This, apparently, was Ford's reward for helping the authorities.

About 7:30 p.m. the detectives from San Joaquin and San Bernardino Counties had arrived, and Freeman organized briefings of the detectives from those departments, including Lenihan, Gonzales and Staggs from San Bernardino and Detectives Mike Jones and Joe Herrera from San Joaquin County. In bringing the other detectives up to date, Freeman said he had read Ford his *Miranda* rights once more at 4:40 p.m., and that Ford had waived his rights and had agreed to speak with the detectives from the other agencies.

The San Joaquin detectives went first.[71] Their case, of course, was that of Lanett White, who had been found in the irrigation ditch near Lodi in September. In his discussion with Jones and Herrera, Ford provided details of Lanett's death that could be corroborated. It appeared, from Ford's statements, that he had picked Lanett up at the truck stop near Cherry and Slover Avenues in Fontana. Ford claimed that while he was having sex with Lanett, he had "accidentally" choked her into unconsciousness. Ford told the investigators that Lanett had been making too much noise, so he wanted to make her shut up. He hadn't intended to kill her. Once again he said he had tried to revive her with cardiopulmonary resuscitation, but failed. He wasn't sure what Lanett's name was; but he remembered that she had a tattoo that he described as "My Madre." Lanett, of course, had a similar tattoo: "Mi Madre Debi."

According to Ford, after he discovered that Lanett was dead, he tied her up in a blue tarp in the rear sleeper portion of his truck. He then drove to Phoenix to make a pickup or delivery for the trucking company, with Lanett's body still in the back. After Phoenix, Ford returned to California, where he passed over the I-5 Grapevine through the mountains between

---

71. This account of the San Joaquin County murder case is drawn from interviews with San Joaquin County detectives, and from People's Response to Demurrer, San Bernardino County, December 2, 1999.

Los Angeles and Bakersfield on the night of September 23. At the top of the pass, the California Highway Patrol stopped his truck for a routine inspection just before 10 p.m. No one looked in the sleeper, of course; the CHP officers were mainly interested in the Kenworth's brakes and tires for the downhill run.

By late that night or early next morning, however, the body began to smell. That was when Ford stopped in Lodi, took the turnoff to Highway 12, stopped in the turnout, and tipped Lanett's body into the irrigation ditch before driving on. Later, he said, he cleaned the truck thoroughly.

The San Joaquin County interview was apparently quite lengthy; the San Bernardino detectives didn't get their first chance at Ford until 12:15 a.m. on November 5, 1998.

"I explained to Ford," San Bernardino County Detective Gonzales wrote, "that I was aware that Detective Freeman from the Humboldt County Sheriff's Office and the two investigators from San Joaquin County Sheriff's Office had read him his rights and he agreed to talk with them. I asked Ford if he would agree to talk to us [material deleted]. I told Ford if at any time he wanted to take a break or needed to go to the bathroom, to just advise me and it would not be a problem."

The interview with the San Bernardino detectives now began. The length of the interrogation remains unclear, but the material deleted by Judge Smith's order comprised eleven single-spaced pages; it thus appears that the interview went on into the early hours of the morning of Thursday, November 5. Because the interview transcript was withheld under Judge Smith's ruling, it isn't possible to tell whether Ford again asked to be allowed to speak to a lawyer that night.

4

The Trailer, the Talk and the Trucks

EARLY THE NEXT MORNING, FREEMAN AND THE REST OF THE detectives gathered to plan their search of Ford's Arcata trailer, which had been under Police guard since Tuesday night. Just after 11 a.m., Freeman and seven other investigators arrived to begin the search.

The search produced a number of items of evidence that would be critical to the prosecution. Among the items seized was a blue hacksaw blade, found on a piece of gray carpet; three pairs of latex gloves; an old coffee can that appeared to contain a yellowish substance; a white plastic bag with a "Flying J" emblem; a pair of pink women's panties; files and papers belonging to Wayne Adam Ford, showing that he had control over the premises; several pornographic magazines and videotapes; various articles of clothing and blankets; and several drivers' logs from Wayne's job with the long-haul trucking firm. Based on Ford's earlier statements, Freeman believed the yellowish substance in the coffee can was probably the renderings from the severed breasts of Jane Doe that Ford had boiled on his stove at some point after her murder the year before.

Detective Mike Jones of the San Joaquin County Sheriff's Department quickly alerted Freeman to the significance of the plastic bag with the "Flying J" logo that had been found in the trailer. A bag with the identical logo had been found at the Lanett White murder site, Jones noted. This was highly significant physical evidence circumstantially linking Ford to

Lanett's murder, because at the time there were only a few such "Flying J" truck stops in the state of California. One was in Eureka, another near Lodi, another at Frazier Park near the Grapevine in southern California, and there was also one in Las Vegas. The chances of two such plastic bags winding up in two such disparate locations was potentially incriminating evidence that existed outside any statements Ford had made in the interviews.

After this initial search, the trailer was hooked up and hauled away to the county's boatyard in Eureka. Two experts from the state Department of Justice soon arrived to conduct a more specialized examination of the trailer. They looked in Ford's freezer, and found traces of material that appeared to match similar substances found on the plastic bags at Ford's campsite near Trinidad, appearing to corroborate Ford's statement that he'd kept Jane Doe's thighs frozen in his freezer for nearly a year.

After the search the San Bernardino detectives returned to the jail to conduct a new interview of Ford, this one lasting a little over an hour. Later Ford provided a sample of his blood, and by 4 p.m., the San Bernardino detectives were at the Eureka airport, preparing to fly home. Detective Staggs was carrying a Styrofoam carton containing the severed breast, surrounded by cold-packs. Over the next few weeks, the tissue would be subjected to a DNA analysis that definitely established it as that of Patty Tamez.

All of this was happening, of course, the day after the *Times-Standard* story about Ford first broke, and as the San Bernardino detectives were flying out, the news reporters were coming in. So, too, were the detectives from Kern County: based on Freeman's teletype, it seemed almost certain that the man who had killed Tina Gibbs was in Eureka. As soon as the San Bernardino detectives were done with their second interview with Ford, the Kern County people began. This was about the time that public defender Jeff Robinson arrived at the jail, demanding to be allowed to see Ford, only to be told that Ford was "unavailable."

In part because of the "gag" order that he himself would soon request, and be granted several days later, Robinson has since been somewhat reticent in discussing the events that took place on the day he tried to see Ford. As we have seen, Ford had been asking for a lawyer from the outset; whether he had subsequently waived his right to an attorney voluntarily, as contended by Freeman and others, was to remain the subject of intense dispute over the following years.

But after being rebuffed in his initial attempt to see Ford, it appears that Robinson may have complained to someone, possibly in the Humboldt County District Attorney's Office. That can be inferred from a telephone call that was placed by Freeman to Rod Ford at 2:38 p.m. on the afternoon of November 5, just after Robinson had been turned away by the jail staff, and the Kern County detectives were starting their interview with Wayne. In making the call, Freeman's purpose seemed to be to make a formal record of what had actually happened on the night Wayne had turned himself in.[72]

"Okay," Freeman told Rod, once he had him on the telephone, "just, what I wanted, Rod, was . . . remember last night [actually the night before that, November 3], after I saw your brother the first time? And he indicated he wanted an attorney and stuff? And then, then I interviewed you, and we got through the thing of how you ended up at our department . . ."

"Right," Rod interrupted.

". . . and everything," Freeman continued. "And then I mentioned that . . . that I couldn't talk anymore because he told me that you had suggested . . . he should get an attorney and stuff . . ."

"Yeah, that's correct," Rod said.

"Right," said Freeman. "And . . . a short time later, the way I recall it is, that you sort of approached me in the office and asked . . . asked me if I wanted you to go talk to him."

"Basically I told you I wanted to talk to him," Rod said.

---

72. Transcript of telephone conversation between Detective Freeman and Rod Ford, November 5, 1998, included in documents filed in support of the arrest of Wynn Adam Ford in San Bernardino County on June 29, 1999.

"Yeah," Freeman said.

"Because I wanted him to do the right thing, and if there was anybody that needed help, they needed to be helped and, at that point I wanted to talk to my brother to try and convince him to do the right thing . . ."

"Okay," said Freeman.

Rod started to say something else, but Freeman broke in.

"And then," Freeman said, "I kind of responded, well, I don't—it's not, I'm not telling you to do that. I don't . . ."

"Right," Rod said.

"I'm not asking you to do that," Freeman said, meaning that it wasn't his idea that Rod go see Wayne to get him to change his mind about talking.

"Right," Rod said.

"Is that right?" Freeman asked.

"You—you—you did not ask me, you did not coerce, you didn't . . . I did this on my own free will," Rod said.

"Okay," Freeman said.

"Ah, that's what happened," Rod added.

"Okay," Freeman said. "That's good and, you did, eventually, while I arranged it so you [could] visit with Adam, and so you went over there and visited with him, and then . . . is that correct?"

"Yeah, that's correct."

"Okay," Freeman said. "And then later on you were sitting in my lieutenant's office . . . at the sheriff's department and I was called in there, and then, then you told me I should talk to him."

"Yes, that's correct," said Rod. "That's correct."

"That he, that your brother, wants to talk to me now."

"Yes."

"Okay. Very good," said Freeman. "I just wanted to get all that settled, and on the record, on tape because, just this, actually our conversation was one of the more important things that has gone on in this case," Freeman said. Freeman already suspected that he would be accused of using Rod to manipulate Wayne into confessing without a lawyer being present, and he wanted to make sure that he had some sort of proof that Rod's surreptitiously bugged talk with Wayne in the jail had been all Rod's idea.

"Right, right, I understand," Rod said.

Now Freeman had other important tasks to attend to. Because Wayne had told him that he had picked up Jane Doe while driving the 1985 El Camino that his father had given him, and he'd used the small truck to get rid of Jane Doe's torso, Freeman wanted to locate that vehicle and subject it to forensic tests. Wayne had told him that he'd given the small truck back to his father. Freeman tracked down Wayne's father Gene, who told him that Wayne had returned the El Camino in perhaps May of 1998 because it didn't run well. Gene offered to drive the truck up to Eureka, but Freeman assured him that he'd have it picked up by the Napa County Sheriff's Department instead. Freeman didn't want to run any chance that evidence that could lead to the long-sought identification of Jane Doe might be compromised. And as for the other victims, a civilian employee of the San Bernardino County Sheriff's Department was flown in to pick up the semi-tractor from Wayne's long-haul employer. It was seized, and immediately driven south to be subjected to a thorough forensic analysis. The detectives might have Ford's confessions on tape, but they weren't about to just take his word for it. Some physical evidence would also be extremely useful.

5

Media and Madness

BY THE NEXT DAY, FRIDAY, NOVEMBER 6, 1998, THE WORD of Wayne Adam Ford's alleged misdeeds had spread from coast to coast. By the time Wayne was brought in for his first appearance before Judge Watson, the Humboldt County Courthouse was jammed with newspeople; the clerks at the courthouse later said they'd never seen anything like it. As we have seen, Ford was introduced for the first time to Kevin Robinson, who entered the plea of not guilty, and asked Judge Watson for the so-called gag order. Although the judge set the next appearance for November 12, the weekend's explosion of news coverage prompted Robinson to ask the judge to rule immediately on his gag order request.[73] The judge agreed, and on the following Monday ordered that anyone having anything to do with "this case"—including representatives of any law enforcement agencies anywhere in the state of California—refrain from making any public comment about it, on pain of contempt.

This had the effect of putting the stopper in the bottle, at least as far as the official sources were concerned. It did not deter the news media from branching out to Wayne's em-

---

73. As Freeman later described the events of the weekend, when newspaper and television reporters were turning Eureka upside down to find out more about Ford, nearly everyone in town was giving interviews of one kind or another—all except him. "I was keeping my mouth shut," he said, later. And indeed, even more than two years later, Freeman steadfastly refused to discuss the case because of Watson's gag order.

ployer, his relatives, and even the neighbors in the Arcata trailer park where the Airstream had so recently resided. The trailer park residents got so fed up with the intrusion that some reporters were threatened with physical violence.

That previous day, unbeknownst to the madly scrambling news media, still more technicians went through Ford's Airstream. This time Freeman wanted to make sure the techs sprayed portions of the trailer with Luminol, a chemical that reveals blood traces when subjected to ultraviolet light. According to exhibits eventually placed into evidence against Ford, first in Humboldt County and later in San Bernardino County, the floor of the trailer's bathtub had at one time been awash with blood.[74] The same procedure was used on the El Camino, which also showed positive for the presence of blood. Meanwhile, Freeman arranged for state fingerprint technicians to come in and process both the Airstream and the El Camino, in the hope that Jane Doe might have left a stray print behind that might help identify her.

Eventually, of course, the media clamor in the matter of Wayne Adam Ford died down, as new and more immediate subjects of journalistic interest arose; soon all the reporters who had flooded into Eureka flooded back out, leaving only Rhonda Parker of the *Times-Standard* and a local cable television channel as the last, involuntary hold-outs. With all of the official sources clammed up by court order, the *cause celebre* largely faded away.

Still, as November turned into December, Freeman invested a great deal of effort in trying to assemble the threads of Wayne Adam Ford's past. He'd almost immediately made a call to the Las Vegas police after arresting Ford, and thus forewarned, Lucie's police officer father was able to prepare her for what was to come, and to take steps to protect her privacy. Within two weeks, Freeman interviewed Lucie. Later,

---

74. Grand Jury photographic exhibits, *People* v. *Ford*, San Bernardino County. Case #FSB027247, as inspected by the author.

Freeman was also able to track down Leigh, and interview her, and then Anaya. Freeman also located Scott and Linda, Ford's old friends from San Clemente, and was able to determine that Ford had actually stopped for the night at Scott and Linda's house in southern California on Friday, August 21; it was apparently on his way north from their house that Wayne had picked up the surviving woman in Santa Rosa two nights later. Scott and Linda were both horrified to learn that the man they'd known for so many years had been accused of such crimes.

And Freeman heard from others who had either known Ford in the Eureka or Arcata area, or who claimed to know him; one such was a woman named Wendy; Wendy told Freeman that she'd given a hitchhiking Ford a ride to the Trinidad area just before he had surrendered, and that Ford had told her he'd killed a lot of women, and was thinking about killing himself. Wendy told Freeman that she'd talked Ford into turning himself in instead. Wendy added a great number of lurid details to the story of her encounter with Ford; eventually, she would compose a lengthy memorandum of Ford's supposed confession to her, and submit it to both the prosecution and the defense. Neither side, however, put much stock in her account; as Canty put it later, to have heard that much detail from Ford, Wendy would have "had to spend three days with him," when the ride from Arcata to Trinidad took less than thirty minutes. Freeman, for his part, concluded that there was little in Wendy's first description of her encounter with Ford that she couldn't have learned from the news media; he decided to discount it altogether.

Freeman's counterparts in San Bernardino County were likewise busy. The day after Ford had been arrested, Freeman called the owner of the long-haul trucking firm Ford had worked for, and made arrangements to have the tractor taken out of circulation to prevent possible evidence contamination.

On the same day that the San Bernardino detectives flew out of Eureka with their precious Styrofoam carton, a San Bernardino County Sheriff's Department civilian employee, accompanied by SBSO forensic specialist Richard Dysart, went to Arcata to pick up the tractor rig, and drove it south to San Bernardino. During the following week, the San Bernardino detectives' search of the truck cab and sleeper yielded a large amount of material, much of it trash, such as old cigarette butts, paper cups, various papers and other things one might expect to find in a well-traveled tractor rig.

But there were several other items that caught the specialists' attention, including a broken acrylic fingernail, various lengths of rope and rubber tie-downs, rolls of duct tape, another "Flying J" plastic bag, a piece of cut carpet that tested positive for human blood, and various articles of clothing, most of them appearing to belong to Ford. The specialists then vacuumed the rig thoroughly; the gleanings included yet another acrylic fingernail, various hairs and fibers, and bits of other pieces of trace evidence. Tests of the floor of the sleeper portion also proved positive for blood, as did the emergency exit door. The tractor was eventually returned to the owner in Arcata, but not until almost two months had elapsed. The owner was not happy.

That wasn't all. Ever since Ford's arrest, people from the state Department of Justice had been poring over Ford's truck logs, trying to see where he had been, and when, over the previous year. Soon someone noticed that between October 21 and October 23, Ford and the truck had been in the Victorville area.

By this time, of course, train conductor Larry Halverson had called in with his account of seeing Patty Tamez climb into the large black truck that had quickly turned east on "Happy Trails Highway" 18, on what he believed was Thursday, October 22. Ford's log showed that he'd made a plywood delivery to a construction yard in Barstow on October 22, 1998, and a pickup the same afternoon at the Mitsubishi Cement Plant in the Lucerne Valley some fifteen miles east of Victorville on Highway 18.

On November 12, 1998, San Bernardino Detective Jeff Staggs visited the Mitsubishi plant in Lucerne Valley, where he interviewed a security guard at the plant gate, Roy Angeles.

After Angeles looked at a pick-up order form that had been in Ford's possession after his arrest, he told Staggs that he remembered both the truck and the driver. Angeles went to a cabinet and retrieved a bill of lading for the cement load. According to the paperwork, Ford and his truck had arrived at the plant at 3:51 p.m. to collect pallet loads of bagged plastic cement, altogether weighing almost 46,000 pounds. The truck left the plant two minutes before 7 p.m. Ford had signed the pick-up form.

Angeles also remembered that the driver of the truck was acting "extremely strange," according to Staggs.[75] When he first pulled up to the plant, Angeles told Staggs, the driver had appeared confused. He stopped short of the gatehouse. Usually, Angeles said, drivers familiar with the plant's routine would drive up to the gatehouse, and get out of the truck to go to an open window at the side, where the driver would receive a plastic audit card used to gain access to the plant. Then the driver would swipe the card through a time punch system at the warehouse area. At that point, the normal procedure was for the driver to use a forklift to load the bagged cement pallets onto his truck. Once loaded they would return to the time punch system, and swipe the card once more. Back at the gatehouse, the driver would return the twice-swiped card, get the bill of lading and leave.

All of this normal procedure seemed too much for Ford to handle, Angeles told Staggs.

"Angeles noted that this particular driver . . . appeared to be having a great deal of problems," Staggs wrote. "He appeared to be frustrated upon their initial contact. He said the driver stopped short of the gatehouse, and then eventually pulled up alongside of the gatehouse.

"Angeles said the driver appeared to be extremely reluctant to get out of his truck. Angeles opened the window of the gatehouse and directed him three different times to get out of

---

75. Detective Staggs' investigation report, San Bernardino County Sheriff's Department, December 11, 1998.

the truck and come over to the gatehouse where he could give the audit card to the driver."

Wayne finally got out of the truck and approached the guard, explaining that he'd never been to the plant before and wasn't sure what to do. Angeles explained the procedure with the cards. Angeles told Staggs he never looked inside the truck, but he certainly didn't see a second person in the front portion of the vehicle.

When Angeles told Ford that he'd have to use one of the plant's forklifts to load his own truck, Ford grew "very agitated."

"Well," Angeles said Ford told him, "we'll see what happens."

Once Ford was through the plant gate, two other trucks arrived; both left with their loads long before Wayne had finished loading his. Angeles thought this meant that Ford was having difficulty getting the load evenly distributed over the trailer's axles.

"Angeles said according to the time stamps on the bill of lading, the driver was in the plant for 3 hours and 7 minutes," Staggs noted.

When he finally left, Ford told Angeles that he'd had a hard time getting the load right. The order called for fourteen pallets, but Wayne had only managed to get thirteen on the truck. He complained about having to load the truck himself, and predicted that he was going to be underpaid for the trip. He also told Angeles he would never come back to the plant again.

According to his truck logs, Wayne delivered the cement load to a company in Los Banos, California, on the following day.

Of course, by the times Staggs conducted this interview, Wayne had already told the San Bernardino detectives the details of his fatal encounter with Patty Tamez—details contained in his statements to the investigators in the early morning hours of November 5, 1998, and later in the early afternoon of the same day. As a result, Staggs knew the significance of Angeles' observations.

However, if train conductor Halverson's observation of Patty getting into the black truck about 3 p.m. on October 22, 1998, is correct,[76] that simply doesn't leave enough time for Ford to contact Patty in downtown Victorville, make the deal, drive to a secluded location, have sex, kill her, conceal her body and make it to the cement plant more than fifteen miles away by 3:51 p.m. It appears entirely possible that she was still alive when Ford's truck first arrived at the Mitsubishi plant.

This then raises the possibility that Ford, rather than having trouble adjusting his load, was actually busy sexually assaulting Patty Tamez in the truck while parked at the plant. That may have been why his time punch card showed he was in the plant for more than three hours, when later drivers had easily obtained their loads and left before Ford.

Under this theory, the agitated Ford would finally have left the plant in darkness, driven back to Apple Valley, then driven to the place where he had finally killed Patty, severed her breast and dumped her body into the aqueduct, all before driving on to Los Banos to deliver his load of cement.

So why didn't Patty get out of the truck at the plant, if she was still alive? The chances are, based on everything else that is now known about Ford, that Patty was tied up and gagged, helpless to escape the doom she probably knew was awaiting her.

It also appears that Ford, in his conversations with the San Bernardino County detectives in Eureka, had told them that he had picked Patty up in Victorville and had initially taken her to a dirt field just south of a convenience store at the intersection of the "Happy Trails Highway" and Apple Valley Road; he may have told Patty, who normally went north of town for her "dates," that he was on a schedule, and had to

---

76. If Halverson's sighting is correct—and the cement plant documents seem to corroborate it—it may be one of the extremely rare cases where there is an actual, verifiable witness to a serial killer's contact with his randomly chosen victim.

go to the Lucerne Valley to make a pickup, which is why she might have agreed to a location off the highway. As it happens, this store was directly across the highway from the National Guard Armory where Patty had gotten in all the trouble the year before. It seems likely that this was the place where Ford first attacked Patty, tying her up, much as a spider weaves its deadly web around its prey, to come back to later. It likewise appears that Ford had never expected to have to load his own truck at the Mitsubishi plant, which may have upset his intentions.

While we don't know what Ford actually said to the detectives, it appears that the investigators were interested in this convenience store. Detective Staggs went there in late November and asked the manager if he recalled seeing a large black semi-tractor with an empty flat-bed trailer parked in the dirt field on October 22, 1998. The manager replied that full-sized black trucks parked in the field on a regular basis. Staggs showed the clerk a picture of the truck driven by Ford, but the store manager couldn't identify it.

A few days later, Detective Staggs went to the Barstow construction yard, where Ford had stopped early on the morning of October 22. The yard manager there, George Mayer, checked the records and told Staggs that he had indeed received two truckloads of plywood that day. One of the drivers was surly, and had long, shaggy hair; the other had shorter hair and was pleasant. The second man helped Mayer unload the plywood, and mentioned that he had just driven down from Oregon the night before. Staggs showed the yard manager a photo array, but he wasn't able to pick Ford's face out of the lineup of pictures. Then Staggs showed Mayer an enlarged Humboldt County booking photo of Ford alone, but he was still unable to make a positive identification.

Next Staggs checked with a clerk at the construction yard's office, who was able to produce a shipping order for October 22 that had Wayne's signature at the bottom.

Later the same day, the clerk asked Staggs to call her back; she'd remembered something else. When she had come to work at 6:45 that morning, there were already two trucks in the driveway waiting to make deliveries. One of the drivers was extremely impatient, the clerk recalled.

"The driver told [the clerk] that he had just gotten through driving from Oregon and wanted someone to immediately unload the lumber on the back of his truck," Staggs wrote in his follow-up report.[77] The clerk had then contacted Mayer by radio, who apparently took his time arriving at the office. This appeared to make the driver impatient.

"While waiting she said the driver continued pacing near the front door and the window area of the construction office," Staggs reported. "He appeared to be more and more annoyed the longer he had to wait. Eventually [the clerk] said she asked him to wait outside. She said at first he ignored her and then she asked him again to wait outside. He then started to leave and then spun around and stared at her almost in a rage-type glare. [The clerk] told me, 'I had never seen a more frightening look from a truck driver. I thought that he was going to kill me.'"

The driver then went outside the office and waited for Mayer to show up to help with the unloading; as we have just seen, Mayer thought Wayne was a very pleasant fellow.

---

77. Report of Detective Jeff Staggs, San Bernardino County Sheriff's Department, December 11, 1998.

6

Jail and Justice

BY EARLY DECEMBER OF 1998, ALMOST A MONTH AFTER HIS arrest, Ford had already exhibited several behavioral traits that made the jail staff nervous. Around the time of the anniversary of his son's birth in December, Wayne began banging on the bars of his cell. When the corrections officer asked what the problem was, Wayne told him that he needed to see a mental health officer right away, because he might "hurt himself." The mental health people came in and talked to Wayne for about an hour, after which he calmed down. And as the winter turned into spring, Wayne began showing more and more aggression toward the corrections officers, warning them that he sometimes had "blackouts," and that he was capable of hurting them if they made him too angry. On yet another occasion, Wayne warned them not to let him into the same area with another prisoner, who had apparently been accused of child abuse. "Ford stated that he had blackouts during which he causes trouble," the jail officer's report read. "He said he thinks his blackouts are caused from problems with his child[hood?]. Ford did not explain the problems with his child[hood?]. I took Ford's explanation to mean there may be a problem due to the nature of [deleted's] charges."[78]

* * *

---

78. Humboldt County Jail incident report package, covering November 1998 to September 1999, exhibit in San Bernardino County's *People* v. *Ford*, FSB 023161.

The case made a brief return to the news on the last day of December, when it was reported that a new law, authored by State Senator Richard Rainey—himself the former sheriff of Contra Costa County—would allow authorities for the first time to combine murders committed in various counties into a single case. This was the so-called "Serial Killer, Single Trial" law, which had first been introduced by Senator Rainey in February of 1997, well before Ford had apparently killed anyone.

The idea, as Rainey expressed it, was to save on the costs of bringing serial killers to trial. He cited two examples of multiple trials of serial killers in the past that had to be held in different counties, because the victims were killed in different places; the cost of multiple trials added millions to the legal bills of the proceedings, Senator Rainey said, and besides, it gave the defendants multiple shots at future appeals. Even worse, Rainey said, the practice of serial trials of serial killers subjected the witnesses and families of the victims to arduous financial and emotional burdens. The logical thing to do, Rainey maintained, was to permit the consolidation of all such serial crimes into a single case, to be tried in one county.

As a result, Senator Rainey offered an amendment to California Penal Code Section 790, initially by providing a new section, (b), which read, "In any case in which a defendant is charged with a special circumstance [legislativese for a crime punishable by death] . . . the jurisdiction for any murder charged in the complaint, information, or indictment shall be in any county that has jurisdiction . . ."—"jurisdiction" being defined as the place where a murder or injury took place, or where a body was found. This had the effect of broadening possible jurisdictions rather considerably.

Senator Rainey's amendment, however, quickly ran into opposition. While the police and prosecutors of the state were all in favor of this change, the defense bar was aghast. The defense lawyers contended that such a change would allow police and prosecutors to "venue shop," that is, look for a plausible jurisdiction where the chances of conviction and death were greater.

Predictably, the debate soon broke down along partisan lines, with the Republicans generally favoring Rainey's proposed amendment and the Democrats opposing it.

The proposal meandered its way through the various legislative committees for most of 1997 and well into 1998, as the two sides tinkered with the exact language of the amendment. In the end, by July of 1998, the proposal permitted the consolidation of murders committed in different counties "as long as the charged murders are 'connected together in their commission' . . . and subject to a hearing in the jurisdiction where the prosecution is attempting to consolidate the charged murders." This seemed to leave it up to a court to determine whether consolidation was legitimate.

"Connected together in their commission" was language taken from another Penal Code Statute, 954, which wasn't much help for those who wanted a more meaningful definition, since that section simply permitted prosecutors in one county to consolidate cases in which the offenses were of the same "class of crimes or offenses."

In earlier cases, the courts had held that "connected together in their commission" meant that the defendant had either planned or performed some sort of "overt act" in one jurisdiction that was inextricably linked to a crime in another. That seemed to imply there had to be something more than murder itself as a connector, although the proponents declined to concede that; they contended that motive alone could be a connector, as well as, possibly, the *modus operandi* of the killer. That was, after all, the purpose of the amendment: to allow for the trial of serial killers whose crimes had taken place in scattered jurisdictions to be tried in one place.

The amendment was finally passed by the legislature in the summer of 1998; then-Governor Pete Wilson signed it into law on September 17—as it happened, three days before Lanett White was murdered. The law was supported by virtually all of the state's law enforcement lobbying groups, including the state Attorney General's Office, the California Police Chiefs Association, the California District Attorney's Association, the Sheriff's Association, and a number of individual elected law enforcement officials. Predictably, the amendment was opposed by the American Civil Liberties Union, and California Attorneys for Criminal Justice, the lobbying arm of the criminal defense bar.

There things rested until the last days of December 1998, when someone realized that Wayne Adam Ford had allegedly killed women in as many as four different counties. A reporter for the *San Francisco Chronicle*, Kevin Fagan, gave a quick synopsis of the newly approved amendment, and then noted that Ford was likely to be the first test case of its constitutionality. A legislative analyst who worked for Senator Rainey, and who also had helped draft the amendment, David Quintana, agreed that Ford seemed to fit the bill.

"He'd be the likely one," Quintana told Fagan.

And Quintana was right, because even as Robinson was preparing to defend Ford on the single Humboldt murder— the Torso Case—a move was underway in San Bernardino County to take jurisdiction for all four crimes. There, Deputy District Attorney David Whitney had already communicated such an intent to representatives of the San Bernardino County Public Defender's Office, which would eventually have to defend Ford in at least the Patty Tamez case if the charges were not consolidated.[79]

Whitney's reasoning was that since it could be argued that Ford had killed both Patty Tamez and Lanett White in San Bernardino County, his county at least had jurisdiction in those two cases; and further, because the crimes showed a number of commonalities—prostitutes as victims, sexual assault, strangulation, depositing the victims in bodies of water—his county had as good an argument as any to be the place to consolidate the other cases as well, under the theory that the new law arguably permitted motive and *modus operandi* as evidence of crimes "connected together in their commission."

---

79. Whitney's intent to ask for consolidation was clear as early as January 1999, when he sent an e-mail to the public defenders' office informing them that he would be seeking multiple murder charges against Ford under the new law, according to Canty.

Exactly what Whitney communicated to the elected district attorneys of the other counties—Humboldt, Kern and San Joaquin—to convince them that San Bernardino should take over their cases remains secret as a result of Judge Smith's rulings, as we have seen: first, that whatever criteria advanced by Whitney to the other counties was irrelevant to Ford's defense in San Bernardino County, and thus not discoverable to his defense attorney; and second, that any communications between Whitney and the other district attorneys was not subject to public disclosure under the state's Public Records Act.

It would nevertheless be interesting to know what these communications consisted of, because it appears that Humboldt County, at least up until April of 1999, intended to try Ford separately in the Torso Case.

On April 6, 1999, Ford was indicted by a grand jury of nineteen citizens in Humboldt County, charged with a single count of murder. Almost before the ink was dry on the indictment, a member of the jury gave an interview to the *Times-Standard*'s Rhonda Parker. The grand jury had listened to Ford's tearful confessions to Freeman, and had been shown the horrifying photographs of Jane Doe's torso, and promptly voted to indict him for first-degree murder.

"It was very hard," grand juror Shayne Gaxiola told Parker. "There was a lot of crying. He kept saying he wanted to help. He wanted to help the family."

In his confession, Gaxiola continued, Ford had said he'd picked up Jane Doe while she was hitchhiking near Bayshore Mall in Eureka on October 14, 1997. That, of course, was one day after Ford had been visiting at Scott and Linda's house in southern California, when he had last seen his son and Lucie. In his confession, Gaxiola said, Ford said the young woman had died while they were having sex. Ford said he'd tried to give the woman CPR, but had failed to revive her.

Gaxiola told Parker that the grand jury had voted 18–1 to indict Ford. Gaxiola had been the only one to vote against the first-degree indictment; he didn't think Ford had intended to kill the woman. He thought the charge should be less than first-degree.

Gaxiola's blabbing about the grand jury testimony created consternation among the officials in Eureka. The jurors had been warned not to discuss the case as it was being presented, but Gaxiola didn't think this applied once the indictment had been returned.

Robinson now went back to Watson's court and got another gag order; this one applied to the grand jurors as well. But one of the main effects of the indictment was that it deprived Ford (and Robinson) of a preliminary hearing, where the evidence would have had to be presented to establish probable cause. Now, because of the indictment, they would go directly to trial, set for September 1998, and all Robinson had to work with was the investigative file that Detective Freeman was continuing to add to as the spring wore on. Robinson hired some psychology experts to examine Ford; the experts concluded, as Ford later was to contend, that the brain injury he'd suffered while he was in the Marines was a critical factor in his behavior.

In the immediate aftermath of Ford's indictment, Wayne appeared to have another mental crisis while in jail. Two days after the indictment was voted, a corrections officer at the Humboldt Jail—whose name was deleted, but who was possibly a woman—began a routine search of Ford's cell.

"He seemed aggressively agitated," the officer reported. "Ford walked over to a chair and aggressively threw his sweatshirt down. Ford turned and walked back toward me. I asked Ford to please stand up against the wall . . . Ford stared me down and only turned left at the last second. Ford stood at the wall and asked me, 'Why do they have women work up here with me? They know there's a problem.' I told him that women do the same job as male officers. He said, 'What does it take for them to see there's a problem? There are four dead already.' "

Ford went on to protest about problems with medical treatment at the jail, and complained again about the guards, contending that "they" had sent the particular guard up to search him because "they" knew Ford and the guard did not get along. Several other officers came to watch as the search was completed. One of them asked if Ford was "having a bad day."

"He stated yes and he was upset about what was written in the paper. Ford was rehoused and we continued the search. As we were searching the next cell, Ford yelled, 'I'm not going to give you the satisfaction of killing myself. You'll have to do it yourself.' "[80]

Later, Ford was given a written disciplinary reprimand for threatening the jail staff. In response, he wrote, "I did not threaten staff. I told [corrections officer's name deleted] that if I am going to be written up for warning staff, then I won't warn staff anymore. I have never threatened staff. I have a known mental condition, and that is what I was warning staff of. This is not a threat to staff."

From this point forward, two officers were detailed to accompany Ford during any movements, while he was regularly placed in belly chains and leg irons. "Remember to use extreme caution," the jail staff was advised.

---

80. Humboldt County Jail incident report package, covering November 1998 to September 1999, exhibit in San Bernardino County's *People* v. *Ford*, FSB 023161.

X
SAN BERNARDINO

1

Venue and Vicinage

ON JUNE 29, 1999, THE COUNTY OF SAN BERNARDINO FI-
nally did what it had been talking about doing for almost
six months—it moved to have Wayne Adam Ford arrested and
charged with all four counts of murder, including the Humboldt County victim.[81]

Wayne's attorney, Kevin Robinson, was outraged. He
quickly drafted a motion for the Humboldt County court to
oppose Ford's transfer to San Bernardino County. Robinson
contended that moving Ford to San Bernardino at that point
would make it impossible for Ford to defend himself in the
trial on the Torso Case that was supposed to take place in
September of 1999, just two months away; further, Robinson
said, using Senator Rainey's new serial killer law to charge
Ford with the Humboldt murder would be unconstitutional, in
that it would violate Ford's rights under the Sixth Amendment,
which states that "the accused shall enjoy the right to a speedy
and public trial, by an impartial jury of the State and district
wherein the crime shall have been committed . . ."

San Bernardino County, said Robinson, hardly qualified as
"the district wherein the crime shall have been committed,"

---

81. In connection with the San Bernardino complaint against Ford, virtually
all of the police investigative reports completed to that time were filed with
the San Bernardino court—1,529 pages. These were the documents that both
Whitney and Canty believed were not publicly disclosable, which were the
subject of the author's intervention discussed in the first portion of this book.

since it was another county entirely, and was nearly 750 miles away, to boot.

The Sixth Amendment guarantee, Robinson contended, meant that Ford had a right to a jury drawn from the area where the crime had taken place, not some other, far distant place that had no demonstrative connection to the crime; indeed, said Robinson, all the courts had so far ruled that the right of "vicinage" meant that Ford had to be tried for the Torso Case in Humboldt County, and nowhere else.

"In this case," Robinson wrote in his brief to the Humboldt court, "California prosecutors have conspired and the San Bernardino prosecutor has agreed to attempt prosecution of a Humboldt County offense in San Bernardino County, some 650 miles from the county in which the crime is alleged to have been committed."[82] [Robinson was apparently measuring distances the way crows fly.]

It was beyond the power of the state legislature, Robinson added, to eviscerate the right of vicinage contained in the Sixth Amendment, especially when there was no "nexus" to connect the Humboldt County murder with anything that took place in San Bernardino County.

The Humboldt County Deputy District Attorney in charge of Ford's case, Worth Dikeman, Jr., simply responded that the way the legislation had been written, it was up to the San Bernardino County judge to decide whether the case should be tried there. That was the purpose for having the hearing that had been written into the amendment.

Robinson's arguments, which were eventually to be repeated by Ford's San Bernardino County public defenders, were rejected by Judge Watson. Dikeman was right, Judge Watson said: the question of whether Ford should be tried for the Torso Case murder in San Bernardino would be up to the courts there to decide, because that's what the state legislature had approved.

"This court," Watson added, "finds nothing prohibiting the

---

82. Motion for Order prohibiting removal of defendant, filed by Kevin Robinson in Humboldt County Superior Court, Case CR991539, July 19, 1999.

legislature from making the determination and therefore finds the Superior Court of San Bernardino County as the proper forum for a motion prohibiting joinder/consolidation."[83]

As a result of Watson's decision denying Robinson's motion, preparations were made to transfer Ford to San Bernardino. This made Ford very unhappy, once again, in jail: not only would he have to learn the ropes in an entirely new jail system, he would no longer be able to have as many visits from his brother and his relatives.

Four days after Watson's decision, Ford decided to try to get rid of Watson as his judge, and fire Robinson at the same time. In two handwritten motions, Ford filed a peremptory challenge against Watson, alleging that the judge was prejudiced against him; in the other, he asked for permission to proceed as his own attorney, claiming that Robinson had failed to provide adequate representation.[84]

Both motions, however, were moot, since Watson had already transferred the case to San Bernardino County.

But there were some other problems lurking beneath the decision to move Ford's Humboldt County case south. Now that the move had been ordered over Ford's objection, there was a potentially serious, practical problem: If, for example, the San Bernardino judge eventually found that the Humboldt Torso Case was *not* "connected together in its commission" with the other crimes, taking Ford south might well have violated Ford's right to a speedy trial under the same Sixth Amendment. After all, Ford had never agreed to go to San

---

83. Judge Watson's order approving Ford's removal to San Bernardino County, Humboldt County Case CR991539, filed August 6, 1999.

84. Ford's handwritten motions were meticulously lettered, and extraordinarily well-written for an untutored jail inmate, citing appropriate grounds for being allowed to proceed as his own counsel, and even including relevant precedents by court citations. If anything, Ford's ability [whether coached by Robinson or some other person or not] demonstrates what Professor Lishman had long ago concluded: diminution of intellectual capacity often does not indicate the presence of brain damage, especially to areas of the brain controlling emotional behavior, since those with such damage can often reason abstractly just as well after the injury as before.

Bernardino; he'd been taken there over his strong protests, and the ever-more-vehement protests of his lawyer; and in the aftermath of the decision, Ford had attempted both to challenge the judge who had made the decision, and to represent himself to no avail. Here indeed was a possible substantive appeal issue.

Ford arrived at San Bernardino County's West Valley Detention Center—the same place where Patty Tamez had been jailed in the years prior to her murder—early in September of 1999.

Sometime in the last week of September, after Wayne had been transferred and was awaiting arraignment, someone at *The Los Angeles Times* noted his recent arrival for trial in San Bernardino, and suggested that this first attempted use of Senator Rainey's serial killer law might make a good story. The reporter selected to cover the story, James Rainey, (no relation to the senator) did the basic research on the new law, then headed out to Rancho Cucamonga to try to get an interview with Ford himself.

More than two years afterward, James Rainey's recollection of the events that led to his interview with Wayne was a bit hazy; he could not, for example, remember whether he had tape-recorded the interview or not, and several other potentially significant details were no longer clear in his mind. On the other hand, Rainey's recollection might have been deliberately vague; by interviewing Wayne—a person already in custody, charged with a crime—it remains possible that the reporter himself might be called as a witness if and when the Ford case ever comes to trial. That's one reason reporters must take care when interviewing prisoners in custody; arguably everything said between a reporter and a prisoner is not subject to any so-called media "shield laws," which ordinarily allow a journalist to protect the confidentiality of his sources. The chances are, also, that the interview was surreptitiously recorded by the jail staff; this often happens with such jailhouse interviews between prisoners and visitors, as we have already seen in Humboldt County with Wayne and his brother Rod.

As Rainey recalled the events, he simply drove out to the jail, identified himself at the front and asked to be allowed to interview Ford. He recalled identifying himself as a reporter to the jail staff, and providing identification. Then he was directed by the staff to a part of the relatively new building where he was to meet with Ford.

Rainey's most vivid memory seems to have been the walk through the facility, which went on for what seemed to him to be at least a mile. He was accompanied by a group of people admitted to visit other prisoners; as they passed through various checkpoints of the jail, individuals and pairs of the visiting group "peeled off," as Rainey put it, to meet the people they had come to see, and by the time he reached the end of the long walk, Rainey was all by himself.

There, in the jail's "administrative segregation" unit, where prisoners at risk of violence from others were housed, Rainey at length came to a sort of cubicle, which was empty. At first Rainey wasn't sure what to do next; then he noticed some sort of communication device on the wall; he couldn't recall whether it was an intercom system, or a handset. In any event, Rainey operated the device, and someone responded. Rainey said he'd come to interview Wayne Ford, and a few minutes later, Ford was escorted into a closed cubicle separated from Rainey by a thick wall of Plexiglas.

To Rainey, Ford seemed composed and in control of himself. In a story published the following Monday, October 4, 1999—**Accused Killer of 4 Links Any Misdeeds to Brain Injury**—Ford claimed that he wasn't guilty of murder, or, at least not murder as it was defined by the law.

"The 38-year-old Ford," Rainey wrote, "repeatedly declined to discuss specifics of the charges against him during the interview at the West Valley Detention Center. He hinted broadly, however, that he believes he is entitled to a defense of insanity or diminished capacity for allegedly killing four women he picked up as he drove the state in his big rig in 1997 and 1998. His trial is expected to begin in about a year."

Rainey quoted Ford in several passages.

"I'm not saying I should be set free," Rainey said Ford told him. "Maybe I should spend the rest of my life in a hospital. This should have been treated medically from the very beginning."

Ford told Rainey about the Myford Road accident, and removed his upper dental plate to demonstrate that his injuries in the accident had been real.

Then Wayne, according to Rainey, claimed that following the accident he had been in a coma for nine days.

Of course, that wasn't right; in Leigh's recollection, Wayne had been conscious the day after the accident. When questioned as to whether he could recall if Ford had really claimed to have been "in a coma for nine days," rather than merely in the hospital for nine days (which *was* accurate), Rainey would only say, "If that's what's in there [the story], that's what he said." This was the point at which Rainey said he couldn't remember whether he had tape-recorded his interview, or whether it was even technically possible to do so.

None of this is to question Rainey's integrity in the slightest. It's only that, if Ford actually claimed to have been "in a coma for nine days," he seems to have been either lying, or at the least exaggerating, a factor which would almost certainly come into play at some point during his trial as a measure of his credibility. The only other alternative is that Rainey misunderstood Ford, which Rainey rejects.

The interview, after it was published, drove Ford's new San Bernardino lawyers into a frenzy. They asked the court in San Bernardino to issue an order to the jailers to prohibit any future contact between Ford and the news media. The order was denied; additionally, efforts by Kevin Robinson and Joe Canty to have Ford shipped back to Humboldt County for trial on the Torso Case were rejected. Ford was in San Bernardino and there he would stay.

"It's in God's hands," Ford told Rainey in the controversial interview; but it was also in the hands of the San Bernardino County District Attorney's Office, which held the record for the most death penalties sought per capita of any county in the state.

2

"Can't He Ever Get This Case To Trial?"

AS THE FALL OF 1999 UNFOLDED, FORD'S DEFENSE LAWYERS began their work to spare him the death penalty that the San Bernardino County District Attorney's Office had already told the court it would be seeking.

Leading this effort on Ford's behalf was Joseph D. Canty, a courtly man of many years' experience (or, "many, many years" Judge Smith was to jest, much later) in the San Bernardino County courts, both as a prosecutor and as a defense attorney.

Just like any other good defense lawyer, Canty was determined to make sure the legal system provided every single one of the defendant's rights, as the question of whether to kill Ford went forward. That meant employing every possible defense, and every possible challenge to the charges. This was Canty's style, and his forte. His ability to elongate legal proceedings for weeks, months, even years was legendary in San Bernardino; at one point, in fact, he was given a nickname by the law enforcement people in San Bernardino County: "Joe Canty Ever Get This Case To Trial?"

Defending and prosecuting criminal cases has much in common with two related but disparate pursuits: chess and warfare. In all three disciplines, one side is on the attack, and the other side is on the defense. And in each pursuit, each side arranges its forces accordingly.

For a good defense lawyer, the guilt or innocence of the client is not really a relevant question, at least morally; instead, it is a tactical issue. To a large extent, the defense lawyer is less defending a specific individual than he is defending the person's rights under the Constitution; thus, the Constitution is, at least in the eyes of most competent defense attorneys, as much a client as the person accused.

As any defender might, whether in chess, warfare, or the legal arena, the first objective is to erect a series of perimeters—walls or moats or barricades—that the attacking forces have to breach or surmount in order to close in on their objective. In the case of Wayne Adam Ford, Canty had a number of concentric defenses: first, was Ford properly charged with all four crimes in San Bernardino County under Senator Rainey's "serial killer" law? If not, that meant some of the counts would have to be dismissed, and as we have already seen, conceivably could put the prosecution of the Torso Case in Humboldt County at jeopardy, since the "speedy trial" guarantee might have been violated.

Inside that ring was the issue of Ford's statements to investigators on November 3, 4, and 5, 1998, and the related question of whether he had been denied access to an attorney. It was clear that Ford had from the start asked for legal representation; what wasn't clear was whether he had ever knowledgeably waived that right. Canty claimed Ford hadn't; Whitney claimed he had. If Ford was denied representation, did that mean that the statements he had made should be thrown out?

This was indeed a critical question. As we have seen, as October of 2000 ended, Canty had moved to throw out the charges against Ford on the claim that Freeman had somehow "coerced" Ford's cooperation on the night of November 3. Whitney's position was that Ford's initial demand for a lawyer when he first arrived at the Humboldt County Sheriff's Department was unavailing, because he wasn't yet "in custody"; in fact, Whitney would claim, Ford wasn't actually put into custody until *after* Rod Ford had told Freeman that his brother was willing to talk. And, said Whitney, it was at that point that Wayne had waived the right to a lawyer, and so therefore, the statements were admissible.

This was a critical issue for Whitney, because without Ford's statements, the prosecutors had precious little evidence to link Ford to Tina Gibbs' murder; and while there were witnesses who seemed to place Lanett White getting into Ford's truck in Fontana, and the evidence from the Lodi crime scene was incriminating, again Ford's statements about Lanett White's murder were critical to proving the case beyond a reasonable doubt.

If the statements were thrown out, that left only the Torso Case—where authorities had the physical evidence of the severed limbs and the luminol findings—and the Patty Tamez case, where, of course, they had the severed breast that had been in Ford's possession. But the problem then became whether the two cases were "connected together in their commission"; Canty could well argue that they were not, since the *modus operandi* in the Torso Case was significantly different from the other cases, as well as some of the circumstances.

If these two remaining cases were separated, then the problem of the speedy trial in Humboldt County again became significant; and also at that point, as Whitney put it, the prosecution would be left with insufficient grounds to ask for the death penalty, since he would have only one murder to prosecute in San Bernardino County, that of Patty Tamez.

So the issue of Ford's statements—those redacted by Judge Smith's order in June of 2000—was critical to both sides, more than two years after Ford first presented himself for arrest.

Inside those rings there was yet another potential defense issue. In the aftermath of the release of the investigative reports in June of 2000,[85] the authorities in San Bernardino County decided to dispense with the preliminary hearing that had been scheduled to begin in September of 2000, and obtain a grand jury indictment instead.

The district attorney's office blamed this on the release of the documents, which they contended had led to a flood of

---

85. See "Contending," earlier in this book.

publicity that was prejudicial to Ford.[86] Besides, they said, Canty had already indicated that a preliminary hearing might last as long as four or five months. Again, the catcalls about "Joe Canty Ever Get This Case To Trial?" were heard.

On July 27, 2000, the San Bernardino County District Attorney's Office presented evidence to the county's civil grand jury, which issued an indictment of Ford for four counts of murder the following day, along with a special finding that the crimes were "connected together in their commission." To that end, Whitney had presented a former Los Angeles County Sheriff, John Yarbrough, who was an expert in criminal profiling and crime scene analysis. Yarbrough brought charts showing the commonalities between all four of the murders and the Sonoma rape case. The grand jury then voted to find that the four murders were indeed "connected together in their commission." Whitney moved to have both the indictment and the transcripts of testimony before the grand jury sealed to prevent more publicity.

Thus, Whitney hoped to skip the preliminary hearing and go right to trial with a minimum of public hoopla. He was impatient to get moving, he told the court; the case had already been delayed long enough. Besides, Whitney said, he already had two other death penalty cases pending.

Canty said he couldn't possibly be ready for trial so soon; besides, he, too, had another death penalty case pending. But then when Canty inspected the indictment, he realized that Whitney hadn't used a regular grand jury to get it, but had instead pressed into service the county's civil grand jury. In California, by law, every county must annually impanel a grand jury charged with examining the workings of the county government, a sort of blue ribbon panel of citizens whose job it is to watchdog the county government's operations; rarely,

---

86. Several area newspapers indeed wrote articles based upon the release of the information in the wake of the author's motion; and virtually all of the published articles focused on Ford's peculiar behavior with his ex-wives and girlfriends, omitting much of the information about Ford's Marine Corps record, and entirely missing the issue of Ford's possible brain damage.

if ever, was such a jury used to issue a criminal indictment, and as far as anyone could tell, it had never been done before in a murder case. This, Canty said, was patently unfair: virtually all of the members of the civil grand jury were acquaintances either of district attorneys or judges; in fact, the members of the civil grand jury were appointed to their posts by the San Bernardino bench. That meant there was an inherent conflict of interest, Canty contended, and Ford had been denied his right to a grand jury drawn from all segments of the community.

So here was another possible area of legal challenge; and as the year 2000 came to a close, a special judge from outside the county had to be brought in to determine whether the indictment should be thrown out because of the alleged close relationship between the grand jurors and the judges, and whether the whole process should be started over, all over again.

Finally, inside all those rings of defense was at least one other, as noted by reporter James Rainey: the issue of Ford's mental competence.

Was Ford's head injury in early December 1980 relevant to his actions? Was he legally insane at the time the crimes were committed? Here the issue of "times" was important. Was it possible that Ford's claims of blackouts were true, and that his killings were in fact accidental? That, in moments of stress, he lost any semblance of conscious control over his actions, and was thereby unable to form the intent of murder? Would that make him innocent of premeditated murder, or any kind of murder except, perhaps, manslaughter? At those instants when he claimed to have blacked out, was he legally responsible at all? Could he even be found not guilty by reason of insanity? At the very least, even if found guilty of some or all of the murders, would the fact of his head injury weigh in a jury's decision on whether to give him the death penalty?

All of those convoluted questions also had to be examined; and finding actual, hard, documentary proof of the severity of Ford's head injury in 1980 was difficult for the defense, because so much had been tossed out over the intervening years.

As a result, it might be that Ford's only chance would rest on the expert testimony of psychiatrists and neuropsychiatrists; not a happy prospect for Ford, because, as my shrink friend in Seattle put it, juries usually hate hearing head doctors testify—they almost never agree with one another.

All of these issues, and others, continued to swirl around the Ford case. By December of 2000, the most optimistic estimate had Ford finally facing a jury in perhaps July of 2001; but no one was willing to bet that it would actually happen.

EPILOGUE

THERE IS, OF COURSE, ANOTHER COURT INVOLVED IN EVERY criminal case, and it is not one with railings or robes or clerks or bailiffs, but the court of public opinion, which is where *this* case is being tried, the case of the *Shadows of Evil.* In effect, the readers are the judge and the jury in this court; and in their own minds they have the power to be, at various times and as the occasion demands it, also the prosecutors, the police, the witnesses, the victims, the defenders, and even the accused. That is the power of the imagination, when coupled with the facts, and with a clear intent to see the matters fairly.

But in this case, the court of public opinion does not have all the facts; and is actually lacking some of the most crucial of them: the statements of Wayne Adam Ford himself, made on the emotional night of November 3, 1998, and in the days that followed.

The judge, relying upon his interpretation of the law, kept those statements out of the public record, from a concern that their publication might prejudice Ford's right to a fair trial, whenever it takes place.

And while the statements could clarify exactly what Ford said he did and did not do, or whether he was afforded his constitutional rights, there is more, much more, that might have been gained in the court of public opinion by their release.

For we do not really know Wayne Adam Ford. Without his exact words, spoken under stress on that strange night, we can gain no image, no insight into the quality of his character. We know him only by what others have said about him, and not at all by what he has said about himself. We cannot hear him speak: about what happened, why it happened, and how he truly feels about it. Whether he has remorse, or is feigning; whether he lies when convenient or tells the truth even when it is most painful; what he really thinks about himself, and what he would wish for if he had his life to live over. In short, we know nothing of the soul of Wayne Adam Ford; that is what remains in the shadows.

Was Wayne, as his first wife Leigh eventually came to believe, simply an amoral man, who took whatever he wanted, no matter who he hurt? And if this was true, was this something that was inborn in Wayne, or something that he learned? Or was it the result of the accident in which, while acting as a good Samaritan, Wayne was knocked spinning headfirst into a ditch and left to die, only to live for another two decades without the biochemical phenomenon the rest of us know as compassion for the feelings of others?

Those are the questions Wayne's jury will have to face, as we in the court of public opinion also try to consider them. And there are other questions as well, some as immediate as they are profound.

Why didn't anyone care enough about Tina Gibbs, Lanett White and Patty Tamez to help them, when they so obviously needed it, before it was too late? Why, even when they were dead, did no one care enough about them to learn what had driven them to such desperation?

Should Wayne Adam Ford be executed if he is found guilty? Should he be strapped to a gurney and injected with a lethal substance that will soon paralyze his ability to breathe, forever taking his life from this world, as he has been accused of taking the lives of others?

Is this justice?

Will it do any good?

And there are still other questions, the answers to which, so far, still lie in the realm of the shadows.

Who was Jane Doe?

Who was her mother, her father, her baby? Where did she come from? Where was she going? Why has no one missed her?

And, if she could: would *she* kill Wayne Adam Ford?

BITTER MEDICINE

Two Doctors, Two Deaths, and a Small Town's Search for Justice
Carlton Smith

Port Angeles, Washington seemed like the perfect place to live...until two local doctors made headlines. On a chilly January night, Dr. Eugene Turner hastened the death of a three-day-old baby boy who had been pronounced brain dead. Two months later, ER physician Dr. Bruce Rowan hacked his wife to death with an ax, then tried to kill himself—claiming he snapped after witnessing Dr. Turner's act of euthanasia. What really happened? Now, bestselling true crime writer Carlton Smith reveals the never-told-before facts and the stunning truth behind two doctors, two deaths, a surprising trial, and a picturesque town standing in the shadow of a ghastly killing...

BM 3/00